To Dr Covey

The lady with a wonderful, story Garland Thompson

D1374130

UNHERALDED BUT UNBOWED:
BLACK SCIENTISTS & ENGINEERS WHO CHANGED THE WORLD

ISBN 1448673836
EAN-13 978-1448673834

i

*To my daughters Connie and Grace, to Hassana the
Intermediary, to my grandson Dovante, and to all the young
technology butt-kickers of the next generation.*

A Note to Readers:

The main material for this book -- reports of discoveries,
inventions and innovative processes -- was culled from the
extensive archive of Candidate Biographies, support letters
and technical papers compiled by Career Communications
Group from corporate citations to the Selection Panel for the
Annual Black Engineer of the Year Awards. In these,
corporate officers made the strongest arguments each could
muster about the value to their companies -- often to entire
industries -- of the achievements of the Black go-getters
driving their product lines and profits, to show the candidates'
worthiness for recognition.

And other than at the Awards Gala itself, or in the pages of
US Black Engineer & Information Technology, there are very
few places the general public can learn of these amazing
intellectual accomplishments, or of Blacks' new access and
clout in U.S. industry: Not in the annual Black History Month
rehash of *Great Discoveries by Blacks Long Dead*; not in glossy
science magazines trumpeting *The Latest New Thing*; and
certainly not on the Discovery Channel -- nor even on Public
TV. That impels this work, which could not exist without the
permission of CCG for me to spend months combing those
archives. My thanks to CCG and its leaders, Tyrone Taborn
and Jean Hamilton, without whose generous assistance this
work would have been still-born. -- *Garland L. Thompson*

UNHERALDED BUT UNBOWED:
BLACK SCIENTISTS & ENGINEERS
WHO CHANGED THE WORLD

CONTENTS

UNHERALDED BUT UNBOWED:
BLACK SCIENTISTS & ENGINEERS WHO CHANGED THE WORLD

AUTHOR'S INTRODUCTION
CONNECTING THE DOTS IN BLACK HISTORY

This book might be called "A Comprehensive History of Black Technology Exploits in the 20th Century," but that would miss the mark by a wide margin. More comprehensive listings of Black inventors and their patented innovations already exist, such as Ray Webster's encyclopedic listing[1], or Mike Brodie's excellent work[2],

---

[1] Webster, Raymond B. *African American Firsts in Science and Technology*. 178 pages. Detroit: Gale Group.
[2] Brodie, James Michael, *Created Equal: The Lives and Ideas of Black American Innovators*,
Copyright 1993, by Bill Adler Books, Inc., William Morrow and Co. Inc., New York.

which also traces the records of the Baker's Dozen of Black scientists who worked in the Manhattan Project. This book does survey the sweep of technological and social change over the last 100 years – it could not help but do so, considering its principal subjects' life spans – but it really has a different focus.

The targets here are entirely different. I'm trying to answer very different questions: What happened in history to lead up to openings for a John Slaughter, ridiculed for wanting to be an engineer but persevering to become a seminal figure in American science?

Who were the Blacks who went before, disproving the myth of intellectual inferiority even as it was being promulgated? How did others manage the climb up the difficult pathways those pioneers established? What could motivate an Arnold Stancell, a Guion Bluford, a Shirley Jackson to push on into uncharted spaces in Corporate America, outer space and nuclear power despite 100 years of express national discouragement for Blacks seeking to step onto the Big Stage of world-shaking performance in the sciences?

What affected the lives and attitudes of an Art Carter, a Linda Gooden, a Rodney Adkins or Wanda Austin, as they climbed to executive power and influence as technology leaders at some of the biggest and most powerful corporations in the world? What legacy will they leave behind?

Readers will note the regular intrusion of discussion about civil rights and the push to open up pathways to success through affirmative action, and no apologies will be offered for that. None of the careers described here could have happened without a continuing push by Black people to overturn the barriers put in place by white supremacists at the close of the Civil War.

Lest We Forget

Lest anyone forget, many of the people who fought and lost that war to keep Blacks enslaved were alive and still kicking about it well into the 20th Century. Margaret Mitchell, author of "Gone with the Wind," the best-selling, teary-eyed remembrance of days better forgotten, modeled Scarlett O'Hara after her own mother, a plantation *belle* who had watched her artificially privileged lifestyle reduced to ashes in the Siege of Atlanta. Large numbers of those former Confederate soldiers, political leaders, planters and their hangers-on moved elsewhere after the Civil War, especially to the West, spreading bitter memories of their paradise lost and ramping up racial animosity everywhere they went.

Another source of racial animus was the drive of European immigrants to block job competition by the newly freed Blacks. Beginning even before the Civil War with the Irish who battled in the streets to drive emancipated Blacks away from jobs in the burgeoning factory enterprises of the Northeast during the 1840s, and continuing with the waves of white immigrants pouring into big-city industrial centers in the late 19th Century and through the first half of the 20th, these new Americans used every tool available to keep Blacks from becoming effective competitors for the jobs they came here to get.

Cowboy movies sometimes portray gunfighter-heroes battling and escaping "Red Shirts" and "Regulators" without revealing that these groups, like the League of the White Camellia, rumored to be secretly led by former Quantrill's Raider Jesse James, all were founded by ex-Confederate soldiers riding as masked terrorists, struggling to re-impose the pre-war white dominance.

This book briefly reprises some of the atrocities of that shameful era, not as any attempt to rake up old antagonisms or drag out old guilts, but to cast into sharp relief the depths of repression existing in the racially restrictive environment in which the Black forerunners of today's high-achievers lived and worked as they fought their way past the caste prohibitions enslavement and post-Reconstruction segregation imposed. It also serves to remind everyone why affirmative, deliberately compensatory efforts still are badly needed today, to overcome the legacy of racial domination that so severely restricted Blacks' progress over so many generations in the past.

It requires retelling today that even though the first successful organized labor groups urgently sought Black support to win the right to negotiate contracts at the turn of the 20th Century, many of the newly won labor contracts featured clauses expressly barring Blacks from the best job titles, and often from having jobs and union membership at all. That happened in the genesis of railroad unions during the late 1800s, ultimately requiring Black Pullman Car porters and postal workers to organize unions of their own, and in particularly in the building of construction unions, which 100 years later still largely exclude Blacks despite decades' worth of successful lawsuits and federal Labor Department efforts to eliminate the *de facto* segregation the construction tradesmen have enforced.

Thus, it was not on just a whim that Blacks in Baltimore formed the Chesapeake Maritime Railway and Drydock Company in 1879 , in but one example of the lengths Blacks had to go to win employment in shipbuilding and repair over the hostility of the forerunners of today's construction trade unions, which used strike actions and contract negotiations to keep Blacks out of lucrative shipyard and construction jobs. Those early unions were dominated by European immigrants who were deeply resentful of the competition represented by newly freed African Americans, who had learned to ply their crafts in the malignant enterprise of enslavement and now wanted to be paid commensurate wages for work they had earlier done without any compensation ever being offered.

Where that kind of organized effort failed, there was always the resort to street riots and brutal pogroms. The violence began in the 1830s and intensified with the mob rampages in Philadelphia of 1842, when Irish immigrants attacked a Black temperance parade and then ran through the streets, burning Black homes and beating and killing any Blacks they could catch. It continued in New York during the 1860s' "Copperhead" protests and riots against the draft and, pointedly, against Emancipation, and in Chicago just after the turn of the 20th Century, when a mass transit company tried to put Blacks into streetcar jobs "reserved" for whites.

By the middle of the 20th Century, discrimination in the North and West had become less violent but far more subtle and comprehensive: With the need to keep Blacks from ever thinking they could be "equal" to whites a widely accepted priority, eye-winks and blatantly displayed personal prejudice were often all that was needed to keep even very highly qualified Black applicants out of prestigious schools, better-paying jobs and lucrative career fields conferring professional standing.

Bucking the Tide

Such a thorough-going, longstanding refusal to permit Blacks to enjoy the economic mobility other Americans took for granted mandates thorough-going efforts at eradication. Those efforts were kicked into high gear at the end of the 1960s by Assistant Labor Secretary Arthur Fletcher, whose "Revised Philadelphia Plan for Construction Labor" forever changed the game in union contracting, with a stroke of Fletcher's pen wiping some of the most odious tactics off the plane of legal contracting action. Fletcher, building on the success of Pullman Car Porter union leader A. Philip Randolph in forcing President Franklin Roosevelt to set up Fair Employment Practices Committees during World War II and the continuing drive of the Kennedy-Johnson-era Office of Equal Opportunity, followed with his own well-organized program for changing the complexion of the American workplace. The success of those efforts, and those of many other committed activists inside and outside of government, provided the structural supports beneath the career access and technical achievements chronicled here.

Top Honorees to the Front

Also noticeable in this work is the preponderance of Black Engineer of the Year Award Winners among the pioneers discussed. That is no accident, either.

Beginning with my days commenting on technology policy on the Editorial Board of *The Baltimore Sun* during the late 1980s, I spent a quarter of a century volunteering as a member of the Selection Panels for the annual Black Engineer of the Year Awards, sponsored by Career Communications Group Inc., publishers of *US Black Engineer & Information Technology* magazine, and the Council of Deans of the Historically Black College and University Engineering Programs, and I am mightily grateful for the insights gained during that labor of love. Judging the contests, writing about the winners in *USBE* and other publications, and meeting those impressive individuals at the annual Awards Galas and in conferences afterward helped me build up a body of knowledge that otherwise would have been missed as I worked a decades-long career in journalism, bouncing back and forth between "mainstream" media and the Black press.

Among other goals, this book represents an attempt to share some of that inspiring information with a broader audience.

For I could not help but be struck by the absence of these Black world-beaters' names from the headlines of the newspapers, magazines and broadcast outlets for which I wrote or against which I competed, when I looked over the stories those same media were reporting about the industrial market successes their achievements made possible. I kept meeting white corporate CEOs, men whose names were making big headlines every day, who took time off to show up in Baltimore and stand up before audiences of thousands to extol the virtues and accomplishments of these Blacks, but I kept seeing even those loud proclamations of recognition left out of the news about the fortunes of American companies.

The News You Didn't Know

It was as if Black engineers and business leaders important enough to set product lines and run major operating units of *Fortune* 500 companies did not exist, even in the pages of *Fortune*, which should have known better. Its writers, and those working for such publications as *Forbes, Business Week*, the *Wall Street Journal*, the *Journal of Commerce*, and the *New York Times* Business Section, have access to the top executives of every country in the world, and there is no excuse for their continued blindness. Those writers, exemplars who set the tone of news coverage for publications and broadcast outlets across the country, also have inside access to see in gestation the very latest technologies and newest products, and to talk at length to their creators, many of whom, over the last several decades, have been Blacks.

Somehow, the Blacks always seem to get left out of the excited reportage about the new discoveries, further promoting the notion that all of the important intellectual work in America is done exclusively by whites, with a few token Asians sprinkled in for leavening.

I knew better, and I tried many times to get my colleagues, Blacks as well as whites, to recognize that these Blacks, their success and access, and the responses of their corporate employers represented major changes in the industrial workplace. It took a civil rights rebellion, lasting decades, to force open enough doors to let Blacks compete in the "meritocracy" so mythologized in the rhetoric of opponents to desegregation and affirmative action. But once in the arena, with the education long denied their forebears, the Blacks' own merit and drive worked its own revolution in the American workplace. And now they were being ignored.

My frustration at other journalists' refusals to even come to look impelled this work. How can we tell our children to strive to be the very best if no one ever shows them what real success looks like when someone does perform? How can we put an end to the prejudice and discrimination that continue to thwart Blacks' best performances in many fields, if no one ever shows the masses of white Americans how outdated their preconceptions really are?

Even Excellence Needed Some Help

I would be remiss if I left out the fact that none of those corporate dossiers the Selection Panel considers mention that "we hired [this candidate] because of affirmative action," or "we wanted to get out from under a barrage of criticism by civil-rights activists, so we hired so-and-so." As is shown when you read these winners' bios in *USBE*, or on the Career Communications Group Web site, those dossiers contain recitations of extreme excellence, demonstrated over and over again as the award nominees moved from posting to posting, resulting in multi-million-dollar payoffs – often *billion-dollar* payoffs – for their employers. Praiseworthy in itself? You bet!

But as stated before, in this complex, multi-ethnic, competitive society of ours, there is so much more to the story. Civil rights always plays a role, even if people who should know better downplay it. One oft-repeated comment at the aforementioned annual Selection Panel meetings, in which 20 or so engineers from across industry spend days dissecting corporate leaders' competing claims about their candidates' winning qualities and achievements, is that so many of the people with the best experience, running the biggest projects, tend to come from the military-industrial complex.

That is not happenstance. Lyndon Baines Johnson's Executive Order 11246, requiring all contractors doing $50,000 or more worth of federal business to demonstrate "affirmative action" to open their workforce ranks to disadvantaged minorities, has teeth, nearly half a century after Johnson issued it. Defense contractors are the biggest recipients of federal contract dollars, and their staffing tables show a level of balance and opportunity for minorities that is starkly different from the scene in strictly private, civilian-oriented industry.

The Fair Employment Practices Committees began that

push, and Secretary Fletcher put new horsepower into the drive. Working in a Nixon Administration assembled in the wake of the Kennedy assassinations and under intense fire from its left, Fletcher seized on Johnson's order. Starting with his "Revised Philadelphia Plan for Construction Labor," Fletcher proceeded to construct an entire apparatus of equal-opportunity enforcement.

Broad Enforcement

The federal Equal Employment Opportunity Commission gets the headlines when it goes to court against companies that unfairly hold back opportunities so freely granted to whites and treat Blacks, women and other minorities differently, or permit other discrimination on the job. But the work of Labor's Office of Federal Contract Compliance Programs has had a much more comprehensive effect in the modern workplace.

OFCCP staffers, often called "faceless bureaucrats" when mainstream news reporters take note of their work at all, use the horsepower Johnson's order provides to delve deep into corporate staffing policy. OFCCP people meet with Human Resources types and corporate leaders, negotiating pragmatic agreements for hiring, training, and assignments for minorities, and the agreements, once signed, are enforceable in court. Or, in cases of truly bad-faith behavior, in administrative orders debarring uncooperative contractors from doing business with government agencies.

Double-Barreled Success Stories

Thus, two propositions are simultaneously true: The first is that the innovators put forward for Black Engineer of the Year Awards have arrived at their lofty corporate positions by dint of their own brainpower, discipline and, very often, prodigious efforts. The second, equally powerful truth is that the insistent drumbeat in the background of all their careers is the progress of civil rights drives, directly or indirectly. For without civil rights and – *gasp* – affirmative action – knocking down barriers, opening up doors and demanding that technical merit, whether found in a Black, Hispanic, female, Native American or Asian professional, be given truly equal opportunities to succeed and rise, few of these men and women would arrive at such eminence. One has only to look back to the bad old days of segregation to see that.[3]

---

[3] In but one telling demonstration, the records of the Manhattan Project, universally held by Americans to be an exercise in genius, show that Ralph Gardner was one of more than a dozen Black scientists who played key roles. Gardener, a University of Illinois chemistry grad, worked at Chicago's Argonne National Laboratory under Enrico Fermi, along with fellow Blacks Lloyd Albert Quarterman, Harold Delaney, Jaspar Jefferies, Edward A. Russell, Benjamin Scott, Moddie Daniel Taylor, and J. Ernest Wilkins. In New York, other Blacks including William Jacob Knox, George Warren Reid Jr., Sydney Oliver Thompson, George Dewitt Turner, and Cecil Goldburg White worked on the Manhattan Project at Columbia University.

Enrico Fermi and his white colleagues are justifiably enshrined in the pantheon of American science – Fermilab is even named after him – but the Blacks promptly became academic footnotes after World War II. That's despite achievements that not only helped win the war, but launched a new industry – Nuclear Power – and developed methodology later used by Hyman Rickover to build a Nuclear Navy that is the envy of the world.

In addition, those Black pioneers, particularly Moddie Taylor, J. Ernest Wilkins and the non-nuclear scientist Otis Boykin, created the

So this is a connect-the-dots book. Rather than a book of profiles, useful in itself during Black History Month but set aside the rest of the year, the main attempt here is a work that shows how the activities and achievements of Blacks brought to prominence by peer-reviewed contests like the Black Engineer of the Year Awards connect to the rest of Black History – indeed, to the history of the world.

For if American history truly is a tapestry, woven from many different strands and with colors and textures assembled from many competing directions, the history of Black struggle in America is a tapestry of its own, interwoven, affecting and deeply affected by everything that affects American society.

Looking Closer at Science Pioneers

The role of the Black scientist or engineer will never be fully understood by examining it in narrow, limiting ways, as if science and technology somehow existed apart from the tumult and clash of social policy, played out in the larger arenas of society. The Black scientist or engineer is every bit as much a part of the Black community as the Black athlete, entertainer or preacher, and every bit as much a player in the scramble to boost its progress.

Too frequently, however, Black achievement in science and technology is treated as some kind of special case, to be

---

underpinnings of the electronics technology with which Americans amazed the world during the 1960s, '70s, and '80s. But as Brodie explains, Gardner could not find an academic position in his field when he left Argonne Laboratory in 1947, amid the booming expansion of university education prompted by the G.I. Bill, an expansion never matched in world history. His other Black colleagues were likewise forgotten.

ignored unless and until it is time to engage in feel-good rhetoric in February, with no real relevance to the everyday lives of Black people. This book is an attempt to rectify that, to show that not only is technology relevant, its study and career paths open vistas of continuing success for the active, questioning minds of Black youth.

Now, enough of the introductory commentary. Time to read the chapters, and find out for yourself if I've really managed to connect those dots. . . .

— Garland L. Thompson
Philadelphia, Pa., August 2009

Supplemental Notes

4. Scholars say Mitchell's 1,037-page 1936 novel, actually written during the 1920s, was based on the memories of her mother, who spent the rest of her life being bitter at Confederate General Joseph F. Johnston for the loss of Atlanta. The book, which romanticized life in the slave-holding antebellum South, sold 1.5 million copies even before it was republished as one of the best-selling movies of all time by David O. Selznik in 1939.
See also *www.filmsite.org/gone; www.newline.com/sites/gonewind*.

5. "The Memory Books of Amos Webber," the reprinted notes, weather recordings and newspaper clippings of a Black Philadelphian who lived through those hard times and later fought with the 5th Massachusetts Cavalry in the Civil War, tell much about the lives of Black Americans before the war. Discovered in the Harvard University archives and brought to light by historian Nick Salvatore, the Memory Books discuss many events, including the riots led by Irish immigrants in 1831 and 1842, during which the immigrants made it clear what their real target was: driving off the Blacks. That 1842 riot saw the blazing destruction of Pennsylvania Hall, a newly built meeting place for abolitionists. It had been kicked off by angry

white mobs who confronted peaceful marchers in a Temperance parade for having the temerity to display a banner depicting a Black man bursting free from his chains in front of a rising sun the mobs interpreted as a city in flames. Pointedly, Salvatore notes that Philadelphia's Black population immediately stopped growing while the white population boomed.

6. As Ken Burns' excellent documentary *The Civil War* brought out, whites in New York reacted hotly to Abraham Lincoln's Emancipation Proclamation, rioting against the military draft because they did not want to fight to free Blacks, who would then become competitors in the job market.

7. See also *www.ccgmag.com; www.blackengineeroftheyear.org*.

8 See also "Affirmative Action Pioneer Advised GOP Presidents," The Washington Post, July 14, 2005 By Joe Holley, Page B01.

Chapter 1

John Slaughter's Triumph
Counselors laughed, but his drive won respect

A quarter of a century ago, John Brooks Slaughter was an oddity, a Black man heading a major, "mainstream" institution. The man now stretching the performance curve at the National Action Council on Minorities in Engineering, ramping up scholarship dollars and pushing out reports challenging the intellectual *status quo* in our technology-driven society, in 1982 was chancellor of University of Maryland at College Park, flagship of the University of Maryland system.

Dr. Slaughter was used to being the "First Black" wherever he went, mainly because the discrimination so rampant in his day prevented other Blacks from showing off their natural ability in so many fields.

Counselors at Slaughter's high school in his hometown, Topeka, Kansas, actually laughed[1] in his face when he told them he wanted to be an engineer. They had never seen or even heard of a Black man being an engineer, so they told the young John Slaughter to wise up and learn a trade -- a taunt that would still be heard a generation later by the young Shirley Jackson, in undergraduate school at the Massachusetts Institute of Technology.

1

Slaughter, undeterred, persevered. The trade he wanted to learn was engineering, and learn it he did. And now, a generation later here he was, chancellor of a campus that was a wellspring of engineering talent. The counselors had stopped laughing a long time before that, but America still had lots to learn about the drive and creativity of Blacks in the technology enterprise. The Maryland academic community, for its part, probably had its own unvoiced doubts about John Slaughter.

College Park, with 38,000 students during the middle 1980s, was the nation's sixth-largest public university. It still is a major producer of American science and engineering talent; and it had never experienced a Black top administrator. Nor had most of Maryland, which had to be occupied by Union troops to prevent its secession during the Civil War.[2]

Maryland Before Slaughter
During most of the 20th Century, Maryland had refused Blacks admission to most of the colleges in its state-supported system of higher education. In addition to supporting three Black colleges -- Bowie State, Coppin State, and Morgan State -- during the decades-long desegregation fight, Maryland gave Blacks scholarships for out-of-state study to keep them out of its own public institutions. The state's only law school, the University of Maryland in downtown Baltimore, could not offer admittance to Thurgood Marshall in 1929 when he got home with his degree from Pennsylvania's historically Black Lincoln University.

Segregated education was a fact of everyday life in

2

Maryland. Marshall himself had been an honors graduate at all-Black Frederick Douglass High School in his home city, but in Baltimore County, outside the city limits, there was no Black high school. Blacks had to pass a special test to gain county scholarships to Douglass, the city's Black high school, or go without completing their educations.

Not surprisingly, the 1934 lawsuit of *Donald Murray vs. Maryland*[3] was only the first complaint young Attorney Marshall brought in the Maryland courts, fresh from recording one of the highest-ever scores on the state Bar Exam. Marshall, called "the Best Lawyer of the 20th Century" by the time of his death, completed his Constitutional Law apprenticeship under Howard Law School Associate Dean Charles Hamilton Houston, who trained an entire cadre of lawyers to challenge the Supreme Court's rationale for its 1896 ruling in *Plessy v. Ferguson*[4], which legalized racial segregation -- "separate but equal" was the law of the land.

To the surprise of many white Marylanders, the state courts upheld Marshall's challenge in *Murray* because Marshall showed the state had no "equal" facility for Blacks.

Murray and his classmates, the first four Blacks ever to graduate from the Maryland law school, formed their own firm to fight discrimination cases. Marshall and Houston, fresh from their success in *Murray*, filed suit against Baltimore County, demanding an opening for a Catonsville girl to attend all-white Towson High School. Whites did not have to pass tests to get into Towson High, while county Black students had to win scholarships to go to Baltimore City's all-Black Douglass High. Still later, another Marshall

3

lawsuit attacked segregation in the city public library system.

Still Battling

In 1950, in the appeal of *Sweatt v. Painter*,[4] Houston and Marshall won again in the federal Circuit Court, with a complaint that eventually forced establishment of a law school at Houston's historically Black Texas Southern University to make "Separate but Equal" look more "equal" for Blacks. Back in Baltimore, even after the Supreme Court had overturned the *Plessy* ruling with its 1954 decision in *Brown v. Board of Education*, it took another series of lawsuits by the late Juanita Mitchell, an NAACP lawyer and the wife of the legendary "101st Senator" Clarence M. Mitchell Jr.,[6] to open schoolroom doors and break down the segregation in other public facilities that had so constricted the lives of Thurgood Marshall and other Blacks in Maryland.

In recognition of that unruly past, in 1973 the NAACP Legal Defense and Education Fund included Maryland as a principal offender in a lawsuit against the federal government for permitting states to continue to maintain segregated systems of higher education. The resolution of the lawsuit, *Adams v. Richardson*, required the Office of Civil Rights, a Kennedy-Johnson-era enforcement agency now part of the U.S. Department of Education, to issue a number of demands to Maryland and other states with dual systems. Among other things *Adams* demanded enhancement efforts at state-run historically Black colleges and universities to attract a more diverse student body, more open admission standards for

Blacks applying to "mainstream" graduate and professional schools, and it barred the duplication of the enhanced programs at mainstream white state institutions. The lawsuit also compelled the granting of "other race" scholarships to desegregate historically white and Black state colleges.

Maryland's Massive Resistance

Maryland's resistance to the end of the Jim Crow era was so bitter that it caused widespread resentment. Comparisons with events elsewhere are telling:

• While Maryland slept unchanged, Lyndon Johnson named Robert C. Weaver the first Black Cabinet secretary in 1964, and named journalist Carl Rowan head of USIA, the agency that spread America's message to the world.

• Howard University graduate Edward Brooke was head of Boston's City Finance Commission in 1961, then was elected attorney general of the Commonwealth of Massachusetts before moving on in 1966 to become the first Black elected to the U.S. Senate since the post-Civil War Reconstruction.

• Cleveland, Ohio, made Carl Stokes America's first Black mayor in 1967, and Richard Hatcher made similar news in Gary, Indiana. But Baltimore, Maryland's biggest city, did not get around to electing its first Black mayor, Kurt L. Schmoke, until 1987, 20 years later and more than a decade after Blacks, a quarter of the state's population, had become an outright municipal majority.

It thus should have surprised no one that in 1968, when news arrived that Dr. Martin Luther King had been assassinated in Memphis, the pent-up frustrations of Blacks in Baltimore exploded in one of the worst of the riots that

5

erupted across the country.

Baltimore Sun editorial writer Daniel Berger, then a young reporter honeymooning with his English bride after an overseas posting, recalls standing with her on the roof of the Belvedere Hotel downtown, watching his city burn through the night. In commentaries written in 1968 and later in the 1980s, Berger and others poignantly questioned the logic of the riots: *Why?*

But the answer is that the long-ignored injuries imposed by a bitterly segregated society eventually overwhelm all logic, provoking a rage that boils over in very predictable ways. Harlem Renaissance author Langston Hughes, Marshall's Lincoln classmate, implied as much in a famous poem, more than a decade before the outburst. Hughes asked, even more plaintively, "*What happens to a dream deferred?*" The author, a consummate *raconteur* and human observer, asked presciently whether the answer would be a slow descent into despair, or perhaps, "*does it explode?*" Many commentators remembered that poem as smoke and embers from the 1960s "Riot Seasons" blanketed cities across the nation.

The Steep Odds Slaughter Overcame

The social and economic dreams of Blacks continued to be deferred in Maryland, even after the riots. Even in academia, the refusal to grant equal status to Blacks was apparent. For instance, at historically Black Morgan State University, state lawmakers' hostility was clearly demonstrated when they eviscerated the university's budget, beginning a pattern of historic underfunding in the 1970s that continued until the late 1980s. Change came only when Morgan scholars took matters into their own hands. University researchers badly embarrassed the gubernatorial administration of former Baltimore Mayor William Donald Schafer with a major report exposing the disparities between Morgan's funding and the moneys allocated to majority-white state institutions, and the governor himself was put on the defensive on campus, confronted by angry student demonstrators when he arrived to make a speech dedicating its then-new Clarence M. Mitchell School of Engineering Building.

Morgan's president, Earl S. Richardson, had already begun to deploy another strategy to good effect: Going after major grants from federal agencies -- such as the U.S. Department of Education, National Science Foundation, and the National Aeronautics & Space Administration -- to erect all-new facilities. State support was then guaranteed by the federal requirements for so-called matching funds.

Thus, at the University of Maryland at College Park, Dr. Slaughter, a highly regarded scientist and a leader in every endeavor he'd ever begun, must have seemed a man from another planet when he arrived from the National Science Foundation in 1982.

Getting there may have looked easy from afar, but it could not have been. American legal segregation had officially ended in 1954 with the Supreme Court's ruling in *Brown v. Board of Education of Topeka, Kansas*, the city where Dr. Slaughter grew up. But the social mores of segregation still prevailed, nowhere more prevalently than in higher education. Many whites considered Blacks constitutionally incapable of the highest levels of achievement, despite the record of Yale physicist Dr. Edward Alexander Bouchet and

7

Tuskegee's better-known "chemurgist," George Washington Carver. That made Dr. Slaughter's accession to the Maryland chancellor's office even more remarkable, a high point in a career that had consistently overturned preconceived notions of inexplicable deficiencies in Blacks' intelligence.

How Dare *He?*

Dr. Slaughter, a product of Topeka schools still segregated during the 1940s, had met stunned laughter when he told high school counselors he wanted to be an engineer. The counselors had ever seen a Black engineer, and they tried to steer the young Black man into vocational education courses.

Perhaps they had never heard of Dr. Bouchet, who became the first Black science doctorate holder when he finished his physics Ph.D. at Yale University in 1876, or they had forgotten the Scottish-trained engineer Elijah McCoy, who invented a lubricating system that made it practical for steam-powered railroad engines to go long distances without dismantling for maintenance, and for the booming factories of the Industrial Northeast to run non-stop. Imitators abounded in McCoy's time, but it is instructive to recall that those seeking quality products years later looked for "the Real McCoy" while managing to ignore the *real* McCoy behind the sobriquet.

Unwelcome in the Lab

Dr. Bouchet, a victim of the same segregationist obstacles that littered the career path of the young John Slaughter three generations later, gave up his quest to become a career scientist. Instead, he went to Philadelphia to head the Institute for Colored Youth – now Cheyney University of

8

Pennsylvania – and began a lifelong career as an educator.

The young John Slaughter went on to a distinguished career as an educator, too. But first he had to overcome the skepticism of his teachers and counselors and get to engineering school, three-quarters of a century after Dr. Bouchet, generations after Elijah McCoy and the two "Black Edisons," Granville T. Woods and Garrett Augustus Morgan, proved that Blacks had the brains. Slaughter graduated from Kansas State University in 1956, two years after Marshall's compelling endgame in *Brown v. Board of Education* brought a successful conclusion to Dean Houston's decades-long campaign to rip out the legal underpinnings of race discrimination in America.

The *Brown* decision electrified Blacks everywhere – including a young John Slaughter – setting the stage for a national uprising waged in the streets, in university classrooms, government offices and corporate workplaces, that reshaped every facet of American life in the 20th Century.

Dr. King, who began the successful Montgomery Bus Boycott, just one year after *Brown*, then proceeded to shake up the nation with his speeches, his book, "Stride toward Freedom," and his clarion call of leadership in the decades-long street fight against the mores of segregation. That fight won him the Nobel Peace Prize, but ultimately led to his death at the hands of a gunman on a Memphis motel balcony.

Science Still Had Obstacles, Too

There were many kinds of struggle in the battle to open up a society as closed as America was to Blacks. Dr. Slaughter, following in the steps of such pioneers as the early 20th-

Century ocean biologist Ernest Everett Just[7], biophysicist and nuclear researcher Herman Branson and the brilliant chemist Percy Julian, fought his battles in the pristine confines of the research laboratory. Even there, logic and the laws of nature, ostensibly supreme, still too often were subverted by prejudice. His campaign, waged without marching feet or blaring bullhorns, was nonetheless essential: it put flesh on the bare bones of legal equality in the science and technology job market for Blacks climbing out of the deep well of social disadvantage in an economy proclaiming openness to all.

Beginning as an electronics engineer for General Dynamics, a company that made everything from supersonic airplanes to nuclear submarines, the young John Slaughter moved steadily up the ranks, crossing the lines from industry to government to academia and back again.

But not without painful battles. As Bonnie Winston reported in a 1987 *US Black Engineer* story, in 1960 when Slaughter joined the Naval Ocean Systems Center in San Diego, Calif., he was refused a supervisory position because whites would be "uncomfortable."

Two years later Slaughter was running a department with 250 researchers, a team that included the man hired for the supervisory post that had been denied to Slaughter.

Multi-Tasking, from the Beginning

Slaughter simultaneously stood duty as director of the Applied Physics Laboratory at the University of Washington, pushing the curve all the way. His scientific team developed some of the early theory for computer control systems in naval weapons systems. Another Slaughter-led initiative delved into underwater acoustics research and applications that had critical implications in the decades-long confrontation between U.S. naval forces and submarines from the Communist-led Soviet Union.

Down the Pacific Coast at the University of California, he completed studies for his master's and doctor of philosophy degrees in 1971. Six years later Dr. Slaughter, then one of only three Blacks elected to the prestigious, 1,100-member National Academy of Engineering, moved east to Washington, as assistant director of the National Science Foundation. In 1979, President Carter named him director.

Lighting Up those Shadows

A look at what went before shows how significant that appointment was. Joe Louis, following the turn-of-the-century precedent set by the great Jack Johnson, K.O.'ed the German Max Schmeling during the 1930s. Jackie Robinson desegregated big-league baseball in 1947. Althea Gibson upended the tennis world in the mid-1950s, defeating all comers at Wimbledon twice. Wilt Chamberlain reinvented basketball in the 1950s and 60s, and a long line of Blacks had since overwhelmed all claims of inferiority on athletic fields.

But recognition of intellectual capacity was still a stopping point. Pioneers as far back as Benjamin Banneker had fought to prove that Blacks could match white competitors in science and technology, only to be forgotten after their deaths.

Much of that proof actually came to public light in the dangerous pursuits of warfare, for during the first half of the 20th Century, the military, where technology advance moved most rapidly, also was one of the few arenas in which Black

11

achievements could catch the public eye.

Warriors as Tech Pioneers

Eugene Bullard, "the Black Swallow" of the *Lafayette Escadrille* in World War I, had journeyed to France as a stowaway early in the 20th Century to escape the segregation that later constricted the world of the young John Slaughter. Bullard joined the French Foreign Legion to fight *"les Boche,"* and became a hero as a soldier and as a pilot. Wounded on the ground and three times in aerial combat, decorated with the two highest honors France bestows on a soldier – the Cross of War and the Legion of Merit – Bullard was ignored in the United States after the war while other heroes such as Eddie Rickenbacker flew around the country, displaying their skills before thousands of adoring fans.

Lesson Ignored

Bullard, later wounded again battling Germans after the invasion of France in World War II, returned home in 1940, and watched from the sidelines as the Army ramped up its Air Corps. Bullard stood by, dismissed and forgotten while the Tuskegee Airmen battled stereotypes to fight where he had flown before, because American whites still chose not to believe Blacks had the brains or the verve for aerial combat, notwithstanding his own distinguished example. Even Blacks did not know of Bullard's exploits until Eleanor Roosevelt wrote about him in mid-20th Century newspaper columns.

Bessie Coleman, a Chicago manicurist determined to fly during the Roaring Twenties, had to go to France to obtain her pilot's license. After her death in a tragic air accident in

1927, the Chicago School aviators inspired by her courage campaigned tirelessly for the integration of the new Army Air Corps, meeting steely silence from official Washington.

Flying in the Face of Hatred

Thanks to First Lady Eleanor Roosevelt's intervention – and the strident championing of Black newspapers led by the Baltimore *Afro-American* and the *Pittsburgh Courier* – the Tuskegee flyers won their wings in 1942, along with a now-forgotten Black Civil Air Patrol lieutenant named Willa Brown, who had earned her civilian license in 1937, the year Amelia Earhart disappeared into the Pacific.

The Tuskegee Airmen, defying all obstacles, wrote a new chapter in the annals of air combat over Europe while "Patton's Panthers" – the 761st Tank Battalion – were on the ground, charging through the bloodied fields of France and Belgium in iron chariots to show that the technological savvy and courage of their comrades in the sky was no fluke, despite the doubts even Gen. Patton had privately expressed.

'Brothers' Who were Overlooked

Themselves mostly forgotten today, the 761st spearheaded the breakthrough at Bastogne memorialized in the hit TV miniseries "Band of Brothers,"[9] although they managed to get left out of that story, too. It took half a century after the war, when many of the Black World War II veterans had gone to their graves, before a sweeping Army review of Blacks' wartime record, led by researchers at historically Black Shaw University, could see to it that the heroism and sacrifice of "Patton's Panthers" and their Black brothers in arms, some

13

long dead, were recognized with appropriate decorations.

Segregation Even in the Labs

Despite that wartime heroism, the segregation in federal offices put in place by Woodrow Wilson a generation earlier was still in force. Thus, at the beginning of the Space Race the National Advisory Committee for Aeronautics, forerunner of NASA, launched into the competition to beat Soviet Russia to the Moon with a segregated workforce. NACA also had an ace: Kathryn Johnson, beneficiary of a scholarship to all-Black West Virginia State College, arranged by President Franklin Delano Roosevelt in response to her teenaged plea. Johnson joined her Black colleague Sally Richmond in a hurriedly assembled, off-the-books spaceflight team after President John F. Kennedy said in a famous speech that Americans would be first to go to the Moon.

There initially was no budget for the spaceflight initiative, so NACA leaders simply created a "Skunk Works": they drafted the best specialists from many departments to build a team that worked in the bureaucratic dark make it happen. [10]

Johnson, one of the very best mathematicians, calculated the orbits for Alan Sheppard's and Virgil "Gus" Grissom's first sub-orbital flights as well as John Glenn's historic first American orbit of the Earth, and worked under Orbital Computation Team leader Richmond's direction to put Neal Armstrong on the Moon.

Central players in a drama watched by the whole world, Johnson, Richmond, and another Black colleague, Robert Shurney, who designed the "Vomit Comet" zero-gravity training flights, nevertheless worked in obscurity. The public face of science and technology advance in America was expressly and exclusively white.

So what if a Baker's Dozen of Black scientists had joined the Manhattan Project, playing key roles in ushering in the Atomic Age? So what if NACA's own Linwood Wright had just revolutionized jet engine design with the super-efficient turbofan he and his co-developer invented to make air travel cheaper, and therefore practical for average Americans to join the "Jet Set"? So what if Blacks had played key roles in every area of American scientific and technological advance since Benjamin Banneker?

Never mind George Washington Carver. Blacks were not to be seen or heard, no matter how vital their contributions, and even Blacks who should have known better went without learning about Black professionals' huge contributions to mankind's greatest exploits.

Thus Kathryn Johnson, a member of the Alpha Kappa Alpha sorority, stood silent, unknown and unrecognized at the back of the crowd at a national gathering while her sorors cheered before a TV set one night in 1969, watching Neal Armstrong step off the spaceship Eagle's ladder and walk into history treading on the Moon.[11]

Stepping Out in Front
That began to change when John Slaughter stepped up to the leadership of the major federal agency driving American science, first as assistant director in 1977, and then, three years later, the first-ever Black director. It's hard to ignore Black intellectual capacity when the Black intellectual in question is head of the agency providing funding for

15

university and private corporation research, support for science education from public schools through college and post-graduate school, and initiatives to boost the capabilities of research-dependent enterprises across the country.

Clearly, Dr. Slaughter was not a figurehead. Like his protean older contemporary, Lincoln Hawkins, whose 147 patents at AT&T Bell Laboratories made him the first Black elected to the National Academy of Engineering, Dr. Slaughter became a mentor and driving force for promotion of Blacks and other minorities in the research establishment. The legion of people he helped during his climb to the top of American science stood up and cheered when, after he moved on to be chancellor of the University of Maryland at College Park, *US Black Engineer* magazine named Dr. Slaughter the first Black Engineer of the Year in 1987.

Critical Achievements

Dr. Slaughter, a Fellow of the American Association for the Advancement of Science, had served on the Committee on Minorities in Engineering for the National Academy of Engineering. In 1977, he had served as editor of the *International Journal of Computers and Electrical Engineering*, and he still chairs the Action Forum on Engineering Workforce Diversity. He's also a Fellow of the American Academy of Arts and Sciences and the Institute of Electrical and Electronics Engineers, and in 1993 the American Society for Engineering Education inducted him into its Hall of Fame.

But that's getting ahead of the story. Dr. Slaughter left Maryland during the late 1980s to lead Occidental College.

Still More Giant Steps

After a long, distinguished tenure at Occidental College, Dr. Slaughter moved back East to in 2003 to take over as president and CEO of the National Action Council on Minorities in Engineering, founded three decades ago out of a National Academy of Engineering inquiry Dr. Slaughter had led, to address the low status and small numbers of Blacks, Latinos and Native Americans in the engineering profession. A 2003 commemorative banquet at New York's Waldorf Astoria Hotel raised new moneys for NACME, which reported that it had spent more than $100 million to boost some 18,000 new minority entrants into the technology workforce, paying their college costs and sponsoring internships to prepare them, dramatically changing the face of engineering.

Triple Threats

Today, American industry faces the triple whammy of an aging workforce, steep shortfalls in federal financing for research in physical and mathematical sciences and engineering, and a steady decline in interest in engineering careers among the young white males who traditionally have filled out engineering class lists. Thus NACME's role in providing scholarship aid to minority degree candidates is ever more critical. An April 30, 2005 *New York Times* column by Joseph E. Stiglitz, a Nobel Prize-winning economist at Columbia University, sketched out reasons that should ring alarm bells across the country:

1. Asian countries, especially China and India, produce eight times as many B.S. degrees in engineering as the United States. To understand the power of his point, note that during

the late 1980s the U.S. was producing 90,000 bachelor's degree engineers a year; during the first part of this decade, the U.S. struggled to produce 63,000 engineers a year.

2. The share of foreign-born Ph.D.s in the U.S. science and engineering labor force has risen to 38 percent. As other observers have shown, what's scary about this is that the rapidly improving economic climate overseas is making it harder and harder to recruit and keep foreign professionals in the United States. And among those who do come, many now return to their home countries, taking with them the knowledge of America's manufacturing skills, its marketing style and the financial potential of markets in which their own products can be sold at very competitive rates.

3. Federal research funding in math, physical science and engineering has declined 37 percent as a share of Gross Domestic Product since 1970. Other countries, notably China, India and Japan, are pouring money into state-of-the-art research centers while the United States, flush with success after persuading most of the nations of the world to rewrite their patent, copyright and trademark laws to work the way they do here, is sitting on its laurels.

Add to that the signing of 13 agreements at a 2005 summit between the prime ministers of India and China, at which the Chinese prime minister proposed a marriage of India's software expertise with China's burgeoning manufacturing prowess to take over world leadership in information technology from – *ahem* – the United States. Coming after the sale of IBM's personal computer business to state-owned Chinese company Lenovo, it was clear the Chinese leader was not engaged in puffery, but was announcing a serious drive to dominate an industry Americans think of as their very own. Americans, long accustomed to world leadership in science and technology, would do well to take note.

John Brooks Slaughter, the original Black Engineer of the Year, thus works at a critical nexus in the industry-government-higher education partnership. His organization, NACME, is accelerating scholarship spending at a time when real dollars of federal assistance for minority college students are falling. In the 2004-2005 academic year, NACME recorded a 40-percent increase in scholarships, to 733 students, 36.6 percent of whom are women. Latinos increased 9 percentage points, to 44 percent of the total, while Blacks represent 49 percent and Native Americans 3 percent.

NACME at the Crux

But NACME is not only a scholarship agency. It also is a prodigious producer of research analyses on the state of the technology workforce and the situation of minorities in industrial America, serving as sounding board and advocate for initiatives to increase the share of minorities in the workgroups and career tracks responsible for some 50 percent of the country's economic growth. Its new Research Council, composed of respected leaders in engineering, is designed to maintain and strengthen NACME's role as a provider of information on minority performance in math and science at the secondary school level and on their success in university-level engineering programs.

Thus, Dr. Slaughter has come full circle. From a young black man battling segregation to fulfill his own engineering destiny, he now is an elder statesman, providing a legacy to help many other young minority men and women fulfill their own. Because of his drive NACME continues to be the agency at the crux.

Supplemental Notes to Chapter One

1. See also "NACME Symposium Highlights Crisis in Science, Technology, Engineering and Math (STEM) Education," at www.nacme.org.

2. Maryland, a slave-holding state before the Civil War, was occupied by Union troops after rioting mobs tried to block soldiers marching from Camden Station next to the Inner Harbor to another rail line a mile away, on their way to fight the war. Ultimately, Baltimore's mayor was arrested by Union troops, as were anti-Union members of the state General Assembly and other officers.

See also

Browne, Gary Lawson. *Baltimore in the Civil War*. (Baltimore, MD: University of   Maryland   Baltimore   County,   198-);

Callum, Agnes Kane. *9th Regiment United States Colored Troops: Volunteers of Maryland, Civil War, 1863-1866*. (Baltimore, MD: Mullac Publishers, 1999);

Cottom, Robert I. and Mary Ellen Hayward. *Maryland in the Civil War: A House Divided*. (Baltimore, MD: Maryland Historical Society: distributed by Johns   Hopkins   University   Press,   1994);

Denton, Lawrence M. *A southern star for Maryland: Maryland and the Secession Crisis, 1860-1861*. (Baltimore, MD: Publishing Concepts, 1995);

Sheads, Scott S. and Daniel Carroll Toomey. *Baltimore during the Civil War*. (Linthicum, MD: Toomey Press, 1997).

3. Another sorry chapter was the state's attempt to re-enslave the children of emancipated Blacks after the close of the Civil War. A *habeas corpus* battle between the Baltimore Circuit Court and the Orphan's Court, extensively covered in news stories in *The Baltimore Sun* archives, revealed the Apprenticeship law passed after the war to be an almost word-for-word copy of the antebellum enslavement act. It required the children of freed men and women to provide free labor for the property owners who had held their parents in bondage, under the baldly ridiculous claim of unpaid debts for the care and feeding of those formerly enslaved. Noting that the state had enacted a new constitution after the war expressly prohibiting slavery, the Circuit Court voided the law.

4. (Page 2.) See *Murray v. Maryland*, 169 Maryland 478 (1937).

5. See also *Plessy v. Ferguson*, 163 US 537 (1896).

6. *Sweatt v. Painter*, 339 US 629 (1950)

7. See *Brown v. Board of Education of Topeka*, 347 US 483 (1954)

8. See Brown, Luther, The New Crisis, "Clarence Mitchell Jr.: The 101st U.S. Senator," December 1998

9. *Adams v. Richardson*, 480 F.2d 1159, 1164 (DC Cir. 1973)

10. (Page 3.) See Hughes, Langston, *Montage of a Dream Deferred* (1951)

11. (Page 6.) See *www.georgiaencyclopedia.org/nge/Article.jsp* See also Lloyd, Craig,

Free Man in Paris: Eugene Bullard, a Black Expatriate in Jazz-Age Paris. University of Georgia Press, 217 pages.

12. (Page 15) Few young Black women know about Willa Beatrice Brown (1906-1992) today, but many could take counsel from her performance.

Beginning as a schoolteacher in Gary, Indiana, and later a social worker in Chicago, Brown became one of two Black women in a segregated flight-training class, then became the first woman of color to earn a commercial pilot's license. Brown, who also was at one time the only woman in America to be certified as a commercial aviation mechanic, married her instructor, Cornelius Coffey, and together they ran the Coffey School of Aeronautics at Chicago's Harlem Airport, teaching other Blacks to fly. With her husband and Enoch P. Waters, Brown formed the National Airmen's Association of America in 1939, with the express goal of getting Blacks into the Army Air Corps. As national secretary and president of the Chicago branch, Brown lobbied for integration of the Air Corps and for Black inclusion in the Civilian Pilot Training Program, instituted to prepare U.S. airmen for service in the war brewing in Europe. Brown, who became the first Black woman commissioned as a military pilot as a Civil Air Patrol lieutenant, also saw her Coffey School chosen as a preliminary training center for the Black Air Corps groups being trained at Tuskegee, Alabama. She became Civilian Pilot Training Program coordinator for Chicago, and eventually became war-training service coordinator for the Civil Aeronautics Authority. Brown later was a member of the Federal Aviation Administration's Women's Advisory Board. See *www.aeromuseum.org/History /IlAveHist/Willa* for an excellent report on her.

13. See Kareem Adbul-Jabbar and Anthony Walton, *Brothers in Arms: The Epic Story of the 761st Tank Battalion, WWII's Forgotten Heroes*. Broadway Books, New York. 302 pages. (2004).

See also Sasser, Charles W., *Patton's Panthers: The African-American 761st Tank Battalion in World War II*. Pocket Books, New York (2004) 354 pages.

14. (Page 7.) Winston, Bonnie, Johnson interview, *US Black Engineer*, Fall 1996.

Chapter 2

Erroll Davis Climbs to the Top in Power
Following in Lewis Latimer's Footsteps

Years ago Eileen Shanahan, then a *New York Times* financial reporter, rushed breathlessly into a journalists' skull session at the University of Arizona.[1] Shanahan had arrived in Tucson fresh from interviewing a young *Fortune* 500 top executive, and the surprising answer to how the man so quickly arrived at the CEO's chair was intriguing. It went something like this:

"I went to the Wharton School for my MBA," the man said. "When I was about to graduate, I had an exit interview with the dean, and he asked me how I'd enjoyed Wharton.

"I said I liked it a lot, but I hadn't learned what I came to learn: How to be a CEO.

"The dean chuckled and said, 'Oh, you can do that in a few steps. Here's what you do:

'1. After you graduate, take your first job – anywhere – in, say, manufacturing. Learn manufacturing. Quit.

'2. Take the next job – anywhere – in sales. Stay long enough to learn sales well. Quit.

'3. This last job is important. Go to work in finance, for a

23

company that is not tottering, but will face serious challenges down the line, say, in a few years.

'4. When the challenges become apparent, and the board of directors is casting about, looking for a new leader who knows the whole picture – manufacturing, sales and finance – step forward. You're ready.'

"So that's what I did," the executive told Shanahan. "And here I am."

Davis Followed Similar Steps

Careful observers might use Shanahan's template in looking over the career of Erroll B. Davis, Jr., who rose to be chairman and Chief Executive Officer of Madison, Wisconsin-based Alliant Energy before moving on to another top job as Chancellor of the Georgia State University System. Davis, a B.S. degree-holder in electrical engineering from Carnegie Mellon University in his native Pittsburgh, won an IBM Fellowship to complete his MBA studies at the University of Chicago in 1967 before launching a career that made him the highest-ranking Black American executive in the utility business. How he got there, treading over the trail of the historic Lewis Latimer, is an interesting story on its own.

Davis, like most young Blacks during the 1960s, had a military obligation to complete. After his Carnegie Mellon studies, he served at an Army Tank Automotive Command maintenance facility in Warren, Michigan from 1967 to 1969. He jokes that the Army sent him there because of his poor eyesight, and there could be truth in that. There also could be happenstance. The Vietnam conflict dragged on during the late 1960s, but men and women in uniform all knew that

24

getting sent off to fight in Southeast Asia could sometimes be just the luck of the draw. Davis spent his time Stateside, learning how to manage a multi-million-dollar technology organization and digging into what it took to keep his complex hardware running at optimal levels.

The Next Step: Corporate Life 101

He didn't go far from his Michigan posting when he mustered out. After fulfilling his ROTC active-duty obligation, Davis signed on with Ford Motor Co., an outfit whose reputation for opening up career opportunities for minorities goes all the way back to Henry Ford's leadership in hiring Black factory hands during the 1920s and 1930s, at a time when other industrialists – and the nascent manufacturing unions – were working hard to keep them out.

"Learn finance"? Davis did, in spades. But clocking four years in the Finance Department of a comprehensive, integrated manufacturing enterprise like Ford Motor Co. teaches more than how to count paper clips, and Davis paid close attention to what it takes to keep the bottom line black in the making of products sold to millions of consumers.

Davis left for a slightly longer stint at Xerox Corp., another integrated manufacturer. Again, he served on the finance staff, moving up as he learned what it takes to keep Xerox humming in a sales environment populated by hard-nosed business users and tough offshore competitors. Xerox faced daunting challenges as Asian and European manufacturers poured high-quality products into its core American market during the 1970s, but by the mid-'80s had beaten back its major competition, bringing to market office machines that streamlined business practices all over the world.

It is significant that the business model for producers of large, expensive products such as Xerox office equipment involves long-term leasing. To make that work, suppliers must provide efficient maintenance of equipment and affordable resupply of consumable items, things that are as important to profits as turnkey sales of production gear.

To stay successful, a Xerox must maintain a corps of technical professionals among its support staff as well as salespeople, marketing professionals, scientists and product developers in its other operating arms, and it must manage relationships with a far-flung network of suppliers as well as key customers. And a Xerox financial manager must develop a comprehensive understanding of operational priorities: R&D, its costs and benefits; manufacturing effort and the costs and benefits of working the supply chain; marketing initiatives; sales activity; leasing and maintenance programs. Finance officers in a manufacturing enterprise also must keep a close watch on the flow of widgets, washers and solid-state devices that go into the final products.

'Learn Manufacturing' Wherever You Are

That is, a finance officer had better learn as much as he can about manufacturing. Xerox, like other manufacturing giants, competes on factory efficiency as much as it does on product capabilities and quality, marketing and sales effectiveness. It is battling to stem a flow of constantly improving products from companies here and overseas, seeking to capture big shares of the office equipment market, on its home turf in the biggest economy in the world.

Latimer Went Before Him

More than a century earlier, Lewis Latimer had met such challenges as a major contributor to the success of the Edison Electric Co., after his time building the telephone system with Alexander Graham Bell. It's almost forgotten today, but Latimer was the chief engineer who built and managed the central-office power stations that changed the way of life at the end of the 19th Century. Electric light was exciting, but to win in the market the Edison Co. had to produce electric power efficiently as well as find economies of scale in the building of electricity grids that would let it compete on price as well as convenience with municipal gaslight suppliers providing illumination power to cities like New York. Those gaslight suppliers had an installed infrastructure of pipes and pumping stations across the country, delivering "coal gas" to homes, factories and office buildings everywhere. Latimer and Edison still had to install their wired infrastructure to reach those customers, at competitive rates.

Thus Latimer, who designed the plants, wrote the operating and maintenance manuals and directed the construction of electric power systems for New York, Philadelphia, Baltimore, Toronto and London, gained a fair amount of financial savvy as he worked his technological magic across the globe. Similarly, Erroll Davis, the engineer-businessman, learned much about the management of technology enterprises while working in finance.

Joining Latimer's Club

Davis signed on at the Wisconsin Power & Light Company in

1978 as vice president of finance, joining his contemporary Cordell Reed at Chicago's Commonwealth Edison in a tiny class of Black utility executives. Reed, a South Side public housing alumnus who was only the third Black American to complete the mechanical engineering major at the University of Illinois-Urbana, had by 1975 become an expert in the management of electric power grids, and his utility had a heavy commitment to nuclear power. Reed was in 1978 department head for nuclear power, and because of his expertise and high visibility, had become a public spokesman for nuclear energy. Now retired, Reed is a widely respected member of the National Academy of Engineering.

Just up the road in Madison, Wisconsin, Erroll Davis was racing ahead to the front rank, but there were other notable Black achievers also moving the curve in utilities.

Davis joined WP&L the same year a young Anthony James (2004 *Black Engineer of the Year*) signed on as a safety and health supervisor at Georgia Power, adding still another to the nation's small but growing corps of Black utility managers. A few years later in 1984, Widener University electrical engineering graduate George A. Williams began his career at the Philadelphia Electric Company, adding his considerable talents to the Black utility executives' cadre.

Living in 'Turbulent Times'

Unlike the Northern-born Davis, Reed and Williams, Anthony James grew up in the South, in Lake Alfred, Florida, on what he called "literally and figuratively on the wrong side of the tracks" from the better-known Winter Haven, in central Florida. James grew up in a poor and under-served farm

28

community, during what his employer the Southern Company called "frightening and unpredictable" times of demonstrations, boycotts, lawsuits, occasional mob violence, and threats of even worse.

Recall the movie "Rosewood," about the real-life burning of a Black town by whites angered over the business success and independence of Blacks in rural Florida a generation before James' youth, or the bombing of "Black Wall Street" in Tulsa, Oklahoma, in 1929, and the phrase "frightening and unpredictable" comes into sharp focus. James also faced additional hardships on the economic front.

He began working the fields as a youth, picking oranges and loading watermelons for shipment North. Then James' father lost an arm in an auto accident, straining the family fortunes even more. The young James offered to quit school to work full-time, but his family would not hear of it. So James worked part-time and during summers, worked two day jobs. In one, he dug laboratory samples for the U.S. Department of Agriculture; in the other, he unloaded 50-pound cargo bags from a railroad boxcar. In the evenings, he found other work. He washed dishes and mopped floors in restaurants, and even found time to bag groceries at a local supermarket.

Times became more unpredictable when a desegregation order moved James from his all-Black high school to a formerly all-white school, whose population was unprepared for integration. As the Southern Company documents accompanying James' nomination for Black Engineer of the Year put it, James was "luckier than many of his classmates, because he was encircled with support of his caring parents, a benevolent scoutmaster, and a charitable, compassionate

29

community." James graduated with honors from Winter Haven High, and moved on to community college.

Seeing a New World

After finishing his associate's degree, James enrolled in electrical engineering at the University of South Florida. A cooperative education assignment at NASA's Kennedy Space Center opened up a new world to the former farm laborer, exposing him to cutting-edge technologies such as Doppler radar, minicomputers and then-new laser printers. Unlike the engineer-manager and bean counter Erroll Davis, James made his climb in the utility industry strictly as a hands-on technology professional.

In 1973, degree in hand, James first joined Procter & Gamble Co. as a production supervisor at an Albany, Georgia, plant whose staff was assembled as an experiment in integration. *"Learn manufacturing,"* the Wharton dean told a young CEO-to-be. But along with his expertise in manufacturing, James had much to learn about managing in an environment built for change. That P&G plant had minorities working in titles and places where no Black managers and supervisors had ever been seen. Gaining skills in a program overseen by none other than Ron Brown -- who later became U.S. Commerce secretary -- and the renowned psychologist Price Cobb, James also gained confidence. So much confidence that James rose through the ranks faster than anyone in the history of P&G's Paper Products Division: Six promotions in a five-year period.

Then, with those five years of experience behind him – and intending to stay in the South rather than move across the country, as he would have to do if he remained with Procter & Gamble – James left to join the Georgia Power Co., a division of one of America's largest producers of electric power, the Southern Company.

Progress at Southern Co.

Quickly, James began to show that his quick climb at P&G was no fluke. James became a plant maintenance superintendent, then assistant manager of a power plant. One he got the attention of Southern Company's top managers, James moved into the jobs that prepare managers to be top executives. His first staff job was as employee benefits manager. Then James won assignment as assistant to the senior vice president of wholesale power marketing – "*Learn sales,*" the Wharton dean said – and that job gave him a broader view of the business. That prepared James for bigger posts, and he moved on to plant manager for two production facilities: the Arkwright Plant and Plant Scherer, where James began his utility career in 1978.

James continued his rapid progress. He won appointment to vice president for power generation and senior production officer for Savannah Electric and became central cluster manager for Georgia Power. Now James was managing five major generating facilities, including the nation's largest fossil-fueled plant and a combustion-turbine "peaking" plant inside the perimeter of a major defense facility. When he was named Black Engineer of the Year in 2004, James, the first Black American to reach plant manager status in the Southern Co., was Chief Executive Officer of Savannah Power, the first Black to hold such a post in his company and

31

in his adopted city. After that James was promoted still higher, to Corporate Vice President, with sales, manufacturing and finance all under his thumb.

Entergy's Traveler

Another Northerner was making a similar climb. George A. Williams began his career two decades ago at Philadelphia Electric Co.'s Limerick Nuclear Generating Station, near Norristown, Pa. Williams, armed with his Widener University electrical engineering degree, went to work as a nuclear reactor operator, and quickly qualified as a senior reactor operator and a shift technical advisor in an enterprise in which every decision is critical, every logbook closely read by federal and state regulators, as well as plant supervisors.

The U.S. Navy's nuclear propulsion programs supply many of the operators who run nuclear plants in the utility industry, a fact little known outside the industry. All of those operators – former enlisted personnel as well as officers – are graduates of extensive military training schools and have years of hands-on experience running nuclear powerplants in attack and ballistic missile submarines and in surface craft such as aircraft carriers and guided missile cruisers.

A Classic 'Quick Study'

Civilians such as Williams, coming in from the more generalized collegiate educational programs, have to get quickly up to speed in such an environment or be shown the door. Williams learned fast, and began to move around, taking his hard-won skills with him. Other utilities noticed.

From 1999 to 2001, Williams oversaw plant operations of

seven generating stations as vice president of operational support for Carolina Power & Light. Entergy Corporation, which eventually lured Williams away, says that while at Carolina Power, Williams became the leader in efforts to integrate fossil generating organizations when Carolina Power & Light merged with the Florida Progress Corporation. To accomplish that job, Williams, who had learned the manufacturing end of electric-power production and become more than conversant with how sales affected his operations, also had to follow the Wharton dean's admonition to *"Learn finance,"* too.

Williams, holder of a master's degree from St. Joseph's University and a graduate of executive training at the Wharton School and Harvard University's program for senior executives, returned to Pennsylvania to be general manager of nuclear assurance at Pennsylvania Power & Light's dual-unit Susquehanna nuclear station in Berwick, Pa., for a short stint before heading to Jackson, Miss., to join Entergy Corp. There, at the nation's third-largest supplier of electrical power, Williams became vice president of operations support for Entergy Nuclear's South Region. The South Region provides centralized services for five nuclear units in Arkansas, Louisiana and Mississippi.

Taking a rotational assignment, Williams became vice president for nuclear operations for Entergy's Grand Gulf Station, on the Mississippi River. Expect to hear more from Williams, whose utility, the principal power provider for New Orleans and Gulf Coast communities in Mississippi and Texas, was hard-hit by Hurricanes Katrina and Rita.

Man in a Hurry

Meanwhile, continuing his career up North, Davis showed himself to be a man in a hurry. As Anthony James was climbing the ranks in Georgia, the military veteran Davis was staging a double assault in his adopted state of Wisconsin. Davis, a firm believer in community service, was making his way up the leadership ladder in community activities as he charted a careful charge up the corporate ranks.

On arriving in Madison, he volunteered in local United Way activities and the Madison Art Center, and he and his wife established a college scholarship fund for Black students. *"Learning finance"* could be accomplished in the non-profit world as well as in the for-profit business environment, along with the invaluable training in human resource management gained in the less hierarchical, not-for-profit world.

By 1987, when Davis rose from executive vice president to president of WP&L – the nation's only Black leader of a publicly held company – he also had reached the rank of chairman of the United Way of Dane County, Wis. In addition, he sat on the board of directors of the Wisconsin Manufacturers and Commerce organization, was a member of the Madison Police and Fire Commission, a director of the Madison Capital Corp. and Madison Development Corp., and president of the Madison Urban League Board of Directors.

Shining at the Top

Black Enterprise magazine took notice: Davis now was the highest ranking Black in any business field. Asked about his new high status by a local Madison newspaper reporter, Davis said he was proud to be Black, but he didn't dwell on race. He had much to do and to learn, to be successful. Or, as he put it, "I could also be the first Black president to be fired."

Davis, now running all parts of the utility's operations, stepped into the top job at a time when then-CEO James R. Underkofler and the board of directors were pushing a complete restructuring of the corporation. Their plan, now complete, created a holding company for utility operations and subsidiary corporations, to pursue new opportunities in such businesses as landfill development and communications.

They had to move fast. WPL Holdings, as it became known, faced growing competition from other gas and electric suppliers, as energy deregulation opened doors to non-utility generators and the selling of excess power from private corporate systems into the public net. Large customers were beginning to buy natural gas directly from its producers, using utilities such as WPL only to transport the gas through their pipelines. *"Learn sales"?* You bet.

Running on the Big Dogs' Track

In other words, WPL, a company employing 2,600 workers supplying power and natural gas to customers spread over a 16,000-mile part of southern Wisconsin, faced large challenges. Revenues had slipped from $170.2 million in the first quarter of 1986 to $157.4 million, only partially because of an unusually warm winter. In Eileen Shanahan's terms, Davis was ready.

Davis was a key player in WPL's transition to a holding company, and then he played even bigger roles in WPL's merger with several other utilities to become the main electric power and gas supplier for southern Wisconsin and parts of Iowa, Illinois, and Minnesota. He was ready for his move up to the last rung of the corporate ladder. As the last decade of the 20th Century closed, Davis stepped up to it.

In 2000, Davis was named Chairman and Chief Executive of Alliant Energy, a *Fortune* 1000 company with 8,500 employees across the country and abroad. Alliant, traded on the New York Stock Exchange under the ticker symbol LNT, had operating revenues of $3.1 billion in 2003, and total assets of more than $7.7 billion. It serves more than 1.4 million customers over a 54,000-square-mile territory that contains nearly 10,000 miles of electric transmission lines and 8,000 miles of natural gas mains.

Alliant operates fossil fuel, nuclear and renewable generating facilities across the upper Midwest, producing more than 31 million megawatt-hours of electric power a year.

Serving a Large Community
Remembering his roots, Davis also sits on the Board of Trustees of Carnegie-Mellon University. As a corporate fast-mover he also sits as a director of B.P. Amoco, PPG Industries and Union Pacific.

Large assignments keep coming to those who can handle corporate reins. In June of 2004, Davis became one of only four independent directors on the board of the U.S. Olympic Committee. Davis was appointed to a six-year term on the 11-member board, chaired by former Los Angeles Olympic Organizing Committee head and Baseball Commissioner Peter Ueberroth. The USOC now says the naming of this board and its reduction from 125 members to 11 represented "the final step in the most sweeping governance transition in the history of the U.S. Olympic Committee."

---

1. During the 1980s Shanahan, later a newspaper editor in Pittsburgh, shared duties with the author as Faculty Editors in the Maynard Institute's Editing Program for Minority Journalists, a mid-career skill-training and placement program for Black, Hispanic, Native American and Asian news professionals. It was based at the University of Arizona

Chapter 3

Cochran Swoops Aloft with The Blue Angels

Donnie Cochran always wanted to fly. Growing up on a family farm near Pelham, in southwest Georgia, young Donnie, the fifth of 12 children, paused while working in the fields to watch Navy jets fly over. In that, he was emulating the thoughts of generations of Blacks who watched the new "flying machines" take to America's skies after the First World War. Unlike those early days, however, Cochran did not have to fight to gain entrance to the military flying corps. A generation of agitation, followed by the exploits of the Tuskegee Airmen[1] in the Second World War, had ensured that Black youngsters with the talent and the education could turn their dreams into reality, as Cochran did.

"I started thinking about flying when I was about 12 years old," he told *US Black Engineer* magazine in a 1987 interview. "Out working in the fields, I had the opportunity to see Navy jets flying over, in what I later figured out was low-level navigation training. And as I'm out there, working in the heat of the day, I see those jets screaming by, and I wondered, 'Now which is better, me down here or those jets up there?

Which is more exciting?' It didn't take me long to realize that if I had an opportunity to pursue flying, that was what I was going to do." Cochran kept on flying, all the way to the top as commander of the Blue Angels, the nation's premiere aerial acrobatics team and recognition as the 1989 Black Engineer of the Year.

Looking to the Skies

Cochran looked to the skies for the same epiphany as his older comrade, Walter Davis, who had watched shiny jet planes crease the sky over the furrows he plowed in Winston-Salem, North Carolina, a generation earlier. Davis grew up and joined the Navy, too. Like the young Donnie Cochran, Davis won his wings at the home of naval aviation, Pensacola Naval Air Station. Davis, who joined when one of the "Golden 13"[2] first Black naval officers was still serving, finished in 1959, when few Blacks even knew there were Black naval officers, let alone pilots.[3] Davis qualified in fighter jets and flew two combat tours in Vietnam, joining his Black Air Force and Marine Corps comrades in daily battles against Soviet-built MiGs, Surface-to-Air (SAM) missile sites and "Firecan" radar-guided cannon before returning to the United States to help develop the F-14 Tomcat, which remained the Navy's top air superiority fighter until the end of the 20th Century..

Vice Admiral Davis retired in 1996 as the Navy's "Grey Eagle" – the active-duty flying officer with the oldest wings – after having served as a test pilot and Class Desk Officer for the F-14, and commanding officer of the USS Ranger during the making of the classic movie "Top Gun." As an admiral commanding Navy task forces at sea, Davis also continued in the cockpit – he flew Tomcats off carrier decks, taking catapult shots and making as many "Tailhook" landings as his fighter pilots did – and before retirement was leader of the Space and Nuclear Warfare Command (SpaWar).

Building the Tools

At SpaWar, Vice Admiral Davis led the team designing the satellite constellation, sensors and communications suites that permit Navy commanders to control far-flung task forces around the world. That includes the Indian Ocean, where carrier planes and Tomahawk missile strikes took the fight to the Taliban and Al-Qaida in Afghanistan after 9/11.

With no U.S. air bases close to the land-locked Afghan border and other nations blocking Air Force overflights to get there – and with a forbidding array of mountain walls serving as a physical barrier – the Navy's carrier fleet provided the only means of round-the-clock support for the U.S. Special Forces troops taking the fight to the Taliban. Navy strike planes like the F-14D Tomcat and F/A-18 Hornet were mainstays, supported by Air Force AWACS command and surveillance planes, KC-10 jet tankers and Navy E-2C "Hawkeye" command and control planes.

The Air Force could, did and does fly long-range bombers such as the B-1, B-2 and B-52 over Afghanistan, but these must fly long missions from bases on the American mainland. F-15 Strike Eagles and F-16 Falcons fly from bases in Southern Europe, but only the carrier task forces had staying power during the critical early months of the war. Navy and Marine Corp planes, directed to their targets by ground-based Air Force Special Forces operators, flew over the mountains from the carrier decks, providing the round-the-clock, quick-response air support U.S. troops needed to dispose of the Taliban, and Admiral Davis' SpaWar crew laid the groundwork for that support.

And unlike the actor Tom Cruise, Admiral Davis was an actual graduate of the Top Gun fighter combat school.

But that's another story. Let it suffice to say that, after the Tuskegee Airmen broke the color line in military aviation during World War II, the U.S. Navy's own "Golden 13" first Black naval officers were the pathfinders who opened the way for younger Blacks like Walter Davis and, a generation later, Donnie Cochran, to reach the highest levels of performance in the naval air service.

Inspired to Join

When an older sibling came home to Pelham wearing Naval Reserve Officer Training Corps whites in 1972, just after Donnie Cochran finished high school, he was hooked. Three brothers had gone to historically Black Savannah State College and majored in engineering technology, and when young Donnie saw his oldest brother "wearing this real sharp white uniform," The younger Cochran decided, "this is pretty neat." To make it even better, the older brother "was going traveling," Cochran said, "something I hadn't done. I hadn't traveled out of the state of Georgia."

Cochran majored in civil engineering technology, and might well have continued the tradition begun by pioneers such as Archibald Alexander, an internationally known Black architect and bridge-builder. Alexander, who took advanced training in bridge design in Great Britain, is responsible for the reflecting pool at the Jefferson Memorial, Washington's Whitehurst Freeway, and his consulting company built the Alabama airfield where the Tuskegee Airmen got their wings.

But flying was in Donnie Cochran's blood.

"Coach" Roscoe Draper would understand that implicitly. "Coach" Draper, a colleague of the now-legendary Chappie James and "Chief" Anderson in teaching the Tuskegee Airmen how to fly, himself learned to fly in the pre-World War II Civilian Pilot program[4]. The U.S. Army had begun the program in response to ominous news of approaching war in Europe, and Congress directed Black inclusion because the Black public, increasingly air-minded, kept demanding that Blacks allowed to join the Air Corps.

Most of its Black graduates were not allowed to put on Army wings even at the height of the war, but Draper, undeterred despite being refused entry to the Air Corps itself, qualified for his instrument and instructor ratings and became a flight instructor, earning the nickname "Coach." Coach Draper, who later returned to flight school and qualified in helicopters as an FAA employee, now lives in Philadelphia and is an active member of the Black Pilots of America chapter that bears his name. During the early part of this decade, more than 60 years after his famous students wrote their names into history, Draper continued to work occasionally as a licensed FAA aircraft inspector.

On His Way in Naval Air

Donnie Cochran enrolled in Savannah State's Naval ROTC corps like his brother, and joined the FLIP program, which put him into the cockpit of a Cessna 152, following a similar path as that followed by "Coach" Draper and Chappie James, who eventually made his way into the Air Force and worked his way up to become the first Black four-star general. By the time Cochran graduated from Savannah State, he had even made a "hop" in a TA-4 tactical jet trainer, and completed 30 hours flying Cessnas. Using his degree and NROTC credits, Cochran skipped the rigorous Aviation Officer Candidate School and graduated into a commission.

After that came flight school at Pensacola, the closest Naval Air Station from which the planes Cochran admired as a youth could have come. It didn't hurt that he'd majored in civil engineering. Military pilot school provides the equivalent of master's-degree education in the dynamics of flight, structural properties of airframes, physics of gas turbine engines, communications, computers and aviation electronics, and airborne weapons systems.

After basic and advanced jet training at Kingsville, Texas, Cochran went to sea, flying RF-8 Crusader photographic reconnaissance aircraft off the decks of the nuclear-powered carrier Nimitz in the Mediterranean Sea.

Meeting the Adversary Up Close
If that sounds like a pleasure cruise, recall that Cochran graduated from college at the height of the Cold War. Soviet Navy vessels were stationed at Odessa, on the Black Sea, ready to steam down the Dardanelles and into the Eastern Mediterranean at a moment's notice, and the U.S. Navy's job was to bottle them up in event of a Superpower military confrontation. Soviet merchant ships plied the strategic waterway, moving through it and up and down the Suez

Canal the way American vessels crossed through the Panama Canal, using the Dardanelles-Mediterranean - Red Sea-Indian Ocean route to tie their vast country together through the Black Sea and the Pacific Coast.

Soviet military authorities were well aware of the U.S. presence in the Mediterranean, and Soviet warships and electronic eavesdropping vessels frequently shadowed U.S. and NATO units on fleet training exercises, frequently breaking into military formations and trying to insert bogus fleet commands into voice radio traffic.

U.S. planes also monitored the Soviets' military activities, trying as hard to prize out the secrets of their technology and practices as the Soviets did with the U.S. fleet.

Add to that the constant tension of the unsettled political and military relations between and among the nations of North Africa, Israel and the Persian Gulf. The Nimitz transited Suez and patrolled the Indian Ocean during the Iranian hostage crisis, when Teheran mobs stormed the U.S. Embassy and abducted the staff.

Photo reconnaissance is critical at such times, when fleet commanders and their civilian leaders at the Pentagon need up-to-date information on the deployments of potential enemy forces and the possible sites of American military incursions. Cochran and his reconnaissance comrades were in high demand and their planes flew almost round the clock.

Cochran shifted to the F-14 Tomcat, the Navy's premier air superiority fighter, for 38 months' sea duty aboard the USS Enterprise. The ship was based just north of San Diego, California, at Miramar Naval Air Station, memorialized in Top Gun as "Fighter Town, USA."

Death is Always Close By

It is not well understood by civilians, but military service is dangerous even in peacetime. That is nowhere more apparent than in the Navy, because warships cruise the oceans loaded with all the weapons they'll need for a full-scale battle, should an international crisis blow up while they are deployed. Conditions aboard differ very little in peacetime or in war, and the high-powered apparatus used by sailors and officers to accomplish their duties on daily and nightly watches can itself take lives.

The conditions under which the Blue Angels fly are even more hazardous. A Summer 1987 *US Black Engineer* story noted that the Angels, the world's most famous precision aerobatics team, have taken the art of close-quarters formation flying to unprecedented levels:

"Sixty-three times a year, flying over 37 different locations, the Blue Angels push the performance envelope in their distinctively painted F/A-18 jets. Swooping over onlookers' heads in their patented Diamond formation, smoke trails streaming behind, the Angels then perform echelon rolls, double farvels, diamond rolls, clean and dirty loops, Cuban eights, four-point hesitation rolls, opposing blivots, their trademark *fleur de lis*, and the complex delta vertical break, which ends with all six planes crossing simultaneously in front of the audience at speeds exceeding 500 nautical miles per hour, at 'minimum separation'."

Just Sit Back and Watch

Non-aviators who have seen the Angels in action know that

you don't have to understand what all those terms mean to be wowed by a Blue Angels performance. From the minute the Marine-piloted C-130 support plane shows up, to the precision drill by the hand-picked ground crewmembers, to the precise second when Blue Angels pilots step out, make their salutes and step into their planes, the Angels put on a show that has no equal. Just lean back and enjoy the sight of some of the best pilots in the world, putting their planes through the most demanding regimen imaginable.

When Cochran joined the group, his very visible presence became its own lesson in dismissing the prejudices and preconceptions of the past. When he took over as commander, selected after rigorous review of his service record and flying capabilities, the lesson was underscored yet again. A Black man was running the show, managing a flight group with combat-capable planes and gear worth hundreds of millions of dollars. How he got there is its own story.

The Door Opens, with a Crash

The dangers of the Blue Angels' work became all too apparent on July 13, 1985, when two Blue Angels A-4 Sky Hawks collided over Niagara Falls Air Force Base. Lieutenant Commander Mike Gershon, of Pensacola, Florida, was killed and Lieutenant Andy Caputi ejected and parachuted to safety on the grounds.

Cochran, then a lieutenant commander, and two other pilots were chosen to replace the two men. On Oct. 4, 1985, Cochran became the first Black man to fly in the Blue Angels' tight formation in the team's 40-year existence. Cochran had flown more than 2,000 hours in jet fighters and completed

469 carrier landings. He was 31 years old.

On July 4, 1986, Cochran and his teammates flew Sky Hawks in a ceremonial celebration to salute the restoration of the Statue of Liberty. The young Black officer, finding himself doubly the center of attraction because of his historic posting, told reporters, "What I am doing is not just a job, it's an opportunity. I would like to show young people the roads that are open to them in America. Nobody said, 'here, Donnie, apply for the team, and they will give it to you.' You have to earn it."

Interestingly, when *US Black Engineer* interviewed him a year later, Cochran didn't seem to think his being chosen was all that unusual:

"They were looking for people who could do the job. . . . I think about 70 percent of all Naval tactical aviators who fly off ships could be trained to do what we do. That says a lot about the way the Navy trains its pilots."

After his two-year tour with the Blue Angels, moving up to the newer F/A-18 Hornet, Cochran went back to Miramar Naval Air Station and joined the "Bounty Hunters" of Fighter Squadron VF-2, deployed aboard the carrier USS Ranger, Admiral Davis' former command. Then he was selected to attend the Air War College in Montgomery, Alabama, also earning a master's degree in human resource management from Troy State University.

Duty called again, and in March 1992 Cochran reported to Fighter Squadron VF-1 as executive officer. The next year, he took command, leading the squadron until it was disestablished, then moved on to command the "Sun Downers," VF-111.

'Tailhooked' Upward

History caught up with Cochran again when the explosive news reports of wild behavior at the Navy fliers' annual Las Vegas "Tailhook" reunion in 1991 caused the grounding of the Blue Angels' leader, Commander Robert E. Stumpf.[5] Comdr. Cochran, 41, was called back to take over as "Boss" in 1994.

"I look at (being the first Black man to lead the Blue Angels) as an opportunity to be the Boss," he said then. "Not Black and white, but an opportunity to command a very special organization," consisting not only of the six formation flyers, but also the ground support team and the Marine aviators flying the C-130 transport that accompanies the group and is an integral part of every Air Show performance. "I am perfectly aware that I am an African American."

Stepping Down, to Take Off Again

In June 1996, Cochran decided to leave the Blue Angels. Painfully aware that 22 Blue Angels pilots had died in training or in air shows before he joined the team and troubled by near-misses on his own watch, Cochran had twice ordered a unit stand-down to strengthen safety procedures. Nearing 43 years of age – much older than the men who flew with him – he no longer felt that he fit in.

"I can hold my head high," he said then. "I have not crashed any airplanes, none of my pilots have crashed an airplane, none of my pilots have been hurt."

Captain Cochran had spent more than 4,350 hours in seven different types of aircraft, had completed 570 carrier landings, and had been awarded the Meritorious Service Medal, the Air

Medal and the Navy Commendation Medal, among numerous other awards. He went first to Florida, as commandant of the Reserve Officer Training Corps unit at historically Black Florida A&M University. Then he retired from the Navy.

But not from flying – it was in his blood. And military pilots' extensive training and experience is a lucrative commodity in the civilian air fleet. So Cochran did what many retired fighter and bomber pilots do. He signed on the dotted line to fly jetliners, at first for a cargo airline. Cochran still wears uniforms, but now he takes to the air as Chief Pilot of an integrated consumer-products giant, flying corporate jets and managing the crews, the maintenance and operation of a transportation unit that moves top executives around the world at a moment's notice.

It's not the same as taking catapult shots in the cockpit of an F/A-18 Super Hornet, but Cochran has been there and done that enough times already. When he looks in the mirror each morning, Cochran can be satisfied that he, too, has moved the bar of achievement upward for Blacks in technological America.

Notes

1. After much agitation by the *Pittsburgh Courier*, the *Baltimore Afro-American* and other Black newspapers -- as well as a vociferous campaign by the "Chicago School" flyers, spearheaded by Willa Brown and her husband, Cornelius Coffey -- the Tuskegee Training Program was established at Alabama's Tuskegee Institute, to prepare Black pilots for service in the Army Air Corps. Nearly 1,000 "Tuskegee Airmen" were trained through this program, and Tuskegee Institute was the only facility

graduating Black warplane pilots into the Air Corps until the program closed in 1946. The 99th Pursuit Squadron was formed as part of this program. It was later redesignated the 99th Fighter Squadron and its pilots fought in campaigns in North Africa and Europe. In one action, the all-Black 99th won distinction when it destroyed five enemy planes in less than four minutes, something that had never been done by American fliers.

The all-Black 332nd Fighter Group, commanded by Lt. Col. Benjamin O. Davis, scored two big distinctions after it began flying in 1944: Escorting bombers over Nazi-held territory, it lost very few bombers to enemy fighters. And flying over the Mediterranean, 332nd pilots attacked and sank a German destroyer with their .50-cal. machine guns. This had never before been done.

In all, Tuskegee Airmen destroyed 261 enemy aircraft and damaged another 148 in 15,533 sorties. Sixty-six of their members were killed in action between 1941 and 1945, the end of World War II. See also *www.africanamericans.com/Military.htm*.

2. The Navy commissioned its first Black officers in February 1944, at the height of the Second World War. It marked the end of a long, intense struggle to overturn the prejudices of a naval service that had forgotten the heroic service of Black sailors such as James Forten in the Revolutionary War, of Black seamen in the Civil War, and the Blacks who served in the Spanish-American War and World War I. Push came to shove when Eleanor Roosevelt, wife of the president, and Adlai Stevenson, then assistant Navy secretary, demanded an end to the Navy's refusals to fully integrate Blacks, and the Navy backed down. The Twelve commissioned officers and a warrant who earned his rank at the same time became known as the "Golden Thirteen": Jesse Walter Arbor, Phillip George Barnes, Samuel Edward Barnes, Dalton Louis Baugh, George Clinton Cooper, Reginald E. Goodwin, James Edward Hair, Charles Byrd Lear, Graham Edward Martin, Dennis Denmark Nelson, John Walter Reagan, Frank Ellis Sublett, and William Sylvester White. See also Paul Stillwell, ed., *The Golden Thirteen: Recollections of the First Black Naval Officers*. U.S. Naval Institute Press (1993) 304 pages.

See also the excellent Defense Studies Series' Integration of the Armed Forces, 1940-1965, by Morris J. MacGregor Jr. of the Army's Center for Military History. It may be found on the Internet at *http://www.army.mil/cmh-pg/books/integration/IAF-FM.htm*.

3.The first Black naval aviator was Ensign Jesse L. Brown, who was killed in a combat mission in December 1950 in the Korean War. Ens. Brown was awarded the Distinguished Flying Cross and Air Medal posthumously. See also *http://www.africanamericans.com/Military.htm*.

4. Congress enacted the Civilian Pilot Training Act in 1939 to create a reserve of trained pilots who could be called up in case of war. Civilian flight schools did the training, and the Act required that at least one of them had to train Black aviators.

5. The Tailhook Association, a fraternal organization composed of sea-based Naval and Marine Corps fliers, held its annual reunion in Las Vegas, with spectacular results. The meeting featured a two-day symposium on Operation Desert Storm, and some 4,000 people attended. Wild partying broke out, and news media carried lurid stories of drunken aviators publicly engaging in lewd behavior, harassing female officers, and fighting. Some 83 women said they had been sexually harassed, as well as a small number of men. The Navy was greatly embarrassed, and major Pentagon and Congressional investigations were launched, resulting in the ends of some officers' careers without fully laying out exactly what did and did not happen.
See also *www.raahistory.com/military/navy/cochran.htm*

See also *www.blueangels.org/Years/1995/year1995.html*, and *www.blueangels.org/Years/1996*.

See also the Pop Quiz on Black American history-makers on Savannah State University's Internet Web site, *www.admissions.savstate.edu/utils/g/Content.Pop.asp*

6. The Norfolk Virginian-Pilot discussed Cochran's decision to resign his

command in a May 30, 1996 news story, "Blue Angels Leader Praised for Tough Choice to Resign," by Paul Clancy.

7. Numerous sites detail the explosive contretemps over wild behavior at the Tailhook Association's 1991 conference. See *www.pbs.org/wgbh/frontline/shows/navy/tailhook* and *www.now.org/issues/military/policie/tailhk.44w.html*, or read the Department of Defense Inspector General's report, at *www.inform.umd.edu/EdRes/Topic/WomensStudies/GenderIssues/SexualHarr assment/*

8. Also see the Tailhook Association's Web site at *www.tailhook.org*.

Chapter 4

Following the Trail of Giants

Here is a story that illustrates the point that a single, committed Black mover and shaker can reorder the landscape on which the lives and careers of millions across the country and, ultimately, the globe, work out. Can you say Ayn Rand? "Atlas Shrugged" was a big story, continuing her depiction of outsized individualists who dominated history in "The Fountainhead": Giants whose single-minded drive reshaped the world in their own desired image. A small army of philosophers and literary explainers grew up to discuss her work and her theory of social "objectivism," and millions of people continue to read her books and essays.

Too bad her central characters were fiction. A better name to conjure with is Leon Sullivan. His giant steps were factual, not fictional, and his drive caused deep changes in the industrial workplace, in America and later across the world. Like a character from an Ayn Rand novel, Dr. Sullivan trod the corporate arena as if it were a stage made for him. But unlike Rand's fictional Howard Hughes look-alikes, Dr. Sullivan's interest was in reshaping the world to make a better life for the less-fortunate many, not in simply creating an empire for himself.

You also could say "Arlington Carter." He is an engineer whose understanding of the lessons taught by people like Leon Sullivan made him take hold of his city's community development programs even as he pushed his own career at the world's largest aircraft maker to unprecedented heights. Carter was working in Seattle during the 1970s, a decade later and 3,000 miles away from Sullivan's gritty Philadelphia parish. And Carter worked for Boeing and not for General Motors, where Dr. Sullivan sat on the board. But the "Lion of Zion" had been roaring about opening up the industrial workplace to broader access for Blacks since the 1950s, and the reverberations from his movement to end job discrimination were rattling corporate cages all over America.

Stretching Out on his Own

To be sure, the Chicagoan Arlington Carter, a brilliant ex-serviceman and engineer, earned his own way at Boeing, writing his own record of superior achievement and resetting the bar of expectations about what a Black man could do with the tools of science and business. But it also is 100-percent sure that without the steadfast contention, agitation and attention-getting boycotts of Leon Sullivan and the ministers and community leaders he inspired, very few Blacks anywhere would have gotten chances to rise like Arlington Carter.

Moreover, Carter and his Boeing superiors could not have been unaware of the Rev. Dr. Leon Sullivan's ringing calls for community involvement by the corporations that gain so much benefit from the communities in which workers and consumers live. For as well-crafted and well-executed as Art Carter's community development initiatives were, they could not have met such a positive response in the executive suite had there not been a national groundswell of Black activism led by urban "social engineers" such as Dr. Leon Sullivan and like-minded groups such as the Saul Alinsky-organized Woodlawn Organization in Carter's native Chicago.

How else to explain the aircraft giant's decision to loan Carter, a rising young innovator and manager, to community development efforts in the Seattle-Tri-Cities area during the height of the Cold War? How else to explain the aircraft engineer Carter's own pressing sense of purpose in accepting and pursuing such assignments when the company employing him was deeply involved in a high-stakes, international competition for supremacy in the skies?

Sullivan's Travels

For an answer, look at the good Dr. Sullivan's own story, and see how it resonated with America's manufacturing giants.

Born in Charleston, West Virginia, in 1922 and educated at historically Black West Virginia State College and the Union Theological Seminary, the young Rev. Leon Sullivan first went to Washington, summoned by A. Philip Randolph to work on the national march he organized to demand equal treatment for Blacks in War Industries plants during the Second World

War. Next Dr. Sullivan moved to New York, where he studied at the knee of the legendary Adam Clayton Powell at Abyssinian Baptist Church. At the time Dr. Sullivan began those early 1940s adventures, Arlington Carter was a only a child, with his own adventures still far ahead of him.

Adam Clayton Powell, a spell-binding orator and New York congressman, was gearing up his precedent-setting campaign to demand better opportunities for Blacks in the American workplace, and the Rev. Sullivan was an eager assistant. Randolph had begun the early steps when he organized the Brotherhood of Sleeping Car Porters after watching Blacks pushed out of other unions they helped start in the railroads, construction and other industries at the turn of the 20th Century.[1] Pullman car porters were the early Black success stories whose income and influence provided the bedrock of the emerging Black middle class, and Randolph's prominence and influence thus extended far beyond the membership of his railroad union.

Randolph's protests, coming as the country was gearing up to fight Nazi racism in Europe and Japanese xenophobia in the Pacific, embarrassed President Roosevelt into establishing the Fair Employment Practices Committees, demanding that defense industry jobs be opened to Blacks. Randolph's famous threat to march on Washington made it possible for many Blacks, supervisors and managers as well as line workers, to get a solid start in defense. After the war, Randolph followed that up with intense negotiations and still more threats to prod Harry S Truman into desegregating the armed forces.

But despite those successes, now that the war against

tyranny and racism in Europe and Asia was over, Randolph and other leaders could see the unspoken rules of racial division of labor re-instituted in factory after factory, company after company, in a wave of bitter reaction to the progress Blacks had made during the war years.

The official claim behind pushing women and Blacks out of industrial workplaces and returning to the *status quo ante* was that room had to be made for returning soldiers, but that rationale didn't count when the returning heroes were Blacks.

There were many other workplaces in which the federal drive for undisturbed war production had not overcome the discrimination that always resulted in Blacks having the poorest-paid, least desirable jobs, excluded from promotion opportunities, pay and respect whites took for granted.

Powell's Bullhorn

Now came Adam Clayton Powell, minister of the biggest church in Harlem, the cultural capital of Black America, using his position as a fulcrum to launch campaigns by consumers – the end-users of the products of industry – to challenge those workplace exclusions.

"Don't Buy Where You Can't Work!" shouted signs and picketers announcing mass boycotts against companies that discriminated in the manufacturing centers and financial districts of New York, generating headlines across the nation. Martin Luther King began his fight against segregation demanding respect for human dignity in the South in 1955, with results that inspired people all over the world. But beginning as a wartime price stabilization and consumer affairs officer a decade earlier in New York, the economic capital of the Free World, the Rev. Powell realized that the subtle and not-so-subtle exclusions and restrictions Blacks encountered in the industrial workplace added up to a *de facto* segregation that had to be fought in other ways.

Armed and Well-Trained

Thus, when the Rev. Dr. Sullivan stepped into his own pulpit at Zion Baptist Church in Philadelphia in 1950, he had already been indoctrinated. Or as he himself put it years later, he had "studied at the feet of giants." When Dr. Sullivan observed Blacks laboring under the same *de facto* economic exclusions that had been chronicled by W.E.B. DuBois in "The Philadelphia Negro"[2] half a century earlier, the young minister could see it was time for a new campaign. Fresh from the increasingly strident – and increasingly effective – initiatives of Adam Clayton Powell, a minister who became a city councilman and then a congressman, Dr. Sullivan showed he had learned well how to use the one-two whammy of an economic boycott supported by the political clout of a bloc of energized voters.

Not only did Dr. Sullivan organize the "Philadelphia 400"[3] ministers to launch sustained "Selective Patronage" boycotts in 1958, he and his fellow preachers also raised the political consciousness of the urban Black public. And Dr. Sullivan's message, amplified by national media headquartered or having major operations in Philadelphia, reached far beyond the city limits of his new home town.

The Midwesterner Arlington Carter, finishing up his Air Force hitch, had not yet decided to become an engineer and join the Boeing Company, where he waged his own decades-long campaign to improve the lot of urban Blacks. But by the late 1950s when Carter returned to his native Chicago, Dr. Sullivan and his mentor Adam Clayton Powell had begun to show the way to get it done, and Blacks in urban communities across America were taking notes.

Political Preaching

The Rev. Sullivan and the "Philadelphia 400" ministers regularly used their bully pulpits to call out troops in the fight against workplace discrimination, producing occasional picket lines but more often headlines across the country. Not stopping there, the "400" also excoriated the failure of the machine politicians who controlled state and local governments in big cities like Philadelphia to serve the real interests of their Black constituents.

Working in the North, they had an advantage. Unlike in the South, where poll taxes and other devices kept Blacks off the voting rolls until the Civil Rights Act of 1964 stripped away those restrictions, Northern leaders such as Powell and Sullivan could regularly call on the voting power of legions of Black Southern ex-farmers arriving as the Great Migration continued after World War II.

Those Black legions, energized by political education delivered from the pulpit and now free to exercise rights other Americans had long taken for granted, provided a bulwark of Black voting clout. They could defeat unsympathetic political candidates, vote down ballot initiatives that did not serve Black interests, and deluge state and federal lawmakers, mayors and governors with petitions, letters and phone calls demanding action on their desired political goals.

That added to the pressure on corporations to open up to Blacks the opportunities for better jobs that had long been denied to them.

And one by one, the manufacturing titans whose plants dominated the Philadelphia landscape discovered the wisdom of making a deal. The list of majors with plants in or near the city was long, and provided plenty of targets: The Budd Co., maker of railcars, transit system equipment, and auto parts for Detroit's big Three. Stetson Hats. Tastykake, the long-dominant pastry-maker. Pepsi-Cola Bottling Co. Daroff Tailoring. Botany 500. Villager women's clothing. Bayuk Cigars. The Philadelphia Bulletin Co., publisher of the nation's largest evening daily newspaper. Midvale-Heppenstal, steel fabricator and boilermaker. Whitman's Chocolates. Nabisco. The Philadelphia Electric Co. General Electric Company. Sylvania. Westinghouse. Breyer's Ice Cream. And on, and on.[4] Ultimately, some 300 corporations decided it was better to sit down and sign agreements than fight the "400" in the marketplace.

Building His Own 'Empire'

But Sullivan, a builder as well as an activist, went even further. The weekly "10-36" investment club he organized at Zion Baptist Church[5] provided seed money for a new kind of public capitalism. This new, church-led capitalism became a model for community-driven economic development across the country when Rev. Sullivan opened Progress Plaza, the first Black-owned shopping center, in the middle of the urban ghetto of North Philadelphia.

Dr. Sullivan had just spent months working with A. Philip

60

Randolph and Bayard Rustin to organize the 1963 March on Washington, reprising the work he did on the original 1941 plan to March on Washington during the war. He had "studied at the feet of two giants," he often said of his time working with Randolph and with Adam Clayton Powell, who recruited him to New York from his West Virginia pulpit, and he, like many Americans, was thrilled when Dr. Martin Luther King delivered his iconic "I have a Dream" speech.

Dr. Sullivan was on his way to becoming a giant in his own right, but his activism took its cues as much from the business-minded Urban League as from the legal eagles at the NAACP and the demonstration leaders down South. And in the Black community of Art Carter's hometown Chicago – rapidly becoming a Black Mecca as busloads, carloads and trainloads of displaced farmworkers arrived to work in its stockyards, packing houses and factories, but also to open businesses in the vast tenement neighborhoods – people took notice.

A Different Dream

Dr. Sullivan, who grew up under segregation, had deep admiration for Dr. King and his Southern Christian Leadership Conference. But living in the urban North, Dr. Sullivan saw that the fight against the more subtle practices and social factors behind urban Blacks' economic exclusion needed a different kind of leadership. So in 1964, the year Congress passed the Civil Rights Act, Dr. Sullivan launched his master-stroke: Opportunities Industrialization Center, built in an abandoned North Philadelphia police station. And after people saw his results, Dr. Sullivan's business plan drew

61

imitators across the nation.

OIC, opened with "sweat equity" and much public fanfare,[6] grew into a massive non-profit enterprise with affiliates in 70 U.S. cities and 15 African countries, the Philippines and Poland. Negotiating with executives and local governments to evaluate the training needs of corporations in or moving into urban areas – and then to meet them with targeted programs to prepare under-served minorities – OIC has provided basic education, job-training, screening and placement for more than 3 million people worldwide. OIC's enterprise development center offshoot, headquartered in Sullivan's home city of Philadelphia, has produced graduates who have become millionaires running the businesses they first conceptualized at OIC.

Moving to the Inside, Widening His Reach

That kind of success draws attention. In 1971, General Motors made Dr. Sullivan the first Black person elected to a *Fortune* 500 company's Board of Directors. Then instead of sitting as a figurehead, Sullivan used his position to learn the inner workings of a major industrial enterprise. Later, he launched manufacturing businesses in Philadelphia, providing not only hands-on training and experience for workers, but also for a new cadre of Black managers, many of whom went on to bigger jobs in Corporate America..

Then Dr. Sullivan widened his reach even further, beginning a new campaign against *apartheid* in South Africa, a country where the multinational GM had major investments. The "Sullivan Principles,"[7] promulgated in 1977, outlined guidelines for corporations and governments doing business with the racist regime in Pretoria, requiring job training and the opening of opportunities for the disenfranchised Blacks of South Africa. The Sullivan Principles, used by corporations, governments and community watchdog groups all over the world, are acknowledged to have been one of the most effective initiatives to end workplace discrimination in South Africa.

By the time of his death in 2001, Dr. Sullivan, the recipient of 50 honorary degrees and the President's Medal of Freedom, had forged personal relationships with every American president since John F. Kennedy. United Nations Secretary-General Kofi Annan, on learning of Sullivan's death, issued a statement expressing "great sadness," but noting that Sullivan's life "shows how much one individual can do to change lives and societies for the better." Sullivan, Secretary Annan said, "was known and respected throughout the world for the bold and innovative role he played in the global campaign to dismantle the system of apartheid in South Africa."

The Rev. Jesse Jackson, seconding Annan's remarks, noted that Dr. Sullivan's work had been a model for Operation Breadbasket, the economic development arm of Dr. King's Southern Christian Leadership Conference, that Jackson later turned into Operation PUSH.[8]

Looking at the Lessons

Ayn Rand may not have noticed Leon Sullivan's success when she began publishing in the middle 1950s, but people like Art Carter could hardly ignore the example. An engineer whose deep sense of commitment took him far beyond the confines of his industrial employment, Carter also learned how to organize and manage community development efforts as he climbed the corporate ladder in Seattle. In so doing, Carter, an engineer leading rapid advances in technology that affected the balance of power in the Cold War, also changed the social and economic environment in which Blacks could evolve in the Pacific Northwest.

Thus, Carter showed how well he imbibed the lessons from the struggles back East, and his own giant steps in aerospace laid down paths many others could follow. Atlas Shrugged? The Black Atlases *shoved*, in the South and in the North, and Art Carter, watching, moved mountains of his own in the Northwest.

But then, maybe engineering was too deep for Ayn Rand and the small army of cultural analysts and pundits who tried to make her the Second Coming of Aristotle.

No Excuses Allowed

Let it be said here: No American can claim he understands history if he or she fails to examine closely this society's history on race. And on race, Ayn Rand's education – and that of her adoring contemporaries and later admirers – clearly was lacking. She might be forgiven her ignorance when she arrived in 1926, because Carter G. Woodson was just getting up the push for a Negro History Week. Asa Philip Randolph had just organized the Brotherhood of Sleeping Car Porters the year before, and had not yet made his fullest mark in American public policy. But over the next quarter of a century, she should have learned.

But she did not, and many in America also did not. Look at

what they overlooked:

"Atlas Shrugged" came out in 1957, three years after Thurgood Marshall's brilliant argument in *Brown v. Board of Education* proved he was the best lawyer in America. In the same year, 1957, the Little Rock Nine[9] dropped a big rock on the segregated mores of the South. Two years earlier, the Rev. Dr. Martin Luther King's triumph in Montgomery, Alabama, had energized disadvantaged peoples all over the world. In 1958, Dr. Sullivan's "Philadelphia 400" ministers were shaking up Corporate America, striding boldly into the national leadership.

Where were Ayn Rand and all her fellow articulators of the American Dream when all that was happening? Where were they looking while those nine brave Black children shook off a century of lynch-mob terror to walk proudly between the lines of federalized, rifle-bearing National Guardsmen, while howling crowds of white Arkansans bayed for their deaths?

Where were they when the Rev. Sullivan's disciplined fellow church leaders were shaming the editorial moralizers at America's best-read evening newspaper, when they were opening up "closed shops" at the factories of some of America's biggest corporations?

Did Ayn Rand's Atlas really shrug, or were she and the literary philosophers trumpeting her values simply asleep while a host of Black Atlases grabbed hold of the world and shook it into a new reality?

Maybe Ayn Rand's coterie never heard of Charles Hamilton Houston, whose prodigious scholarship, teaching and advocacy forged the axe Thurgood Marshall, Constance Baker Motley and a corps of intrepid Black courtroom warriors used

65

to chop out the foundations of racial segregation in America. Which Atlas did they think was shrugging?

More World-Shakers

To be sure, Black America contained plenty of unbridled world-shakers, whether the national cultural leaders were looking or not. Some were still in gestation in Ayn Rand's time, but many others were making very public headlines. Reginald Lewis, the Jackie Robinson of American business, was just a kid then, but Jackie himself was out there shaking up the sports world on which so many Americans set store, mesmerizing sold-out crowds in stadiums across the country.

And in the intellectual arena where Rand and her admirers claimed the high ground, there were other stars she should have known about. The Harlem Renaissance was reshaping the style of American stage, literary and performance arts when she came to this country, and jazz musicians were spellbinding audiences all over the world. W.E.B. DuBois had been challenging the *status quo* in academia and in society since before the turn of the 20th Century. Dr. Woodson, the second Black Ph.D. out of Harvard University after Dr. DuBois, had been attacking the mis-education of the American Negro for the whole of his career, and George Washington Carver, Ernest Everett Just and a host of Black over-achievers were trampling into dust the longstanding image of an ability deficit in Black America for decades before the Russian-born Rand got here.

So let's say it now: It is long past time for the chief arbiters of America's cultural landscape to lose that automatic pardon so many allow, when their "Fountainheads" continue to ignore the giant talents sweeping out of Black communities everywhere, benefitting everyone.

History She Didn't See

By the time Ayn Rand died in 1982, two decades had passed since James West, a Black Southerner who traveled to Sullivan's North Philadelphia for education and opportunity, invented a microphone that became the model for a whole new generation of electronic devices. West joined AT&T Bell Laboratories during the late 1950s as a Temple University physics intern, and stayed to produce a complete family of new inventions that changed communications technologies all over the world. West, now teaching a new generation of engineers at Johns Hopkins University, earned nearly 250 U.S. and foreign patents over his long career, even using his foil electret sensing tools to develop new instruments to detect and treat hypertension, a major cause of death among Blacks and others suffering from diabetes.

Across the country at Boeing, Art Carter's colleague Waymon Whiting had joined Boeing in the middle 1950s. Among other innovations, Whiting invented an automatic escape hatch and slide that made it quick and easy for passengers to get out of a stricken airliner, and had seen copies of it incorporated into planes of all manufacture, including those that whisked Rand to her celebratory writers' conferences and book signings.

Men had walked on the Moon and returned safely, thanks to the incomparable brainpower of two Black women – Sally Richmond and Katherine Johnson – and a Native American, Jerry Elliott, Ph.D., in making the orbital calculations to get them there. Norbert Rilleux, the architect of evaporative processes at the base of everything from modern paint, dye and chemical-making, petroleum refining and yes, sugar production, had been dead for a century. Granville T. Woods, a central architect of modern mass transportation, were he alive at mid-20th Century, would have recognized his own innovations in the subways people admired in Moscow, the capital of Rand's native land.

An Engineer Makes His Move

There also was Arlington W. Carter, a Boeing engineer whose exploits reached far beyond the aircraft and missile plants where he worked.

Born in the Windy City of Chicago, Carter, a prime exponent of the individual drive and excellence Ayn Rand trumpeted – minus the self-absorbed greed of her fictional empire-builders – Arlington Carter did not know what he wanted to be when he grew up. In high school, Carter showed what he called "a reasonable interest toward science, math, physics, and chemistry," and went on to junior college. Then he heard the drums of war, rolling across the Korean Peninsula. In the Air Force, Carter spent four years as a weather forecaster.

After discharge Carter decided to be an engineer. Unsure which field to choose, he "picked EE after reading that electrical engineers made more bucks."

'For Love of the Taste of Potatoes . . .'

Like the characters in the novel "Look Homeward, Angel," Carter's choice may have seemed casual at first glance. But it had outsized portents. For in addition to making money, electrical engineers working in 1961, when Carter finished at the Illinois Institute of Technology, were adapting their new solid-state electronics gear to swing knockout blows at the old ways of doing business. And nowhere was that shift so apparent as in aerospace, where Carter wound up.

Carter joined Boeing because he liked the high-tech atmosphere, but he also quickly got his hands into activities that had nothing to do with his chosen field but everything to do with how life would be lived in the world he was helping to fashion. Starting as a Minuteman strategic missile specialist and moving to the Advanced Surface to Air Missile System, the Safeguard/Sentinel program, and the Strategic Silo Upgrade program, Carter joined community-building programs inside and outside the corporation -- moves Dr. Sullivan would have loved.

Lessons for Wannabes

Interviewed by US Black Engineer in 1989, Carter said that young engineers looking to move up should jump right into community service. Erroll Davis, who was doing exactly that in the Midwest, would agree.

"I believe one of the best places to learn how to manage is through volunteer efforts, such as charities, church activities, and politics," Carter told the magazine interviewer. "If you can learn to manage volunteers, you certainly learn the techniques for managing within your company. You'll learn techniques of how to coach, appraise, model, and inspire. These attributes are critical for moving up, for showing you have the maturity and poise. There are some things you don't learn in school."

Clearly, Carter learned those things well. During the early 1970s he spent two years as a loaned executive for the City of Seattle. There, he established and managed Seattle Housing Development, a not-for-profit corporation that built and refurbished housing for low- to moderate-income residents. He had a $2.5-million annual budget and a staff of 36.

It Only Looked *Easy*

Occasionally, Carter found that the business interests of Seattle Housing Development diverged widely from the business interests of Boeing, which was paying his salary. To complicate matters more, Carter worked for a Democratic mayor, under a Republican governor who often disagreed with the mayor on policy issues.

"I had to learn to walk a delicate line in a situation that was more political than corporate," he told *USBE&IT*. "But it was rewarding because it helped me to learn about politics."

It also, as he says, gave him good management experience. His staff included individuals who frequently had less education and job skills than his corporate co-workers. Worse, when he did get someone properly trained, that person took off for higher pay and benefits in the corporate world. Finally, Carter found that the contractual relationships and lines of authority, so clear and compelling in a corporate setting, often were more diffuse in the not-for-profit environment.

"It was important to be more responsive to community needs, to citizens and various communities. You have to inform what you're trying to do, and try not to offend," he said.

Two-Way Big Payoff

In the end, it paid off at Boeing, as Carter began showing off his new managerial skills. In 1978, when the Rev. Leon Sullivan was cris-crossing the Atlantic campaigning against apartheid in South Africa, Arlington Carter was stepping up into the executive ranks in Seattle, using his influence in more subtle ways but still pushing for change. Carter won promotion to general manager of Boeing's Seattle Service Division, a then-new human resource service branch with more than 10,000 workers. The first Black to serve on Boeing's Executive Management Team, Carter now had significantly broader responsibilities.

Extra Steps Can Count

Earlier, Carter had worked strictly on technology projects, even diverging from aerospace. In one example, in addition to his work on missile systems, he also managed a $25 million R&D contract to test high-speed locomotives for the Federal Railway Administration. "In the overall corporate picture, it was not a big job," he said, "but it was significant for me because I controlled the engineering, purchasing, contract, the whole works."

Putting that together with his experiences managing disparate skill sets and dealing with multiple constituencies through Seattle Housing Development, Carter knew what to do in his new role.

Other Boeing executives had struggled to make the Human Resources Department's processes work better to provide more direct support to the staffing of individual projects.

Under Carter, the department simultaneously staffed two major new airplane programs, the Boeing 757 and 767, mainstays in today's air transport industry. Carter's team hired more than 20,000 people with skills in engineering, computing, business, finance and manufacturing. It showed him to be a first-team player.

Time for Up-skilling

Recognition of his abilities was not long in coming. Boeing nominated Carter to participate in the MIT Sloan School program for senior executives, the equivalent of Command & General Staff Officer School for military types. And like Army War College graduates, Carter kept moving up as his experiences broadened.

Soon, Carter was deeply involved in the Strategic Defense Initiative, a Ronald Reagan program to build a missile defense. The program was derisively dismissed as "Star Wars" by a generation of science writers weaned on the doctrine of Mutual Assured Destruction in a nuclear war, but it produced many new technologies. And as mentioned earlier, Star Wars did succeed in an important objective: It got the Soviet Union ensnarled in a technology race from which it could not emerge victorious.

The news reporters who disparaged Star Wars also routinely, like Ayn Rand, ignored Blacks like Arlington Carter, who worked at the heart of the program and contributed innovation that affected many industries. But Carter was there, leading major technology initiatives. From program manager for the Air-Launched Anti-Satellite (ASAT) program of the 1980s, Carter moved up to general manager of Space

Defense Systems in Boeing Aerospace, adding responsibility for Kinetic-Energy Weapons, Directed Energy Weapons and Space Surveillance and Tracking Systems. Under that flag, Carter also served as Advanced Launch Vehicles Program manager and deputy manager for the Space Systems Division, at a time when the public face of space programs, civilian or military, showed very few Blacks at work.

Visible or not, Arlington Carter was a go-to guy. Organizations under his direct supervision were winning major technology contacts during the late 1980s:

• The Lightweight Exoatmospheric Projectile Program (LEAP) and the building of test high-technology kinetic-energy projectiles for the Strategic Defense Initiative Organization.

• The Neutral Particle Beam-Integrated Space Experiment program, a $40-million procurement to fabricate and test a neutral particle beam device in space.

• The Advanced Launch System, a concept-development effort to determine the system configuration for the Air Force's Heavy Lift Vehicle.

• Shuttle C, a concept-development effort to explore system configurations for NASA's version of a Heavy Lift Launch Vehicle.

Space System organizations under Carter's direction also were indirectly responsible for critical support in Boeing's winning the $750 million contract for the NASA Space Station procurement. That made Boeing the main contractor for the Space Station Habitat Modules, where the astronauts now live and work. In addition, Carter's team played an instrumental role in winning for Boeing a contract to build another Initial Upper Stage used to ferry an Air Force payroll into geosynchronous orbit.

Still Reaching Out

But the societal shifts begun during the civil rights movement of the 1960s still required attention. Black Americans, who rebelled against the restrictions of segregation, *de jure* in the South but *de facto* in many other places in America, were pushing for full inclusion in American society, full equality in public and private life. Community building, a big part of that push, is a lifelong commitment. Thus, further differentiating himself from Ayn Rand's self-absorbed fictional characters, Carter continued his public-service activities, often at his own expense, reshaping his community as he worked to reshape technology:

- Serving as King County (Wash.) Personnel Board Chairman
- Sitting on the Executive Board of the Seattle Hearing and Speech Center
- Being secretary treasurer of the Northwest Illinois Institute of Technology Alumni Association
- Serving as president of the Northwest Area NAACP (Washington, Idaho, and Alaska) and chairman of the Western Region, covering all nine Western states
- Serving as an Executive Board member and Loaned Executive Recruiting Manager for the United Way
- Being Fund-Raising chairman of the Boeing Employees Good Neighbor Fund
- Elected president of the Boeing Management Association

- Serving on the University of Washington Minority Engineering Advisory Board

"I've been outgoing in terms of voluntary assignments," Carter told *USBE&IT*. "They're not always plums, but I work on the basis they'll pay off in other ways, and they usually do."

Take *that*, Ayn Rand.

Carter says that volunteering for non-official functions within the company, such as the United Way, also provides a way of identifying with the company culture and displaying skills that might not be revealed in a person's prime assignment.

"Young engineers have to make an aggressive effort to understand the company, its organization chart and products. Become a part of the fabric of the company and volunteer for activities which further the company's goals. As a senior manager evaluating people," he said in 1989. "I'm always looking for the go-getter, the self-motivated person who is interested in the company. Perhaps things like this are not pointed out in brochures, but they do enhance your potential for advancement."

As they did Arlington Carter's. The enhancement and benefits to the community, as attested by the many letters from community organizations supporting Carter's nomination for Black Engineer of the Year, were enormous. And his career success continued apace.

Movin' Up, Yet Again

In 1988 Carter was named vice president of Boeing Aerospace, appointed general manager of the Defense Systems Division. There, he was responsible for missile

75

systems, Strategic Defense Initiative systems and support services. Among the major programs he led were the Airborne Optical Adjunct system, the Air-Launched Cruise Missile, the SRAM II strategic missile, the Avenger and Sea Lance missile system programs.

In April 1989 Boeing merged two divisions to form Boeing Aerospace and Electronics. Carter became vice president and general manager of the new unit's Missile Systems Division, adding new responsibilities for the Peacekeeper/Rail Garrison, Minuteman Missile Support and system improvements and Small ICBM Hard Mobile Launcher basing system.

At his level, Carter not only had to master and keep up with state-of-the-art space technology, but also the art of political persuasion, a skill he began honing at the Seattle Housing Development Corp. Carter dealt with a wide range of people, within Boeing and in the national polity, from members of the national press corps to members of Congress.

Keepin' It Very Real

To get there, Carter worked hard to balance his work life with his home life. He told *US Black Engineer* that, when he first started working at Boeing, he saw that successful executives maintained excellent physical and mental health.

"I felt there were things you committed to the job, but also things you committed to home, community activities and to leisure," he said. "I saw it as a lifestyle that resulted in prodigious work output, seemingly without effort." Now retired, Carter continues to keep a busy hand in community development programs.

Ayn Rand is long gone, but the admirers of her work are still extant. Time for all of them to listen up about what America really is about.

Endnotes

1. As the Randolph Pullman Porter Museum broadside puts it, Southern plantation owners created a corps of skilled tradesmen among their enslaved Black workers: "Many slave owners trained their slaves" for work as coopers, carpenters, mechanics, cabinetmakers and masons, the museum piece says, "so that they could be hired out or sold for a higher price. There is scant documentation available to estimate the true numbers of slaves employed on the railroads. However, it is possible and likely that there were thousands of skilled tradesmen and manual laborers used in the construction of the many miles of American railroad." For proof, the museum notes that as early as 1838, a Southern railway bought 140 enslaved Blacks for $159,000 to help build a rail line in Mississippi.

As the museum piece dryly notes, "When Abraham Lincoln issued the Emancipation Proclamation Act in 1863, the United States had made few provisions for the future employment of freed slaves. As a result, former slaves who left the plantations found limited opportunities" in the workplace.

As for the skilled tradesmen, the new labor unions, first organized by white and Black workers together, frequently began passing rules to keep Blacks out. One example of the severity of those exclusions – and of the numbers of Black skilled workers actually available after the Civil War – is shown in the story of the Chesapeake Maritime Railway and Drydock Co., organized in the former slave-holding state of Maryland. The shipyard was organized by Baltimore Blacks who, now excluded from the construction industry, decided to pool their skills and bid for ship-building and repair jobs so they could continue in skilled work. The shipyard, opened at the end of the 1870s, operated successfully for 20 years.

2. DuBois, W.E.B., The Philadelphia Negro, 1899. Lippincott, New York Dr. DuBois, hired by the University of Pennsylvania to uncover the sources of criminality in the Black community, instead contributed a seminal American work of social science. Going door to door in heavily Black South Philadelphia, Dr. DuBois found that almost all adults were ex-slaves and that few were allowed to work in the factories and mercantile enterprises of a city that at the time was one of the world's great manufacturing centers.

3. The "400," never as much a formal organization as an organizing idea, generated much attention because their churches had among their memberships a large share of Philadelphia's Black voters.

4. In all, 29 businesses were boycotted, and here's how they did it. A committee of ministers was formed to pick out companies that had no Black employees. The committee visited the firm and, after looking around its shops and premises, asked for jobs in all areas, skilled and unskilled. If the company complied, no boycott. If not, boycotts and loud, media-amplified accusations about the company's discriminatory policies and behavior followed. Stung – and frequently hurt financially by the boycotts – companies fell in line. Eventually, more than 300 businesses had representatives sit down and negotiate agreements with the "400," an ad-hoc group that at times included more than 400 ministers.

5. In 1962 Rev. Sullivan started Zion Investment Associates, inviting his congregation to buy shares in it. Each parishioner was asked to invest $10.00 each week for 36 weeks, and 650 people joined in. Zion Investment Associates then financed four major projects: An apartment complex, called Zion Gardens. Built by Black plumbers, carpenters, electricians and other construction craftsmen, all graduates of the OIC. Next the group built the Progress Plaza shopping center. It was the first shopping center in the United States owned and operated by African Americans.

After this, the Progress Garment Manufacturing Company was started. The most ambitious project of all opened in May 1988. This was Progress Aerospace Enterprises. The government and another group gave money to train 100 unemployed people to become aerospace technicians. General

Electric Company ordered work from the company worth more than $2 million.

6. In 1967 President Lyndon Baines Johnson visited Philadelphia to see OIC and declared he liked what he saw. After that, federal workplace training dollars flowed, and the Opportunities Industrial Centers expanded across the United States.

7.See also *www.aynrand.org*, the Web site of the Ayn Rand Institute, which disseminates information about her books, her work as a Hollywood scriptwriter, and her philosophy of Objectivism.

8. See also *Wikipedia*, the online encyclopedia, which carries a very interesting article on Rand, detailing her early life in Russia, her emigration to the U.S., and her work in Hollywood.

99 . See also the excellent biography of the Rev. Dr. Sullivan, at *www.cbsd.org/pennsylvania/Level1_biographies/* or read the Sullivan Foundation's discussion at *www.thesullivanfoundation.org*.

10. The global reach of Dr. Sullivan's work is reflected in the remarks of Chevron Chairman Ken Derr, praising the retired preacher for introducing his Sullivan Principles at the United Nations. See *www.chevron.com/news/archive/ chevron_press/1999/1999-11-03.asp*.

11. The Shomburg Center for Research in Black Culture maintains extensive records on the Rev. Adam Clayton Powell Jr. and his famous father, Adam Clayton Powell Sr. Visit *www.sci.umich.edu/CHICO/Harlem/text/acpowellhtml* to learn more about the elder Powell. His son, the Congressman, has a biography at www.bioguide.congress.gov. Showtime, the Cable TV channel, produced "Keep the Faith, Baby," a 2002 movie about the life of the flamboyant minister and community leader. At *http://www.adamclaytonpowell.com*, Showtime provides extensive information on Powell's family and the timeline of his activities, as well as a photo gallery.

12. The A. Philip Randolph Pullman Porter Museum and the A. Philip

Randolph Institute maintain good records on the pioneering trade unionist's life and times. Visit *www.aphiliprandolphmuseum.org*, or *www.apri.org*. See also *www.pbs.org/weta/apr*, *www.phila.k12.pa.us/schools/randolph/A_P_Randolph.html*, and *www.georgemeany.org/archives/apr.html*, and *afroamhistory.about.com/cs/aphiliprandolph/p/aphiliprandolp.htm*

Chapter 5

The Cold War Shapes Guy Bluford's Career

Popular media often describe technology as some force of unfathomable Nature, running amok to reshape society. But the truth is that the societal background always influences the development of technology, and the policy decisions of leaders define its direction. Not only do those leadership policy decisions provide such definition, but the personal decisions of individuals – consumers, activists and entrepreneurs – frequently redefine its growth. Conflict in the policy arena often accompanies technological competition – oftentimes prompted by it, but just as often doing the prompting – and the resolution of the policy issue gets played out in the technology. Nowhere is that more visible than in the military dimension.

The career of Guion Bluford, who finished high school in a time of great hope for victory in the civil rights struggle -- but also of widespread insecurity because of the global competition between nuclear superpowers for resources, influence and bragging rights -- provides a case in point.

Educated at Philadelphia's Overbrook High School, the *alma mater* of basketball giant Wilt Chamberlain, Bluford graduated in a time of great portents. Bluford's 1960 class

81

also included future NBA All-Star player and coach Walt Hazzard, who headed for college basketball stardom under the legendary John Wooden at UCLA while Bluford went to study aerospace engineering at Pennsylvania State University. John F. Kennedy was running for president of the United States, promising a "New Frontier" in the fight to extend American democracy and inspiring young people everywhere to dedicate themselves to public service. His potent line, "ask not what your country can do for you, ask what you can do for your country," reached the hearts of people far beyond America's borders.

Black Crusaders

Blacks, electrified by the *Brown* school desegregation ruling, energized by the success of Dr. Martin Luther King's 1955-57 Montgomery Bus Boycott and inspired by the courage of the Little Rock Nine, were pushing hard against the walls of discrimination that had held them in second-class status since the post-Civil War Reconstruction. Newspaper headlines and broadcast news reports informed the world that Black college students had opened a new front against racial domination in the Old South with sit-ins at lunch counters in Greensboro, N.C., and 10 other cities. Sit-ins quickly became a tactic that was repeated in the North as well as the South, including in Philadelphia.

While Bluford was away at Penn State, flamboyant Philadelphia lawyer and local NAACP chief Cecil B. Moore[1] was turning up the heat in Bluford's home city with demonstrations and legal challenges to *de facto* segregation "Up South." Echoing the campaigns of New York minister and congressman Adam Clayton Powell and using a parallel but much more strident approach to that of Philadelphia's own Rev. Dr. Leon H. Sullivan, Moore attacked racial discrimination where it mattered most in the North: at the workplace.

Taking rowdy crowds of under-employed inner-city residents to campaign against discriminatory employment practices at companies such as Greyhound and Trailways and at construction sites for public schools, Moore scored his biggest public-relations coups at places where taxpayer dollars allegedly were being spent for the benefit of all but were carefully kept out of the wage packets of Black workers. Moore also created daily news headlines with picket lines and legal briefs attacking racially exclusive admissions at Girard College, a private school for fatherless white boys endowed by Stephen Girard, one of the financiers of the American Revolution.

Not Fighting Alone

And Moore had important company. Martin Luther King was a towering figure in the South, rushing from place to place because no leaders of comparable status existed in many Southern states. But in the North crusades also were being launched by Adam Clayton Powell, Senior and Junior, in New York, and Rev. Sullivan and the "Philadelphia 400" ministers. Saying "Don't Buy Where You Can't Work," the ministers led parishioners on a sustained campaign to open up the closed shops of large industrial corporations such as the Budd Company, maker of railcars and auto parts, and local bakery giant Tastykake, whose pastries were a Philadelphia staple.

The fiery Moore disparaged the ministers' genteel approach of visits and negotiations after boycotts got corporate leaders' attention, but the churchmen's boycotts did bring many businesses to the table.

The oil shocks of the mid-1970s were still to come and Philadelphia, which had emerged as one of the world's greatest manufacturing centers from the mid-1800s to the 1950s, was still a manufacturing powerhouse. Most of those large manufacturing enterprises had plants located in inner-city neighborhoods – during the 19th Century the manufacturers had caused Philly's rowhouse neighborhoods to be built for their workers – but their best jobs were reserved for the whites, who by now lived elsewhere.

In New York, U.S. Rep Powell, who had trained Sullivan, was generating his own headlines with massive boycotts, picket lines and signs telling Blacks the same message his Philadelphia protégé was spreading: "Don't Buy Where You Can't Work."

Moore's Fellow Traveler

The World War II Marine-Corps veteran Moore probably had more in common with Jesse Gray, a Harlem, N.Y., tailor and former state assemblyman, who was gearing up even bigger populist campaigns. Gray, like Moore, represented the poor and disenfranchised, and his credo was that progress would come on what we today call "human rights" when organizers like himself "got the alley Negroes out into the avenues."

Gray, disturbed at the high rents poor Blacks were paying to absentee landlords for substandard housing, urged his followers to wage massive "rent strikes": Thousands of families paid apartment rents into bank escrow accounts, denying delinquent landlords the right to evict them or to collect the rents without repairing their run-down, poorly heated buildings. Gray succeeded in forcing city takeover of many properties, and brought Housing Code enforcement to life in actions he prompted against many others.

Global Ripples

International events also shaped Bluford's generation. The Sharpeville Massacre of peaceful demonstrators protesting *apartheid* in South Africa – breaking into news headlines in 1960 as well – pointedly brought it home to Bluford and his classmates that racial discrimination existed in Africa as it did at home. That sore point was frequently underscored in the literature distributed by agitators and propagandists espousing Soviet Communism, badly frightening American authorities.

In the former Belgian Congo, the nationalist leader Patrice Lumumba was killed by secessionists amid a post-colonial meltdown of societal order so complete U.S. troops flew in to rescue U.S. citizens and stayed to fight a small, nasty war. Many Africans and outside observers pointed to the role of U.S. intelligence officers, who helped capture Lumumba and turned him over to his political enemies. U.S. forces also joined the European colonialists, supporting a Belgian expeditionary force as it fought bitter battles to restore order, put down dissent and install Joseph Mobutu as the new strongman in that resource-rich African state, forestalling the rise of a more left-wing leader like the assassinated Lumumba.

Superpower Contention Abroad

The real force the troops were fighting to block was the Soviet Union, which emerged from World War II as the arch-enemy of Western capitalism. Soviet *apparatchiks* and development officers ranged across the world, telling the citizens of emerging countries in Africa and Asia that colonialism was racist at its core, but that Soviet-style Communism offered a better model of development, free of the greed and discrimination capitalist rulers had shown.

The Soviet Union had created a colonial empire of its own in Eastern and Central Europe after World War II, when Russia turned the massive armies it raised to fight Nazi Germany on the weakened nations Germany had victimized. Now the Union of Soviet Socialist Republics was making its own industrialization drive, competing for the vast amounts of raw material lying in Third World countries, the former exclusive province of colonial powers and their powerful industrial offspring, the United States of America.

That international political struggle provided a critical backdrop to the American struggle for civil rights, forcing U.S. leaders to answer the complaints of protest leaders such as Dr. King, Rev. Sullivan and Adam Clayton Powell, or see them amplified overseas by Soviet propagandists challenging the validity of "the American Way."

The Politicization of Aerospace

Technology competition, played out frighteningly with the rapid development of military planes, nuclear missiles and naval forces, heightened the atmosphere of tension and fear.

Perhaps a new World War would ensue, putting the lives of every man, woman and child on the planet in jeopardy.

The Soviets did little to dispel that atmosphere of fear, and the Red Scare created by U.S. Sen. Joseph McCarthy and like-minded congressional representatives in the House Un-American Activities Committee, the Subversive Activities Control Board and J. Edgar Hoover's FBI kept many people on edge, long after McCarthy was hounded out of office. Demonstrating its arrival as a global military power, the U.S.S.R. sent Sputnik I blasting into orbit in 1957 while Bluford was in high school, besting efforts by U.S. agencies to send up the first artificial satellite. That sent shivers up the spines of Americans, who realized that the rocket that could orbit a satellite could also loft a bomb.

The Americans, predictably, answered with a demonstration of their own military technology. In 1958 the United States sent aloft a Jupiter-Redstone missile, blasting into space to install Explorer I into low Earth orbit, showing the world that the Soviets were not the only ones who could send a brawny rocket where they wanted it to go.

John F. Kennedy, elected president in 1960, declared in a speech that Americans would be first to reach the Moon, ramping up the priority of aerospace advances as he ramped up the competition.

The Space Race was on, and many in Bluford's generation were afraid the competition in building and testing big missiles would end in a nuclear holocaust. Defense budgets soared, worried commentators argued that the Soviets were outstripping the United States in producing scientists and engineers, and the National Aeronautics and Space

Administration grew into a giant research and development agency, with its own billion-dollar budget priorities and installations around the world. Soviet politicians such as Nikita S. Khrushchev pointedly boasted about the military capabilities flowing out of their supposedly peaceful, civilian rocketry programs, but just as pointedly singled out the military implications of American space exploits.

Bluford, an Air Force ROTC candidate and future rocket scientist, was in college preparing to become a warrior in this political-military technology contest.

Global Proxy Warfare

On the ground, uniformed U.S. advisors were fighting and dying in a far-off place called South Vietnam. Ngo Dinh Diem, regarded by many Asians as a U.S. puppet, survived a coup attempt while trying to marshal forces against the insurgent Viet Cong, led by Ho Chi Minh and the Vietminh guerrillas who had fought the Japanese in World War II and ousted the French from Southeast Asia. Bluford would later see those guerrilla troops through his gun- and bombsights when he flew over the Mekong Delta in an Air Force fighter-bomber. And he, like other U.S. troops in Vietnam, would hear propaganda broadcasts from Viet Cong officers asking why Black victims of discrimination should be fighting for white Europeans' colonial interests in Southeast Asia when their own rights were still denied at home.

In 1959 the Cuban revolution had brought Fidel Castro to power, ending the brutally repressive regime of Fulgencia Battista and putting Americans on the defensive in the Caribbean. Battista had been an American satrap, but the

Soviets scored a political *coup* when Castro declared himself a Communist and threw out Battista and a big crowd of U.S.-based gangsters running the gilt-edged casinos and brothels that had corrupted Cuban society. Castro aligned his government with the Russian-led Eastern Bloc and tried to force the United States to abandon its strategically important naval base at Guantanamo Bay, held on a long lease after the Spanish-American War of 1898.

Tensions intensified three years later when satellite imagery and overflights by U-2 spy planes showed that military personnel were building launch stations for Soviet nuclear missiles. With Cuba lying 90 miles from Miami, Florida, that put the entire United States within range of a devastating attack, and Americans found that intolerable. President Kennedy met the Soviet move head-on, extending the Monroe Doctrine with his new Kennedy Doctrine prohibiting foreign military intrusions into the Western Hemisphere, and sent the Navy to blockade Cuba. The news gripped the world in fear as people everywhere prepared for a nuclear exchange that would bring modern civilization to its knees, but Soviet Premier Nikita Khrushchev backed down.

Amid Disaster, Progress

Guy Bluford, like the rest of the generation of the 1960s, thus lived through an era of stunningly rapid societal shifts. John Kennedy was gunned down while thousands watched in Dallas Nov. 22, 1963, and Lyndon Baines Johnson took over. Diem fell to assassins in a conspiracy many abroad believed was American-sponsored, and the new U.S. president heated up the Southeast Asian conflict further as he beat back a re-election challenge from the even-more hawkish Sen. Barry Goldwater in 1964.

A more significant accomplishment, in the eyes of many, was Johnson's successful drive to pass the Civil Rights Act of 1964, competing an initiative begun under President Kennedy.

In South Africa, Nelson Mandela was sentenced to life in prison for his role in the fight against *apartheid*.

The same year, Bluford finished at Penn State as a distinguished ROTC grad and began his active service with flight training at Williams Air Force Base in Arizona. Pilot's wings in place in January 1965, he transitioned to jet aircraft, qualifying in the McDonnell Douglas F-4C at air bases in Arizona and Florida. But hard news continued to blast into every corner of American life.

Bloody Counterpoint

Malcolm X was shot-gunned to death before his wife and children and a packed, panicked audience while onstage at Harlem's Audubon Ballroom in March of that year, sending shock waves across Black America. While watching the news, the young Guy Bluford was preparing to face death in the skies as he faced off with North Vietnamese MiG pilots and ground-based anti-aircraft crews.

Assigned to the 557th Tactical Fighter Squadron, Bluford flew 144 combat missions out of Cam Ranh Bay, Vietnam. There he joined a small, active corps of Black air warriors that included former Tuskegee Airman Daniel "Chappie" James, whose exploits with World War II ace Robin Olds had admiring comrades nicknaming the pair "Blackman and Robin."

Another warbird slicing the air over Southeast Asia was piloted by future Navy admiral and Black Engineer of the Year awardee Walter Davis, who survived and went home to become the Class Desk Officer driving development of the next-generation F-14 Tomcat and also to play a critical role developing worldwide military satellite communications and surveillance systems.

As the Asian war continued, Bluford flew into increasingly hazardous territory. He flew 65 missions over North Vietnam during Operation Rolling Thunder, but unlike less fortunate comrades shot down to become unwilling guests of the infamous "Hanoi Hilton," Bluford got his planes back to base .

Lessons Learned, But Shocks Continue

The U.S. military approach is to return experienced combat pilots home to train new fighters, a practice begun in World War II. Not only does this prevent the loss of the most capable air warriors, it makes sure their knowledge gets passed on. In July 1967, Bluford joined the 3630th Flying Training Wing at Sheppard Air Force Base in Texas as an instructor pilot in the T-38A jet trainer. He flew as a standardization/evaluation officer and as an assistant flight commander for four years.

Like just about everyone else in the world, Bluford watched with horror the news that Martin Luther King was shot to death by a gun-toting racist in Memphis in April 1968. Then everyone reeled before still-another wrenching blow: Before the nation had learned to cope with the sad reality of Dr. King's assassination, it lost another hero. New York Sen. Robert F. Kennedy, JFK's brother and the hope of renewing the optimism and drive of the Kennedy Years, was shot to

91

death in California, just as he was stepping forth to savor a primary victory that should have been his springboard to success in the presidential race.

Image makers

But the technological race continued. Richard Milhous Nixon, an arch anti-Communist, was resurrected from political oblivion by the assassination of both Kennedys, and ran triumphantly into the White House. The next year American spirits were buoyed watching Neal Armstrong step out onto the Moon on live TV, announcing, "That's one small step for (a) man, one giant leap for mankind." The world remembered the remark as confusing – "one small step for man, one giant leap for mankind."

Joel Shurkin, a former *Philadelphia Inquirer* science reporter, later told this writer the press gang at NASA's Johnson Space Flight Center had advance copies of Armstrong's remarks, and knew that what he said was garbled in transmission. The writers decided to drop the "a" because people watching TV all over the world thought they had heard it right.

Still, the triumph was complete: The Soviets had beaten Americans to the first "soft landing" on the Moon with a robot, but Americans had landed the first man. John F. Kennedy was dead, but his promise had been fulfilled, inspiring space dreams in young people the world over.

The script wasn't the only thing held back. Shurkin and his fellow science writers could have told the waiting world about the Black scientists and engineers who helped make the triumph possible, too. So the critical contributions of Sally Richmond, who led the orbital computations, and Kathryn

92

Johnson, the mathematician whose calculations actually put Neal Armstrong safely onto the Moon, were left for others to describe, many years later.

Back to School, Again

Bluford, who was to make history of his own in the astronaut corps, was busy working his way up to senior flight officer. In early 1971, Bluford attended Squadron Officers School and returned to his Texas base as an executive support officer to the deputy commander of operations and as school secretary to the air wing. Then he went back to school one more time.

In 1972 Bluford entered the Air Force Institute of Technology residency program at Wright-Patterson Air force Base near Dayton, Ohio. Graduating with a master's degree in aerospace engineering in 1974, he won assignment to the Flight Dynamics Laboratory at Wright Patterson as a staff development engineer. He served as deputy for advanced concepts for the Aeromechanics Division and as chief of the Aerodynamics and Airframe Branch of the facility, part of the famed Air Force Research Laboratory. The Vietnam war had ended for Americans in 1973, and Bluford was moving forward as a master of the highest technology: aerospace.

Developments We All Use

Reports on the Air Force Research Laboratory's work may use fancy, esoteric words, but such research affects much of what we do down on the ground. Among other innovations during the late 1950s and early 1960s, Linwood C. Wright, a Black American working in Cleveland for the National Advisory Commission for Aeronautics – NASA's predecessor – was a key leader on the team that developed an efficient high-bypass turbofan engine. The high-"bypass" turbofan was the refinement that made turbojet power practical for civilian aviation while dramatically boosting the output power of military jet engines. Turbojets, introduced by the Germans during World War II, had revolutionized powered flight, but were wasteful of fuel. Most of the energy produced went out the tailpipe as waste heat.

Wright and his colleagues – his wife was one of the "computers" doing the lab's math – figured out how to capture and use that energy: add an extra turbine into the exhaust stream to power a big ducted fan up front, then use the airstream blasting out from the fan for propulsion. The new efficient turbines quickly put an end to the two-track system whereby "Jet Set" movie stars and the wealthy swept through the skies in Boeing 707s while less well-heeled passengers took the boat or the train. The engines also pushed jet aircraft far past the "Sound Barrier" that so occupied the imaginations of aircraft designers around the world. Like many another American aerospace innovation, it was an advance copied everywhere.

The Pilot as Scientist

Expanding his own knowledge base, Bluford the researcher wrote and presented several scientific papers in computational fluid dynamics – whose understanding is critical to rocketry as well as to improvements in powered air flight – at the Air Force Research Lab while studying to complete a Ph.D. in aerospace engineering, with a minor in laser physics.

Flying Above the Curve

That moved him up to the front rank in space exploration. Col. Bluford, who logged 4,000 hours in jet planes, became a NASA astronaut in August 1979, working with engineering systems for the then-new Space Shuttle, which had not yet flown. These included the remote manipulator system, Spacelab-3 experiments, the Shuttle Avionics Integration Laboratory and the Flight Systems Laboratory.

Four years later, the name and face of Col. "Guy" Bluford became famous all over the world when he flew on the Space Shuttle Challenger for three days, deploying the Indian communications satellite INSAT-1B on NASA Mission STS-8.

Red-Tinged Competition

The Soviets had not missed a chance to tweak the United States' nose on race, even in space. Soviet engineers beat Americans getting the first Black man into space when they sent Cuban Col. Arnaldo Tamayo-Mendez into orbit, aboard Salyut 6 in 1980.

The United States had missed its chance to be first with Air Force Col. Robert H. Lawrence, who died in a tragic crash when his F-104 Starfighter plunged from the skies on a training exercise December 8, 1967. Col. Lawrence, who had a Ph.D. in physical chemistry, had just graduated from the Air Force Research Pilot School and was training for the Manned Orbital Laboratory, a Defense Department program that was later canceled. After a long campaign by Blacks for better recognition, Col. Lawrence was granted astronaut status in 1997, 30 years after his death.

Becoming a Household Word

Still, the prestige of the American space program, which was first to land men on the Moon and followed that with the launch of the first re-usable space ship, was undeniable. Guy Bluford, a Black American, was up in the Shuttle, and the ability of America's broadcast news media to put color TV pictures in homes, schools and offices in countries on every continent made all the difference in the world. The Soviets were never able to capitalize on their success in beating the U.S. to yet another space milestone.

Col. Bluford flew into orbit again on Mission STS-61A, a seven-day flight that deployed the German D-1 Spacelab mission and launched the Global Low Orbiting Message Relay Satellite in October 1985. That was the last time the shuttle Challenger went into space before its spectacular destruction in a fireball early in 1986. Caused by a malperforming O-ring seal on the strap-on Solid Rocket Booster that let hot gases burn into the shuttle's external fuel tank, the Challenger accident replaced the image of American competence in space with the picture of a dirty fireball, high in the sky. The shuttle's loss and the death of Ronald McNair, another Black astronaut, schoolteacher Christa McAullife, and five NASA cohorts badly shook the nation's confidence in the competence of NASA, the world's premier space exploration agency.

Timely Warning

Bluford, interviewed by *Pittsburgh Press* reporter Eleanor Chute at a public appearance in May 1989, kept his cool, saying he had full confidence that the United States would recover its balance in space. Delivering a keynote speech at the 40th International Science and Engineering Fair, Bluford told 746 student contestants from high schools in 46 states, the District of Columbia, American Samoa, Guam, Puerto Rico and nine foreign nations that being an astronaut was the "best job in the world."

But Bluford, who grew up in the era of Sputnik and the scare that America was being outpaced in the production of engineers, rang that alarm one more time:

"There's going to be a shortfall of scientists and engineers in this country in the years to come," he told a press conference during the competition. "If we're going to be competitive, the leaders in developing new ideas and new products, we're going to need more scientists and engineers."

That was in 1989, three years after Challenger's blazing fall. Today, with the searing images of yet another, more recent Shuttle disaster burning holes in American confidence, U.S. corporations are racing to establish technology research centers in China and India because of the abundance of scientific and technical talent pouring out of their universities, while U.S. universities produce ever-fewer numbers of engineers and scientists. America's numbers of math and science majors continue to decline – although this country still produces more engineers and scientists per capita – and Bluford looks like a prophet.

Bluford's confidence in NASA proved well founded, though. He went into space again as payload commander for STS-39, an unclassified Defense Department Shuttle flight, in February 1991. Col. Bluford supervised two mission specialist

97

astronauts and monitored all mission-related activities including crew training, payload development, testing and integration of payload gear, mission planning and flight design, flight operations and payload and flight safety. Col. Bluford also served as point of contact for crew-related issues with the Strategic Defense Initiative Organization, a Reagan-era program to develop space-based anti-missile defenses.

The Soviet Empire Falls

The Strategic Defense Initiative – "Star Wars" in the popular press – was roundly criticized by scientists as a wasteful boondoggle that could never work. But the new competition it launched ultimately helped bankrupt the Soviet Union, whose state-controlled industries could not keep up with the innovative drive and market flexibility of industries in the capitalist West.

Meanwhile, the Soviets' 10-year war in Afghanistan turned into a Vietnam-style debacle. In a reversal of the proxy war in Southeast Asia, Afghan *mujahedeen* used U.S.-supplied Stinger missiles to counterpoint Soviet helicopter gunships, stymieing the invaders' ability to protect their troops. On the ground, Afghan warriors whose forebears were raiding caravans in the heyday of the Silk Road ranged through the mountain passes tearing into military columns like so many choice cuts of meat.

Philadelphia *Inquirer* reporter Richard Ben Cramer depicted the *mujahedeen* as silent wolf-packs, preying on the Soviet truck caravans the same way their ancestor had torn into camel trains 1,000 years earlier. Russian women, like their American counterparts during Vietnam, tore the hearts of their countrymen with plaintive wails over the loss of so many of their sons and husbands in a war that could not be won.

The release of Nelson Mandela from Robben Island prison in 1990 finally removed one of the biggest touchstones of Soviet propaganda in the Third World – racist domination by Western colonizers and their descendants in Southern Africa – and heralded a new era of freedom in Black Africa. Bluford, like Blacks all across America, was thrilled when Mandela came to the United States and returned home triumphantly, to become South Africa's first Black president.

Technology Trashed

The Soviet Union had its own technology disasters. One, the fiery blowup at the Chernobyl nuclear power station in Ukraine put a major nail in the Soviet empire's coffin, when Soviet authorities' ham-handed, propaganda-oriented attempts to control the flow of information to the public turned into a political nightmare as well as a public-relations disaster. Soviet authorities had touted the supposed safety of their reactor designs after the American partial meltdown at Three Mile Island in 1979, but now the inherent weaknesses of their own graphite-moderated RBMK-1000 reactor and the unsafe procedures used by its managers were revealed to the world, thanks to aggressive reporting of Western news media and the wide distribution of satellite pictures from the French SPOT-1 ground-surveillance satellite.

The Soviets might have taken a lesson from the business meltdown of the Metropolitan Edison Corp., whose business model and reputation were wrecked by the public-relations disaster at TMI after Met Ed staffers were revealed to be trying harder to mislead reporters and clamp down on news flow than to correct the problems that led up to that near-meltdown.

But the Soviets only learned that lesson the hard way, as had Met Ed. So suddenly, not only the technical competence and environmental stewardship of Soviet engineers, but the very veracity of the Soviet government's pronouncements was called into question. That was the beginning of the end for the Soviet Union.

On to the Next Big Thing

Bluford, who had trained and fought during the contentious era of superpower competition, now watched the enemy nation he prepared to fight pass into history. The skills he developed remain with him, now to be applied in less warlike uses of space technology.

Retired from the Air Force but still deeply involved with NASA space programs, Bluford now heads a civilian engineering group preparing space payloads. His career spanned almost the entire arc of the superpower competition and, like the U.S. military-industrial complex that won the Cold War, he continues to develop new technology initiatives.

Endnotes

1. Cecil Moore, a West Virginia native like the Rev. Leon Sullivan, had with a group of Black servicemen trained at the Montford Point station and participated in the historic desegregation of the Marine Corps during World War II. Discharged at Fort Mifflin in 1947, Moore remained in Philadelphia to

go to Temple Law School at night, working as a schoolteacher by day. Elected president of the city NAACP chapter, Moore immediately began shaking up the city.

Days after taking office, Moore sharply attacked a planned $1.7 million Ford Foundation study of poverty in North Philadelphia. No blacks had been consulted on the project, Moore said, nor was its director Black; he was a white man, former District Attorney Sam Dash (later chief counsel for the Senate Watergate Committee). Perhaps the foundation might rethink its approach if black people refused to buy Ford motorcars, Moore said publicly. In an atmosphere already charged by several years of "Philadelphia 400" boycotts, that received a lot of attention. But instead of brining out dignified church members, Moore called out raucous crowds of inner-city slum dwellers. And his preferred style of negotiation was to do it in the streets, with maximum volume.

Moore also picketed a school construction site in the heavily Black Strawberry Mansion section. Police put the demonstrators down forcefully, and were caught on camera beating some as they arrested them. Moore turned all hearings about the arrests into a public forum, and succeeded in winning agreements for new Black access to the building trades, well before Assistant Labor Secretary Arthur Fletcher's famous "Revised Philadelphia Plan for Construction Labor" mandated broad changes. He picketed the city's Greyhound and Trailways bus depots and won agreements to integrate those companies. He began a loud campaign against blackface minstrelsy by Philadelphia's famous Mummers in their annual New Year's Day parade, backing plans for a mass demonstration, and large numbers of poor Blacks turned out to see if the Mummers would yield. They did. These fights yielded tangible jobs and political empowerment for the city's Black community, its numbers swelling because of the Great Migration.

Perhaps Moore's greatest victory came after a seven-month campaign against the whites-only policy at Girard College, a private school for fatherless boys endowed by Revolutionary War-era merchant and banker Stephen Girard. Threatening to send teen gang members "over the Wall," Moore generated daily headlines. In 1968, the U.S. Supreme Court struck down the whites-only provision of Girard's bequest.

101

See also Salisbury, Stephan, "Moore's Activism Countered Stereotypes," *The Philadelphia Inquirer,* July 7, 2004.

3. Among other gambits, Jesse Gray, a consummate showman as a protest leader, invited 13,000 rent-striking tenants to bring rats to a 1963 session of landlord-tenant court. As Jan Gardner of *The Boston Globe* relates in a April 28, 2004 story,

"People brought dead rats and live rats. People dangled rats by their tails for the newspaper photographers; people displayed rats spread out on newspapers, like fresh fish they'd bought at the market. The tenants won."

Chapter 6

The Struggle to Open Doors for Women
Some Would Brook No Barriers at All

The 1960s-era campaign for civil rights had many dimensions. While the great Drum Major, Martin Luther King Jr., set the image for the era with his dramatic speeches, one equally powerful consequence of the rebellion against society's restrictions was a new impetus for the emancipation of women from the straight-jacket of traditional gender roles.

For Lydia W. Thomas, bent on being a scientist in an era when neither Blacks nor women were thought to have the "Right Stuff" to work on the cutting edge, that meant a campaign waged on two distinct levels.

Dr. Thomas grew up in segregated Portsmouth, Virginia, a sleepy Southern town dominated by its largest employer, the Norfolk Naval Shipyard, and almost overrun by uniformed men prowling out of the nearby Naval Operating Base in Norfolk, Little Creek amphibious naval base and Oceana Naval Air Station in Virginia Beach. Sailors and marines were all over the place, complicating the situation of people struggling to adjust to the changes brought on by the

NAACP's developing attack on the legality of segregation by bringing into the mix men and women raised in other states, where Jim Crow racial divisions were not an accepted fact of life. Confrontations were inevitable in that charged environment, but the military authorities always were there to smooth things out.

Within Segregation, Family Protection

Lydia Thomas, like most youngsters in Portsmouth at the time, was shielded from much of that tension by the protective embrace of her family and the close society of the segregated Black community. But the tensions were always present, in the background, as she grew up.

The military-political situation had other effects on life in the Norfolk/Portsmouth area. Vietnam became a continuing concern as the Kennedy Administration became more and more involved in trying to prevent a Communist takeover, first by sending in U.S. military advisors such as the young Colin Powell to help South Vietnamese forces stem the tide of guerrillas flowing in from the North, and by the ramp-up of U.S. military forces in anticipation of direct participation in increased hostilities. That meant even more servicemen trooping through the streets of Portsmouth, as ships were readied for service overseas.

The Cold War played out directly in the careers of Guion Bluford and Donnie Cochran, but it reached into the life of a young Lydia Thomas in less direct ways. France had lost its colonial hold on Indochina after its debacle at Dien Bien Phu in 1954 when Thomas was in elementary school, and the

Soviet Union launched *Sputnik I* in 1957, just as Thomas was beginning high school. The national hue and cry over the need to produce more scientists and engineers to meet the Soviet challenge benefitted many young people in Thomas' generation, pumping federal dollars into elementary and secondary school math and science education programs and ramping up scholarship support for college science studies.

Black, Proud, and a Go-Getter

Thomas, enrolled in an all-black high school where her mother was the head guidance counselor and her father the principal, was somewhat insulated from the negative pressures that hindered the dreams of other young Black men and women.

"I grew up in Virginia, in segregated schools," she told *US Black Engineer & Information Technology* magazine, "but I had tremendous encouragement for my interest in science – from my teachers and from my parents, who had a great love of learning. They taught me that a book was better than a candy bar."

John F. Kennedy won the race for the White House in 1960, the year before Thomas finished high school. Scientists all over the world completed the first International Geophysical Year the same year, wrapping up the first coordinated, public-private global investigation of what makes Planet Earth tick with a book-length report that electrified high school science students everywhere. Kennedy's launching of the Space Race with his promise to make sure an American was the first man on the Moon provided another heady thrust for science-minded young people.

Howard University, a Center of Ferment

Thus, Lydia W. Thomas arrived at the campus of historically Black Howard University, in segregated Washington's heavily Black Shaw neighborhood, during a time of high excitement: One of the five lawsuits aggregated in the Supreme Court's 1954 decision in *Brown v. Board of Education* had originated in the Washington suburbs, and Howard Law School graduates Thurgood Marshall and Oliver Hill were at the forefront of the battle to put an end to segregation once and for all. James Nabrit, the former law dean who became University President, also had been a key contributor, in a legal go-for-broke attack supported by William T. Coleman, a transplanted Philadelphian and Tuskegee Airman who worked nights after his day job at New York's Paul Weiss, Rifkind law firm to help the NAACP's Constance Baker Motley draft the brief Marshall presented to the high court. Howard lawyers, Howard professors and Howard students were deeply involved in the crusade to end racial domination in the segregated South during the 1960s, and their activism occasionally spilled over into demonstrations and protests in the Washington D.C. area.

Faculty Thunderhead, Close Aboard

In the sciences, Dr. Herman Branson, professor and chairman of the Physics Department, brought his own excitement. Branson, a graduate of historically Black Virginia State College with a Ph.D. from the University of Cincinnati, taught both physics and chemistry at Howard, in addition to handling special projects for the Office of Naval Research and the Atomic Energy Commission.

In 1951, when the young Dr.-to-be Lydia Thomas, in grade school, was just beginning her pursuit of science studies, Dr. Branson had been a co-discoverer with Linus Pauling and Robert Corey of the *alpha helix*, the fundamental structure of proteins. That discovery won Pauling the Nobel Prize, an honor many now believe should have been shared with Dr. Branson, but at Howard during the 1960s, Branson was a giant of science, inspiring students to excel at any task. He specialized in research in mathematical biology and biophysics, subjects of intense interest for the young future biologist Lydia Thomas.

Thomas completed her B.S. degree at Howard in 1965, shortly before Dr. Branson left to become president of Central State University, and launched her own world-beating career. A zoology major, Thomas went across town to American University to earn her master's degree in microbiology in 1971. Two years later, divorced with two children, she earned her Ph.D. in cell biology at Howard, as *US Black Engineer* noted, "just in time to join the technology revolution."

Getting There, the Hard Way

Getting there could not easy, even with the encouragement of her family and the support of the faculty at a traditionally Black powerhouse such as Howard.

After completing her doctoral studies in 1973, Dr. Thomas joined the MITRE Corporation, a not-for-profit R&D lab, engineering consulting firm, and think tank providing services to government agencies large and small. MITRE Corp. does everything from development of new communications technologies to space studies, from developing new weapons technologies to environmental engineering, from research on energy to investigating new ways to manage commercial air flight. In short, *MITRE* does everything, from deeply secret defense R&D projects and projects providing technological support for U.S. intelligence activities, work on information technology and homeland security to environmental and public-safety projects that are not secret at all.

Dr. Thomas, a Black woman from the Life Sciences, had entered an arena filled with electrical engineers, dominated by white males. As Martin Hoffman, board chairman at Mitretek Systems put it in a 2003 *US Black Engineer* interview, at first she was unique because of who she was, but "it wasn't long before she was unique because of what she did – pioneering fields such a environmental protection, product safety, toxicology and risk-based decision-making in governmental programs."

Sloth in the Fast Lane

For an idea of how difficult it was for Dr. Thomas to cut her own swath in such a male-dominated, traditionally oriented engineering organization 30 years ago, consider a report by the University of California at Davis on the situation of women in high technology today.

The report,[1] a study of women business leaders in high technology by the university's Graduate School of Management, looked at the 200 largest publicly held companies in California – many of them national or multinational concerns – to discern the progress of women into leadership positions. Noting that "women play a critical role in the financial health of the nation," the report said women are responsible for 83 percent of some $3.7 trillion in consumer spending. By Wall Street reckoning, women control $14 trillion in wealth and represent nearly half of all investors, the report said. Women today comprise 46 percent of the workforce and hold more than half of all managerial and professional positions. So far so good.

But a look closer into the workings of major corporations, three decades after Dr. Thomas joined MITRE Corp., showed the California business scholars a different picture. Digging into corporate reports and staffing tables in companies covering 11 Standard Industry Classifications – financial services, consumer goods, pharmaceuticals and biotechnology, health care, service, retail, technology, industrial/manufacturing, media and communications, software, and semiconductors – the UC-Davis professors found that despite an overwhelming presence in the professional and managerial workforce, women hold less than 20 percent of the top executive jobs.

Left Behind on the Left Coast

Looking at California, whose 37 million people power an economy ranked eighth in the world, with companies responsible for technological breakthroughs that have dramatically changed the way everyone lives and does business, the UC-Davis researchers compared the Golden State's progress in moving women into executive positions to the progress in seven other regions. California showed up on the low end, its 8.2 percent of women on the executive top rank above only Florida (7.6 percent) and Michigan (5.7

percent).

That is, California women hold only 8.2 percent of the positions as Chief Executive Officer, Chief Operating Officer, Chief Financial Officer, and Chief Information Officer, compared to the 15.4 percent of women who hold such positions in Chicago. Rounding out the group, women in the state of Wisconsin hold 11 percent of the top jobs, women in Philadelphia hold 10.2 percent, in Massachusetts 10.1 percent, and in Georgia women hold 8.2 percent of the top jobs. Dr. Thomas, a zoologist who rose to Chief Executive Officer in an engineering consulting firm filled with male engineers, is thus one of a small sample of American women.

The access of women to seats on corporate boards is another area of concern. For despite their control of $14 trillion in wealth and investment dollars, women hold only a minority of seats on boards of directors: 14.2 percent of board seats are held by women in Chicago, the best-performing region for gender diversity, and California ranked second, with 11.4 percent. Wisconsin was third, with 11.0 percent, Michigan fourth, tied with Massachusetts at 9.9 percent, Philadelphia was fifth with 9.3 percent, Florida sixth with 7.9 percent, and Georgia last with 7.1 percent.

Looks Worse in the Breakdown

Breaking that down further by industry totals, the UC-Davis report found that the highest numbers of women in executive positions were in health care. Some 72.7 percent of the top 200 companies doing business in California had one or more women executive officers, while 50 percent – half – of the companies in retail business had one or more. Service-industry companies followed, with 42.9 percent of the firms having one or more women executives, with financial firms' 42.3 percent close behind. Software companies, which have generated so much wealth and technological progress, were less open: Only 40.9 percent of the companies had one or more women executive officers. In the pharmaceutical and biotech industry, only 33.3 percent of the companies – a third – had a woman in a top job. In industrial manufacturing, the number was 19.4 percent, and in technology it fell to 18.2 percent, with media and communications' 14.3 percent beating out the semiconductor industry's 5.6 percent of companies with at least one woman in a top job.

Working Up the Ranks
Numbers were similarly small in engineering ranks. National Research Council numbers say that women have experienced some growth, but their percentages in the science and technology workforce are still much smaller than their percentage in college enrollment. In 1978, long after equal opportunity programs were supposed to be opening doors for everyone, Labor Department numbers showed women were less than 2 percent of the engineering workforce. That grew to nine percent over the next two decades, and approaching the turn of the 21st Century the National Research Council found that women scientists and engineers finally had risen to 12.3 percent of America's industrial workforce.

Labor Department studies show that women's engineering enrollment had grown also, to some 19 percent of the undergraduate population. But activists such as Lucent Technologies engineer Julie Sheridan-Eng say that even in

111

institutions with relatively high enrollments of women, their percentage usually does not exceed 30 percent. This at a time women are pursuing college studies overall at rates frequently exceeding their male counterparts.

A key problem, Dr. Sheridan-Eng has said in a short online note, is mentoring and support, for women who may feel isolated at school and in the industrial setting, to keep those who are attracted to the engineering profession in the pipeline and on the career track.

Sad Facts Despite Growth

An example of this problem is shown in a "Fact Sheet (De Welde, 2007)" by Kristine de Welde of Florida Gulf Coast University and Sandra Laursen and Heather Thiry of the University of Colorado at Boulder, "Women in Science, Technology, Engineering and Math," which showed that although women earn about half of all mathematics bachelor's degrees, they earn only 27 percent of all doctorates. Noting that women are "well-represented among life science Ph.Ds, approaching equity in agriculture, chemistry and geoscience," the Fact Sheet said, they are nonetheless "more strongly under-represented in physics, computer science, and engineering," according to a 2007 National Science Foundation report. "Across all STEM fields," the three researchers said, "the proportion of women of color is small, and drops with each level of degree attainment."

"Men outnumber women (73 percent vs. 27 percent overall) in all sectors of employment for science and engineering" according to 2007 National Science Foundation figures, the three researchers said, also finding gaps between men and

112

women in business and industry (79 percent men vs. 21 percent) and in federal government jobs (73 percent vs. 27 percent).

Big Growth from a Small Start

Interestingly, they found that for Black men and women, the share of science and engineering occupations had doubled, from 2.6 percent to 6.9 percent, over the last 25 years. For all women, the share also doubled, from 12 percent to 25 percent. White women were 20 percent of the 4.9 million science and engineering workers, trailed by Asian American women with 4 percent of the jobs, Black women with 2 percent, Hispanic women with 1.2 percent, and Native American and Alaskan Native women holding a tenth of a percent. "In general," the researchers said, "across disciplines and sectors of employment, whites outnumber all minorities by almost three to one."

The Fact Sheet offered several explanations for the low numbers of women at all stages of science, technology, engineering and math careers, including:

1. The classroom climate for girls in schools and for women in university departments has classically been described as "chilly." Girls and women are treated differently than males in both subtle and overt ways. For example, everyday ways of conducting classroom discussions can exacerbate inequities when boys are given more attention and praise by the teacher.

2. A dearth of role models also contributes to the underrepresentation of women in science. Women students look to faculty as role models for balancing career and family,

113

and if career demands are seen as excessive, may leave their departments in larger numbers than men. Women benefit from role models and mentors who are cognizant of the differential experiences of women and men in the sciences.

3. Poor preparation and lack of encouragement in STEM subjects in school. Women undergraduates enter their major s highly qualified and competent, but this confidence drops in their first year of science and engineering studies, because of loss of interest in their fields, discouragement at academic difficulties, and poor teaching, all of which can be exacerbated by poorer preparation in high school science and math.

4. A lack of a critical mass of women in a department may lead to dissatisfaction and greater attrition of women scientists.

5. Bias and discrimination in hiring and advancement of women, compounded by salary differences and low organizational status .

Powering Ahead Anyway

Corporate and academic cultural predispositions are one thing, but corporate needs are entirely different drivers of corporate behavior. And high-level scientific performance by a determined individual can put   another dimension into anybody's game.

The great Dr. Percy Julian put exclamation marks after that particular point with his chemical exploits at the Glidden Co. during the first half of the 20th Century, developing whole new classes of soybean products, discovering esserine to treat glaucoma and finding a way to synthesize hydrocortisone to

114

treat arthritis while investigating an accident in his lab, then moving on to discover the synthetic endocrine precursors underpinning today's hormone treatments and birth-control medications.

Women who Didn't Give Up

Lest anyone forget, remember that Katherine Johnson and Sally Richmond doubly underscored that exact same point when they clambered onto the Front Rank of aerospace pioneers, from a start hobbled by racial segregation. The two women began work as female "computers" on the all- Black section of the math calculations team at the National Advisory Committee on Aeronautics, NASA's predecessor in the Space Race. The sections were divided, like other parts of the federal government after Woodrow Wilson's divisive term, but Johnson, who had already spent years teaching in segregated Southern schools, was so good she got drafted to be the main delineator of orbits for the first Mercury space shots, and she got picked again to handle the calculations to take Neal Armstrong and the Spaceship Eagle from the Earth to the surface of the Moon, working under Richmond, who had risen to become Orbital Calculations team leader.

A more contemporaneous exemplar is Nancy Stewart, whose exploits as a computer engineer at IBM resulted in sales of more than $100 million worth of software and hardware for GM's robotized manufacturing plants, earning her promotions up the vice presidential ladder to become chief of global computing networks before she was stolen away by first GM, to blow past a bunch of knotty problems getting a vast Intranet system up and running, then Wal-Mart, where she became chief of large systems. When the Bentonville, Ark., executives got a close-up look at Stewart's capabilities, they quickly moved her up to Chief Technology Officer.

Technology Rings the Register$$$

If being CTO for a retail company sounds like small change compared to the engineering exploits in Stewart's past, recalibrate your count. The biggest retailer on the planet is also one of the most aggressive technology users, and Nancy Stewart is one of the best there is at handling computer technology. She'd have to be, for IBM to trust her with the $2-billion global computing project she managed on her last VP job.

Technology savvy is one of the main differentiators between Wal-Mart and its erstwhile competitors: headquarters systems interrogate store point-of-sale systems frequently, checking to learn what items are selling, in which regions and stores, at what price points, at which times of the day. They also double-check inventory systems, making managers instantly aware of surpluses, shortages and shipping schedules.

Much of Wal-Mart's inventory is already out on the highways instead of sitting in warehouses, and Stewart's team uses GPS location, satellite communications, truck-mounted computers and cell phones to know exactly where each load is, on what pallet, on what semi-trailer, going exactly where. If a consumer product is selling big at a particular store, Stewart re-routes truckloads in transit to get it on the winning store's loading dock in six hours.

116

Wizardry on the Shop Floor

Still another is Sherita Ceasar, who grew up in Chicago's poverty-wracked public housing projects but, refusing to be held back, took her Illinois Institute of Technology degree to Motorola, where she became chief quality control engineer for pager products, then manufacturing chief for all pager products.

Ceasar then was wooed away by Scientific Atlanta to be vice president and manufacturing chief, hired to jump-start quality control initiatives and kick into high gear production of the company's signature TV transmission systems to meet a suddenly burgeoning demand from the broadcast industry.

The industry was gearing up for the government-mandated transition to digital broadcasting, and everything from cameras and transmission equipment to cable-TV set-top boxes would need to be replaced. Ceasar, the wizard who had learned hard lessons about how to make a factory run at Warp Speed, was the right person, in the right place at the right time.

A Post Where She Sees it All

Still another contemporary whose performance is too outsized to be subsumed under the national stereotype of supposed Black deficits is the 2009 Black Engineer of the Year, Dr Wanda Austin, who works in the rarified, security-classified realm of military satellite communications and intelligence. Austin, a B.A. mathematician from Franklin & Marshall College, completed master's degrees in both mathematics and systems engineering at the University of

117

Pittsburgh before taking her Ph.D. at the University of Southern California.

In 1979 Dr. Austin joined the Aerospace Corporation, an outfit working in areas few Americans knew anything about until release of the Will Smith theatrical movie, "Enemy of the State." The Aerospace Corporation builds satellites that work at the core of the U.S. military's C4I (Command, Control, Communications, Computers and Intelligence) network, and if that sounds like a mouthful to you, it's more than a mouthful for potential military opponents to chew on.

In addition to other duties, Dr. Austin is one of that handful of Masters of the Universe who advise the National Security Agency in how to sharpen its intelligence-gathering abilities. A civilian, she holds the Air Force Scroll of Achievement and a Gold Medal from the ultra-secret satellite surveillance crew at the National Reconnaissance Office, among other awards.

Stage Lights, Up!

Work in the shadows of intelligence mostly doesn't come to public light, but when a person rises to command level, it merits public attention.

Dr. Austin's moment came in June 2007, when Aerospace announced that she would succeed Dr. William F. Ballhaus Jr. as President and Chief Executive Officer. Company announcements noted that the Aerospace Board of Trustees actually had hired a national head-hunter firm, Hedrick & Struggles, to do "an extensive nationwide search" for a replacement for the retiring CEO, but in the end, the board members unanimously agreed that Dr. Austin was the best choice to lead the corporation into the future. So said retired the chairman, Air Force Lt. Gen. Donald L. Cromer. And if anyone could argue with that, he or she was not visible on the radar screen.

Taking Her Turn, in Stride

Lydia Thomas, a child of the segregated South and a biologist in an engineer-dominated enterprise, was thus in good company as she drove past similarly daunting challenges, working a career that took her right to the upper - management levels in the high-performance environment of the MITRE Corporation.

It turned out that much of MITRE's work supporting manned space exploration and the remediation of polluted industrial sites required as much expertise in basic Life Sciences -- biology, physiology, hydrology, organic and soil chemistry and the analysis of the interaction of living organisms in closed and open environments -- as in the applied "hard science" of engineering, for one thing. And as Dr. Branson had shown earlier, down at the molecular level, deciphering biochemical activity is a major-league job of basic science research.

So Dr. Lydia Thomas, the consummate zoologist and microbiologist, found her talents a good fit in working with the blended-skill-set teams MITRE needed to complete its contracts with government agencies looking to clean up and move on from the environmental mistakes of the past. And supported by sensitive managers and mentors, she rose to head MITRE's environmental and space developments laboratory.

Then, in 1996, MITRE Corp. spun off the division as Mitretek

119

Systems, concentrating its non-defense technology businesses into one non-profit entity, and named Dr. Thomas its first president and Chief Executive Officer. Mitretek today stands on its own footing as a consulting scientific research and systems engineering organization, working for government agencies at all levels – federal, state, and local – to solve complex technological problems in criminal justice, environment, health, energy, homeland security, space, transportation, and telecommunications. Dr. Thomas runs the whole show.

Broad Advisory Reach

In addition to her work at MITRE and Mitretek, Dr. Thomas has sat on the Environmental Advisory Board for the U.S. Army Corps of Engineers, on the Scientific Advisory Board for the Department of Defense Strategic Environmental Research and Development Program, and chaired the R&D Investment Panel for a Defense Science Board Summer Seminar on technology. She also has been appointed to serve on the Virginia Research and Technology Advisory Commission. In 2002, President George W. Bush named Dr. Thomas to the President's Homeland Security Advisory Council, and she also was elected to the Council on Foreign Relations.

Standing among the Best of the Best

In 1991 Dr. Thomas won a Deans' Award, presented by the Council of Deans of HBCU Engineering Schools to a Black-college graduate for outstanding contributions to industry, at the Black Engineer of the Year Awards ceremony in

120

Baltimore. In February 2003, she went back to claim top honors as *the* Black Engineer of the Year. Later that year, she was selected by the editors of *blackmoney.com* online magazine and *US Black Engineer & Information Technology* as one of the "50 Most Important African Americans in Technology," and returned yet again to be recognized at a special commemorative banquet during the February 2004 Black Engineer of the Year Awards conference.

Through a Different Door...

Like many women now working in the technology enterprise, Dr. Lydia Thomas came into the engineering arena from a non-engineering discipline. But with the constant blending of skills into multi-discipline teams that is a hallmark of the technology enterprise today, the science knowledge and skills Dr. Thomas brought in became premium commodities. Her own drive and accomplishments then moved her to the top rank, in the executive suite and in the arenas of public policy, where government and corporate leaders, senior academics and community leaders meet to decide the direction of developments that affect everyone's lives. In the vernacular, she is one in a million.

Endnotes

1. UC Davis Study of California Women Business Leaders: A Census of Women Directors and Executive Officers, 2005, released February 2006, at *www.gsm.ucdavis.edu/census*.

2. See also *http://www.socwomen.org/socactivism/stem/fact_sheet.pdf*. See also *www.socsec.gov*.

Chapter 7

Stancell Re-Writes the Chemistry Books

Arnold Stancell completed high school at the same time the Supreme Court's *Brown* decision arrived to tear up the sad *status quo* in American race relations. *Brown* had little impact in the North at first, specifically on the education of a young Harlem High student who graduated in 1954, and the young Dr. Martin Luther King's leadership of the Montgomery Bus Boycott had not yet arrived to rivet the nation's attention.

Stancell, named Black Engineer of the Year by *US Black Engineer* magazine in 1992, began his engineering education at the City College of New York, majoring in chemical engineering and chasing a different dream. As with others in this book, however, the high drama brewing during his youth deeply affected him, as they affected Blacks all across the country.

The murder of Chicago teen Emmett Till in Mississippi in 1955,[1] three years before Stancell completed his baccalaureate studies, was a wake-up call for Blacks across the country, igniting the civil rights movement like nothing that went before. *Jet* magazine published gruesome pictures of Till's mutilated body and shocked people everywhere.

The magazine and Black newspapers across the country followed the story of two white men taking the boy from his uncle's home in the middle of the night and the discovery three days later of his broken, bloated body in the Tallahatchie River, generating widespread outrage. Till's mother, Mamie Bradley, kept his casket open during the funeral so everyone could see what had been done to her son, and afterward she embarked on an aborted national tour to raise money for the civil rights fight.

Arnold Stancell was still a teen himself in 1955, and not involved in the storm boiling over the supposedly placid South. But discrimination was rampant not only "Down South," but everywhere during the 1950s, impinging on daily lives and restricting the aspirations of Blacks who, like the young Arnold Stancell, thought the American Dream should be as open to their desires as those of other people. Blacks who lived through that era thus developed a sense of mission, a drive to improve their people's lot no matter what their chosen field of endeavor.

Pushing Against the Curve

Stancell was deeply immersed in chemical engineering studies, but was mindful like all Blacks in his generation of that insistent drumbeat for racial progress. Like his contemporary John Slaughter, Stancell grew up without knowing much about the Black scientists and engineers who went before, for Black chemical engineers were a rare breed.

Rare is not the same as nonexistent, however, and some had to cross his mind. Norbert Rillieux, the son of a Black

124

Louisiana slave and a French mining engineer, had been a clear forerunner 100 years earlier. Rillieux, who studied and then taught at France's famed *Ecole Centrale*, had moved chemical engineering light-years ahead in 1846 – before it was formally recognized as a discipline – with his evaporative sugar refinery. Rillieux found wholly new uses for the thermodynamic analysis skills he acquired teaching steam-engine principles, and his insights put a solid theoretical foundation under modern chemical manufacturing, including the production of dyestuffs and the refining of petroleum. Indeed, former U.S. Agriculture Department chemist Charles Brown once called Rillieux' evaporating pan "the greatest invention in the history of American chemical engineering."

Another forerunner was Elmo St. Brady, the nation's first Black Ph.D. chemist, who graduated from the University of Illinois in 1916. Still another was Edmund Marion Augustus Chandler, a Howard University chemist who took his doctorate at Illinois in 1917, as America was sending its first doughboys off to fight World War I.

The young Stancell may have heard about Rillieux during Negro History Week, but he probably knew nothing about Dr. Brady or Dr. Chandler, who was a plant chemist for Abbott Laboratories during the early 1920s before striking out on his own as a consultant based in Chicago's northern suburbs.

Setting the Pattern

Dr. Percy Julian[2] was the shining light for science-minded Blacks in Stancell's generation. Julian was born in segregated Montgomery, Alabama, in 1899, long before the generation that produced Rosa Parks and Martin Luther King Jr., but not

125

much before E.D. Nixon, the legendary Pullman Car porter, businessman and organizer whose private car service supported the Bus Boycott of 1955. Julian was Black, and integration was a long way off; he was not allowed to go to high school. But Julian, determined to complete his education, persisted anyway and made it into DePauw University as a "sub-freshman."

Forced to take remedial classes, Julian raced to catch up to his peers, then graduated first in his class in 1920. He taught at Fisk University and completed a master's degree at Harvard University. He went abroad to earn his Ph.D. in chemistry at the University of Vienna in 1931, just as the Nazi madness arrived to drop curtains of sorrow all over Europe. Dr. Julian returned to DePauw and began investigating medicinal plant chemicals, making landmark discoveries.

Pioneering biologist Ernest Everett Just returned home from Germany about the same time, as Adolph Hitler's racist campaign for chancellor gathered steam. U.S. audiences learned about the building Nazi juggernaut from a young Eric Sevareid, whose network radio broadcasts of Brown Shirt rallies sent chills up American spines.

Just Getting Started

Undaunted and back in the U.S.A., in 1935 Dr. Julian and his research partner Josef Pikl broke down chemicals from the African calabar bean to synthesize physostigmine, or *esserine*, to reduce the deadly pressure of glaucoma inside the eyeball. In 1939, working at the Glidden Company, Dr. Julian investigated a water leak into a tank of purified soybean oil and learned that an accidental byproduct, soy sterol, could be used to manufacture male and female hormones, useful in treating certain cancers and problem pregnancies. During World War II., the U.S. military adopted Dr. Julian's soy protein-derived chemical foam for the suppression of oil and gas fires, saving many lives. But he was not finished rewriting the history of science.

In 1948, when Mayo Clinic researchers discovered cortisone, which relieved rheumatoid arthritis, Dr. Julian went Mayo one better. Natural cortisone was difficult and expensive to produce, but in 1949 a Julian-led team developed a synthetic substitute at pennies per ounce. It was his crowning glory, but Dr. Julian still kept on working. His more than 100 patents and scores of scientific papers described products that led directly to the development of chemical birth control and medicines to suppress the immune system, required for successful organ transplants. And his earlier discovery of ways to make synthetic hormones led directly to the development of the modern birth-control pill, the precursor of the Sexual Revolution. Without it, that revolution would likely have been still-born.

No Backing Down

The most widely distributed news was bad, however. In 1951 Dr. Julian and his family became the first Blacks to move to Oak Park, Ill., and had their house firebombed twice.

The lesson here was clear: Despite all Dr, Julian's scientific renown, what mattered most to many whites was that he was Black. Dr. Julian faced that bigotry in characteristic fashion, head-on, persevering with grace, drive and a strong component of bare-knuckled courage. Ultimately, the fire-

127

bombers were forced to subside, but not before *Ebony* magazine had painted a vivid picture of the embattled Doctor, his eyes burning brighter than any set blaze, facing down the cross-burners and would-be rioters jeering outside his home.

Coming of Age

But not all the news was discouraging. While Stancell was in college, the Little Rock Nine stood up to the jeering crowds trying to block their entrance to Central High School, breaking the back of segregation in the Deep South state of Arkansas. All Blacks had been inspired by Jackie Robinson's conquest of major league baseball – in New York where Stancell lived – but another New Yorker, Althea Gibson, took the dream of equality to still-higher levels by trouncing the world's best players in the cerebral game of tennis.

In 1957, the same year angry Southerners were screaming hatred at Black teenagers in Arkansas, the 30-year-old Gibson won the singles title at the French Open. Gibson followed that by dominating all comers at Wimbledon and, proving it was no fluke, she repeated as champion in 1958, the year Stancell graduated with his B.S. in chemical engineering and moved up to the Massachusetts Institute of Technology.

Four years later, Stancell began his own career of "firsts" as MIT's first Black doctor of chemical engineering, and joined the Mobil Oil Corporation as a researcher. Initially, he seemed to be following the footsteps of Percy Julian, but as we shall see, Stancell was as much interested in the climb up the corporate ladder as in chemistry.

128

Research Beginnings

During a 10-year stint at Mobil Research Dr. Stancell developed nine patented processes for making plastics: A low-cost, solventless, low-pressure polyethylene process; the first commercial process for making polybutane-1; commercial purification of teraphthalic acid (a polyester intermediate); and rapid bonding of plastic structures at interfaces by use of lasers.

Still in his research mode, Dr. Stancell opened a new field of investigation into plasma reactions at surfaces, leading to ultra-thin (less than 0.5 micron) film deposition for permselective membranes for separation applications. He rose to manager of chemical process development, then took a short break to return to his *alma mater*.

On leave from Mobil, Dr. Stancell served as associate professor of chemical engineering at MIT for the academic year 1970-71. He enjoyed early success mentoring and inspiring a doctoral student, David Lam, who later founded Lam Research, a leading maker of plasma etchers for the making of computer chips. MIT, impressed, offered him a tenured post, but Dr. Stancell was headed for bigger things as a manager back at Mobil.

Executive Action

The pioneering Dr. Julian also had strong business ambitions and a global view. While other Blacks were struggling to come to terms with industrial America, Julian Laboratories, Inc., was setting up research facilities in Mexico and the United States and a chemical plant in Guatemala, producing significant income. The Upjohn Company bought the

Guatemalan plant in 1961, and the Philadelphia-based Smith Kline French took over the other plants the same year.

Dr. Stancell, working inside the corporate structure, would reach even higher levels of access. In 1975 NOBCChE, the National Organization for the Professional Advancement of Black Chemists and Chemical Engineers, recognized Stancell's accomplishments with a Professional Achievement Award, but he really was just getting going.

Working as the general manager of Mobil's plastics business, Dr. Stancell revolutionized the packaging industry with a clear plastic that totally replaced the formerly ubiquitous cellophane. He also developed the plastic base for PVC pipes, a vastly cheaper competitor to copper for indoor plumbing.

Dr. Stancell also played a key role in the communications revolution. Information Technology is widely represented as a triumph of electrical engineers, but the truth is that computer chip-making and the production of optical fibers for data transmission are really massive chemical operations. Dr. Stancell's research in thin-film deposition greatly affected the computer industry, and one of his plastic products became the "cladding," or outer coating, for optical fibers. Without that cladding, light beams moving along the fiber "pipe" would escape at bends, attenuating the signal. With cladding that has the proper refractory and reflective characteristics, most of the energy in the light beam stays within the fiber. This enables the tiny laser beams used in optical fiber communications to travel thousands of miles, still carrying intelligible signals.

In Europe, Dr. Stancell emerged as a regional manager of

marketing and refinery operations, dramatically improving efficiency while learning everything he could about how to put together international deals.

Back in the U.S.A., Dr. Stancell became vice president of Mobil's domestic oil and natural gas business. Then it was back overseas again, as vice president for exploration and production of petroleum and natural gas for the Middle East, Europe, and Australia, with a staff of 5,000 employees and a capital budget of $500 million.

In this arena, small-timers need not apply. Dr. Stancell, up to the task, initiated, negotiated, and successfully signed a joint-venture with the Persian Gulf state of Qatar for natural gas production in the Gulf's North Field, valued at $18 billion during the early 1990s.

Passing On His Lessons

For others, that might have been quite enough. But Arnold Stancell still had something to give to those who would follow in his footsteps, and he chose the education arena. Retiring from Mobil Oil after a 31-year career, Dr. Stancell joined the faculty of the Georgia Institute of Technology as professor of chemical engineering, focusing on polymer and petrochemical processes as well as plasma reactions in microelectronics processing.

Over a decade-long career at Georgia Tech, Dr. Stancell won many honors. In 1993, at the end of his Mobil career, the City College of New York recognized him with a Career Achievement Award, and two years earlier he had been the Invited Marshall Lecturer at the University of Wisconsin. In 1997 he was inducted into the National Academy of

Engineering and won the American Institute of Chemical Engineering's National Award in Engineering Practice. During the same year, Dr. Stancell was named Outstanding Teacher in Chemical Engineering. And in 2004, *Science Spectrum* magazine named Dr. Stancell one of the "50 Most Important Blacks in Research Science," recognizing his lifelong work in making science part of global society.

Leading by Serving

In 2001, Georgia Tech named Dr. Stancell Chair of Servant Leadership,[3] a position created to "ensure that all undergraduates have exposure to leadership. The Chair of Servant Leadership's job, in addition to regular teaching duties, is to teach theoretical courses on leadership and to arrange opportunities for students to apply the principles learned in extracurricular activities.

Stancell was the ideal first tenant of such a chair. Throughout his career, leadership had been his mantra when speaking to young people. Georgia Tech hired him as a teacher of chemical engineering, but it might just as easily have hired the man who affected so many lines of business as a business professor, teaching the principles of executive leadership.

"The world needs technically savvy leaders," said Dr. Lee Wilcox, Tech's vice president of student affairs, in an article in the college newspaper *Technique*. And "with the number of organizations available on campus, Tech is a great place to work on leadership."

Shifting the Leadership Paradigm

Leadership on any college campus is usually seen as reserved for select students. Under the initiative by Georgia Tech President G. Wayne Clough, however, the program was designed to provide leadership training and opportunities to a broader number of students. Dr. Stancell's job would be to add a service-oriented tone to the initiative. "The best leaders are service-oriented," Dr. Wilcox told *Technique*. "They're not there just for the power. They are there to serve."

Dr. Stancell had his own spin: "Servant leaders do not necessarily have to be volunteers. They need to serve the organizations they lead."

Interviewed by the college newspaper, Dr. Stancell talked about the lack of emphasis on leadership in his own professional career. "None of the engineers in my generation even mentioned leadership. If you were smart and bright, that was it."

Coming from a generation that had been inspired by John F. Kennedy and Martin Luther King, Dr. Arnold Stancell could not escape thoughts of the requirements of leadership. When he realized the need for a leadership emphasis among engineering students, he resolved to "get some leadership" into every course he taught.

Discussing Dr. Stancell's selection as first Servant Leadership Chair, Dr. Wilcox noted that "he had been emphasizing leadership components into his courses, including thermodynamics. He realized through a full career at Mobil that leadership was required to be successful."

Thus, Wilcox said, Dr. Stancell "was a natural choice, serving to infuse leadership concepts into the Georgia Tech curriculum, as well as developing a stand-alone focal course on leadership, first offered in the fall of 2002.

Dr. Stancell also was charged with working to make leadership issues "resonate in different parts of the Georgia Tech curriculum. He worked to infuse leadership materials into courses ranging from freshman level to major-oriented classes.

"We would like to start emphasizing leadership right from the beginning of a student's stay at Tech and hopefully reach a vast majority," he told *Technique*. "There is a leadership piece in Psych 1000," Stancell said, referring to one of the required courses for freshmen. He pushed to enhance that portion of the course, and to integrate leadership training into second-year history courses. "American History should include a discussion of historical figures and show good and bad leadership skills in history," Stancell said.

In addition, the Organizational Behavior course, required for industrial engineering and management majors, would expand to cover qualities of leaders in organization. Typical for him, Stancell did not just sit on a committee to create new requirements. He then undertook to personally help the professors in the various disciplines learn how to teach leadership by emphasizing a leadership style that empowered those working under them.

Now retired from Georgia Tech, Dr. Stancell remains active as co-chair of the Board of Chemical Science and Technology, a body established under the National Research Council, which advises the U.S. government on technology issues. Dr. Stancell also sits on advisory boards for chemical engineering at MIT, Carnegie Mellon University and the City College of

New York. Not bad, for a poor kid from Harlem High.

Endnotes

1. See also Rubin, Richard, "The Ghosts of Emmett Till," *The New York Times*, July 31, 2005.

2. See "People and Discoveries: A Science Odyssey: Percy Julian, 1899-1975, *Http://www.pbs.org/wgbh/aso/databank/entries/bmjuli.html*

3. See "ChemE prof to bring servant tone to leadership," Technique, 2001-11-02, *http://new.nique.net/issues/2001-11-02/news/2*

Chapter 8

Dreaming a New Future in Communications
Without Black Colleges, it would have been Impossible

Dr. James W. Mitchell began his academic preparation at historically Black North Carolina A& T State University, and therein lies a tale. Dr. Mitchell, the 1993 Black Engineer of the Year, went onward to Iowa State University, following in the footsteps of the great George Washington Carver, who had journeyed North to the Iowa State Agricultural College more than 70 years earlier. Mitchell graduated to become one of the premier investigators and developers of the ultra-pure optical glass propelling the communications revolution, but what went before is particularly worth retelling.

The Black colleges that prepare the James Mitchells of today still are shouldering a disproportionate share of the work of educating new generations of Black business, science and technology professionals,[1] even though greater numbers of

136

Blacks actually enroll in "mainstream" institutions. How that situation came to be is best discovered by an honest appraisal of the long reluctance of American society to deal with its legacy of discrimination.

We start with Carver himself. Carver is justly revered as the "chemurgist" who almost single-handedly reinvented American agricultural practice, rewrote the menu for American eating habits, and discovered many useful compounds, pigments, plastics and chemical precursors in the fruits and vegetables that are staples of American diets, though he only patented three.

Children in Dr. James Mitchell's generation grew up hearing about Carver's wondrous chemical talents, but it too often gets ignored that only the Civil War spared the plantation-born Carver from a life of "chattel" enslavement, underfed, ill-clothed and prevented from learning to read, write and count by "owners" determined to stunt his marvelous mind with decades of drudgery.

Uncomfortable Truths

Twentieth-Century schoolchildren were dutifully drilled in the reputation of excellence Carver earned in college, even being selected to remain at the Iowa institution as faculty, before he returned South to begin his famous explorations of the hidden values and substances to be found in peanuts and soybeans. But the uncomfortable truth is that Carver had to go North to complete his education because white Southerners were intent on keeping the recently freed plantation slaves down. Immediately after the Civil War, unrepentant Dixie lawmakers tried to re-enslave him and his

137

kind with the infamous "Black Codes," until the federal Reconstruction laws put a stop to that.

Then the Supreme Court published its even more infamous decision in the *Plessy v. Ferguson* railway discrimination case and legitimized Jim Crow segregation in 1896. That was the same year Carver completed his master's degree and began his long career, returning South to teach at Alabama's Tuskegee Institute and help poor Black farmers learn scientific tricks to boost crop yields, combat pests and produce healthier foods.

When many Southerners, Black and white, fled West after the boll weevil destroyed cotton crops and soil exhaustion turned once-rich farmland into a Dust Bowl during the 1930s, Carver stayed behind, working to find solutions and providing inspiration to young people across the country, especially the parents of Dr. Mitchell's generation.

Percy Julian, another chemical pioneer who preceded Dr. Mitchell, was born in Alabama just before the turn of the 20th Century, three years after Carver got his master's degree. Dr. Julian grew up in Montgomery and was blocked from attending whites-only high schools, but did not give up. Julian fought to complete his education in defiance of the obstacles thrown into his path by the *Plessy* decision and the intransigence of the "Solid South." As we have seen, Dr. Julian went North as Carver had before him, beating the odds to become his own landmark success story. But the racial animus that produced segregation did not begin in 1896, nor did it die out altogether in 1954, the year Thurgood Marshall persuaded the high court to rewrite the law of the land in the *Brown* school desegregation case.

'Unthinkable' Education

What had gone before was not pretty. H. Kenneth Bechtel's book, "Blacks, Science and American Education (Rutgers University Press: New Brunswick)," reminds us all that "it was unthinkable" to whites during and after Reconstruction that anything such as equal education for Blacks would be allowed.

"If Blacks had to be educated, white Southerners felt, let that education be suited to their inferior mental capacities and to their proper, subservient place in society. . . . [A]n examination of the data on school expenditures from the mid-1870s to 1930 clearly reveals the massive disparities between the education of whites and Blacks in the South. Data for the state of Alabama indicate the changes that took place over the 55-year period from 1875 to 1930. During the 1875-76 school term, Alabama spent an average of $1.30 per pupil for white teachers ' salaries and $1.46 per pupil for Black teachers' salaries. This difference in favor of Blacks reflects the impact of the Reconstruction administration. By 1885, however, Alabama was paying Black teachers 85 percent of what was paid to white teachers. And 25 years later, Black Alabama teachers still received only $1.10 per pupil while their white counterparts got nearly six times as much ($6.42)."

Violent Underpinnings

That intransigence continued through the middle of the 20th Century, with whites all over the South emboldened by the racial pogrom that had happened in Wilmington, North

139

Carolina, in 1898. A commission appointed by the North Carolina state government now says that the Wilmington violence, for years portrayed as a spontaneous outbreak, actually was coup, in which white supremacists overthrew the government of Hanover County, N.C., at gunpoint.

The 500-page document, the product of a six-year study released in June 2006, said the trouble began when white vigilantes, resentful after years of political rule by Blacks and their Republican allies during the Reconstruction, burned the printing press of Black newspaper publisher Alexander Manly. Roving bands of vigilantes spread the violence all over the city, looting and destroying Black-owned businesses, burning Black homes, killing some 60 people and driving 2,100 Blacks out of the city.

Calling it the only recorded instance of violent government overthrow in American history -- neatly overlooking the earlier racist pogrom and violent takeover of the county seat at Hamburg, South Carolina, and the bloody, large-scale gun-battles former Confederate soldiers waged against police and militia troops to disenfranchise Blacks in post-Civil War New Orleans, detailed more extensively in Chapter 9 -- the 2006 report urged North Carolina's state legislature to consider economic reparations for Wilmington's Black community, which went almost overnight from a political majority whose men had enjoyed voting rights for 30 years to status as a disenfranchised minority when so many Blacks, fearful for their lives, left the county.

Historians say the later violence in Atlanta in 1906, Tulsa, Oklahoma in 1921, and Rosewood, Florida, in 1923 mimicked the Wilmington massacre, with some white leaders using the

140

North Carolina violence to inspire fear in their Black neighbors.

Lead North Carolina researcher Lerae Umfleet described the violence in Wilmington as a "catalyst" for a violent white-supremacist movement around the country, with other states taking note. "Jim Crow had passed in a few other states," Umfleet told the Associated Press staffer covering the release of the report, "but the whole white-supremacy campaign in North Carolina was watched around the country. People built on what happened in Wilmington."

What had happened was that a prosperous port city saw its economic growth stunted as a result of the violence and the institution of voter literacy tests and a grandfather clause to disenfranchise the Blacks, supporting a whole panoply of laws and customs that sharply restricted their aspirations, public behavior and participation in civic life. The result was hurtful to all: Blacks were still such a large part of the community's business and consumer base that curtailing their economic and social access stunted the entire city's economic progress.

Disparities Maintained

That violent legacy was the reason Blacks in North Carolina and other states endured segregation so long, preferring to found their own schools and social institutions. And that terrible example continued to inspire segregationists across the South. In Arkansas in 1957, three years after the *Brown* decision, only President Dwight David Eisenhower's federalization of the Alabama National Guard prevented mass rioting when nine Black children broke the color line at Little Rock Central High School. The Doctor-to-be James W.

Mitchell, just beginning his own high school education in North Carolina in 1957, could not fail to be deeply impressed as the story unfolded on nightly TV news reports, and in headlines around the world.

Bechtel, looking at education in state after state, found lingering disparities that restricted Blacks' access to education over the generations. Tennessee paid Black teachers 63 percent of whites' salaries in 1870 and, six decades later, it still maintained that disparity. South Carolina spent $14 to educate each white child, but only $1.13 for each Black child. Using Washington D.C. as a reference point, Bechtel said spending by the six Southern states on school expenses, school property and teacher salaries fell far short of anything that remotely could be called "equal" education.

Birth of the HBCU

Against this backdrop, the struggle to educate the children of freed men and women took on epic proportions. Northern liberals and philanthropists joined with Black religious and community leaders to open schools across the South. Amid this drive, historically Black colleges such as North Carolina A & T were founded. Some even began before the end of enslavement:

• The Institute for Colored Youth, now Cheyney University of Pennsylvania, was established in 1837 by Quaker abolitionists to educate free Blacks and escapees from enslavement. Beginning as a secondary school, it conferred its first baccalaureate degrees during the 1930s.

• In 1854, the all-male Ashmun Institute at Oxford, Pennsylvania, became the first institution in the modern world founded with the express purpose to offer Blacks higher education in the arts and sciences. By 1926 when the young Thurgood Marshall arrived from his home in segregated Baltimore, it was better known as Lincoln University.

• In 1856, the African Methodist Church established Wilberforce University in Ohio as the first co-educational institution for Blacks.

Pushing into Technology Studies

Today, 13 historically Black colleges and universities offer programs to train tomorrow's engineers. The 13, each credentialed by the Accrediting Board for Engineering Technology, all were established under segregation. But each has dramatically expanded its technology programs, outgrowing the restrictions segregation once enforced:

• Alabama A&M University was founded as the Huntsville Normal School in 1875, and its first principal was a freedman, William Hooper Council. Industrial education began three years later, and was so successful the school was renamed the State Normal and Industrial School in Huntsville. Morrill Land Grant funds boosted its programs and it became the State Agricultural and Mechanical College for Negroes, able to award associates' degrees. It moved up to award its first baccalaureate degrees in 1941, and won university status in 1969. AA&MU began its engineering program with a department of Civil Engineering after showing that the engineering school University of Alabama at Huntsville focused exclusively on the space program. AAMU got to open

143

a complete engineering school in 2002 with the political settlement of the years-long *Wright v. Alabama* lawsuit, over disparate state support for historically Black institutions.

• The Florida Agricultural and Mechanical University was founded in 1887 as the State Normal College for Colored Students. At the turn of the 20th Century its name changed to the State Normal and Industrial College for Colored Students, then in 1906 as the Florida Agricultural and Mechanical College for Negroes, it awarded its first degrees. FAMU won university status in 1953, and operates a joint College of Engineering with its Tallahassee neighbor, Florida State University.

• The Hampton Normal and Agricultural Institute was founded in 1868 as part of a Reconstruction-era push to prepare bright young Black men and women to educate their newly freed people. Awarding its first baccalaureate degrees in 1922, the Institute became Hampton University in 1984. Hampton's School of Engineering and Technology hosts an Aeropropulsion research center and offers majors in Architecture as well as Aviation, Chemical and Electrical Engineering.

• Howard University, founded in 1867 by its Civil War veteran namesake, established its first engineering program in 1911. And until the post-World War II era expansion of Black-college engineering programs, Howard produced a very large majority of the nation's Black engineers. Howard's School of Engineering, Architecture and Computer Sciences offers majors in Architecture, Chemical Engineering, Civil Engineering, Electrical and Computer Engineering,

Mechanical Engineering, and Systems and Computer Science.

• Funded in 1877 as the Natchez Seminary by the American Baptist Home Mission Society, the school now known as Jackson State University moved to Jackson in 1882, and in 1899 changed its name to Jackson College. The state of Mississippi took over support in 1940 and made it a teacher's college. Between 1953 and 1956, the curriculum grew to include a graduate program and B.A. and B.S. programs in arts and sciences. Designated in 1979 as the urban university in Mississippi, JSU won the right to develop its College of Science, Engineering and Technology as a result of the landmark Supreme Court ruling and resulting settlement of the *Ayers v. Mabus/U.S. v. Fordice* civil rights lawsuit during the 1990s.

• In 1867 the Methodist Episcopal Church's Baltimore Conference founded the Centenary Biblical Institute to train young men for the ministry, and later broadened its mission to prepare women as well as men for teaching careers. Renamed Morgan College in honor of Trustee Chair the Rev. Lyttleton Morgan in 1890,the school was purchased by the State of Maryland in a drive to boost opportunities for Black citizens. Now Morgan State University, the institution founded its Clarence Mitchell School of Engineering in 1985, offering majors in Civil Engineering, Electrical and Computer Engineering, Industrial Manufacturing and Information Engineering, and also offers undergraduate and graduate degrees in Transportation and Urban Infrastructure Studies.

• Norfolk State University was founded in 1935, at the height of the Great Depression. Beginning as the Norfolk unit of Virginia Union University, it became the independent Norfolk Polytechnic College in 1942 and in 1944 became part of Virginia State College. Granting its first baccalaureate degrees during the 1950s, NSU became fully independent in 1969 and gained university status in 1979.Its College of Science, Engineering and Technology enrolls 1,600 students, a quarter of the total student population.

• North Carolina A & T State University, Dr. James W. Mitchell's *alma mater*, was established in 1891 as the Agricultural and Mechanical College for Negroes. In addition to a full slate of engineering majors, NCA&T State also hosts a National Science Foundation funded Engineering Research Center.

• Prairie View A&M University, founded in 1876, is the second oldest public institution of higher learning in Texas. Beginning as the Alta Vista Agricultural and Mechanical College for Colored Youth under a state constitutional provision for separate white and Black educational institutions , it became the Prairie View State Normal & Industrial College in 1899, then after the 1947 establishment of Texas Southern University it went through more name changes before settling on Prairie View A&M University. The institution gained the right to grant four-year degrees in 1919 and established its graduate school in 1937. Its engineering program began in 1947 by act of the Texas legislature, during the huge boost to engineering education from the G.I. Bill.

• Southern University, a 129-year-old institution, hosts a College of Engineering begun in 1956. It offers the Bachelor's Degree in Civil Engineering, Electrical Engineering,

146

Electronics Engineering Technology and Mechanical Engineering, a Master's Degree program, and a Collaborative Ph.D. program.

• Tennessee State University, founded in 1912 as the Agricultural and Industrial State Normal School, became a four-year teacher's college in 1922, and won university status in 1951. Settlement of *Geier v. Tennessee*, a 32-year legal fight to dismantle a dual system of higher education in Nashville, resulted in the merger of Tennessee State with the University of Tennessee at Nashville. Today its College of Engineering, Technology and Computer Science offers B.S. degree programs in Architectural and Facilities Engineering, Civil and Environmental Engineering, Electrical and Computer Engineering and Aeronautical and Industrial Technology.

• Tuskegee University, founded in 1881 by Hampton graduate Booker T. Washington, has been producing engineers since the postwar, G.I.-Bill expansion of higher education of the 1950s. Dean Legand L. Burge, noting that HBCUs also routinely enroll greater percentages of female students than traditionally white institutions, said in a 2005 *Graduate Engineer* magazine article that "Of my graduates, over 60 percent are female now. In some majors, such as chemical engineering, females count as high as 75 percent."

• Virginia State University hosts a School of Engineering, Science and Technology that includes majors in Biology, Chemistry and Physics, Nursing, Psychology and Mathematics, as well as in Computer Engineering, Manufacturing Engineering, Electronics Engineering Technology, Mechanical Engineering Technology and

Industrial and Logistics Engineering Technology.

Federal Moves Prompt Expansion

Federal support and encouragement, especially after the 1890 amendments to the Morrill Land Grant Act of 1862, prodded the Southern states which are home to most state-run historically Black colleges and universities to also provide better funding support for them.

The post-war G.I. Bill dramatically ramped up enrollments at HBCUs, as Southern political leaders recognized that federal money flowing into their states benefited their entire communities, even moneys moving through the accounts at Black colleges.

The segregationists also recognized that providing better resources at HBCUs could lessen the pressure to open the doors of the South's flagship state universities to Blacks as veterans of the wars in Europe and Asia returned home, determined to fight for the same Rooseveltian "Four Freedoms" -- Freedom of speech and assembly, Freedom of worship, Freedom from want, and Freedom from fear -- at home that their courage and sacrifice on the battlefields had guaranteed for the peoples of other nations.

Today, according to a 2008 study by the Thurgood Marshall College Fund, the HBCUs -- altogether only 3 percent of the nation's colleges and universities -- enroll nearly a quarter of the African-American college students. In 2006, that amounted to 235,000 students, up from the 206,000 total of four years earlier.

And as Tuskegee's Dean Burge pointed out in that *Graduate Engineer* article, the relatively small number of Black colleges produces outsized results: HBCUs are responsible for 28 percent of all the baccalaureate degrees awarded to African Americans. "When considering degrees in science and engineering," Dr. Burge said, "this percentage jumps to 31 percent. You will find data that shows that of the graduate degrees received over the last 30 years, nearly 25 percent of the doctorates have begun with the bachelors from the HBCUs." Tuskegee, he said, "sends about 23 percent of its graduates on to graduate school."

Legal Redress Demanded

But the popularity of Black colleges, increasing even today, did not stop Blacks from fighting for better openness at the "mainstream" institutions their tax dollars supported. NAACP attorney Marshall's ringing victory in the 1950 Texas case of *Sweatt v. Painter* forced Southern states to greatly strengthen Black colleges, in hopes of maintaining legal segregation. The *Sweatt* court demanded that "Separate but Equal" facilities had to provide opportunities that began to match what whites were offered, so historically Black, state-funded Land Grant institutions had to be beefed up. Four years later *Brown v. Board of Education* doomed such hopes, but that was not the end of the battle.

Southern states went so far as to offer scholarships so their Black taxpaying citizens could attend colleges beyond their borders and stay out of state-funded white institutions, but even that was not enough. In 1973, the U.S. Department of Education's Office of Civil Rights began pushing the still-separate state systems of higher education to comply with desegregation orders and provide enhancement funding, prompted by the NAACP Legal Defense and Education Fund's victory over the federal government in *Adams v. Richardson*.

The lawsuit's resolution, as interpreted by the Office of Civil Rights, required dramatic upgrading of historically Black state institutions, both to address historic funding disparities and to make the colleges attractive to white students and so end their status as vestiges of segregation. Today, the average HBCU's population is 17-18 percent white, with another 13-percent leavening of foreign-born students.[2]

North Carolina A&T, Dr. Mitchell's *alma mater*, is a consistently high producer of Black science and technical degree holders. Its 2001-2002 class, cited on the institution's Web page, contained 20 agricultural and animal scientists, 13 biologists, 48 computer scientists, 159 engineers, 73 graduates in engineering-related fields, five chemists and two physicists. Undergraduate enrollment was 52-percent female.

Bottom-Line Issues

That Dr. Mitchell studied for his B.S. degree in chemistry at historically Black North Carolina A&T State University is thus no accident. *Brown v. Board of Education* was as much a battle about the disparate resources provided to Black children for education as it was about human dignity, and the funding disparities the case laid bare did not simply go away after the Supreme Court spoke.

Doubters have only to look over the voluminous record of *U.S. v. Fordice*,[3] a 20-year lawsuit begun by Mississippian Jake Ayers over the continuing segregation in his home state long after the uproar died down over James Meredith's admission to Ole Miss. Ayers, disturbed over the diminished opportunities for his children because of differential funding for historically Black Alcorn A&M College and Mississippi Valley State University, offered the then-novel argument that differential treatment of the institutions serving Blacks was simply another face of racial discrimination.

Big Surprise?

The Supreme Court found *in 1992*, 100 years after Carver entered the Iowa State Agricultural College, that discrimination still existed in higher education. It kicked the *Fordice* case back down to the federal District Court, which decided, among other things, that historically Black Jackson State University could establish a new engineering school. Next door in Alabama, a less well-known lawsuit, *Wright v. Alabama*, made similar arguments as Jake Ayers. In that matter, the U.S. Court of Appeals ordered enhancements to historically Black colleges, too, including the founding of an engineering school at Alabama A&M University.

Mostly founded after the Civil War, Black colleges have carried the lion's share of duties educating the Black professional elite because, until the last third of the 20th Century, Black students simply were not welcome in the ivied halls of America's "mainstream" colleges and universities, even in private education, even outside the South.

Today's dirty secret is that, despite the success of Carver, Julian and others, Blacks on mainstream campuses still must overcome the stereotypical beliefs of whites, faculty as well as students, that they somehow are less qualified for admission, less deserving of the scholarships and honors they have earned.

Ivy-Halled Exclusions

As Bechtel found with K-12 education, the impetus to discriminate dies hard. Thurgood Marshall's first big case, filed in 1934 after he finished Howard Law School under the tutelage of the great Charles Hamilton Houston, was a battle to open the doors of the University of Maryland School of Law to Black students. Marshall won the case of *Donald Murray v. Maryland* using a rationale the pair later reused in *Sweatt v. Painter* – that "Separate but Equal" could not apply if there were no "equal" facilities for Blacks.

And even after that landmark victory, James Meredith met bitter, violent resistance a decade later when he prepared to enter "Ole Miss." The Meredith story is dutifully recounted during Black History Month, but too few also learn about Autherine Lucy's mid-1950s battle to enter the University of Alabama,[4] a decade before Meredith finished his Air Force hitch and signed up for the University of Mississippi.

Autherine Juanita Lucy, born in 1929, went to Selma University and all-Black Miles College for her B.A. in English. She finished at Miles in 1952, and decided to pursue grad studies at the University of Alabama, the state's flagship institution. "If I graduated from the University of Alabama," she said years later, "I would have had people coming and calling me for a job. I did expect to find isolation . . . I thought I could survive that. But I did not expect it to go as far as it did."

Perhaps no one did. In 1955, fresh from their success in *Brown*, NAACP lawyers Thurgood Marshall, Constance Baker Motley and Arthur Shores won a court order restraining the university from using race to bar Lucy and another Black applicant. Two days later, the court amended its order to open the doors to all other potential Black enrollees, and on Feb. 3, 1956, Lucy, 26, began her curriculum as a graduate library science student.

On the third day of classes, jeering mobs of students, their numbers swelled by townspeople and other whites who come from far and near, threw eggs at Lucy, screamed death threats and tried to block her way across campus. Police escorts got her into her classes, but outside the storied halls the jeering mobs chanted and heckled incessantly.

The university kicked Lucy out, saying it was for her safety and the safety of other students. The NAACP tried for a contempt-of-court citation, but failed and Lucy faded from the headlines. She never went back until 1988, when two Alabama professors invited her to speak about her experiences. Asked whether she'd ever tried to re-enroll, Lucy said no, but that she might reconsider. Faculty members then petitioned to get her expulsion overturned and, in the spring of 1992, 36 years after first trying to enter the university her taxes supported, Autherine Lucy Foster graduated with a master's degree in elementary education. Her daughter Grazia joined her at commencement, getting her own B.A. in corporate finance.

HBCUs' Dual Role

Thus, the existence of Black colleges is indeed an artifact of the discriminatory past. It took a federal court order to get James Meredith into Ole Miss in October 1962, and it took federal marshals and troops to keep him there when a mob led by, among others, retired Army General Edwin Walker tried to storm the campus. Even after that, it took a blistering barrage of lawsuits and demonstrations to open up college doors to Blacks in the North as well as the South. It also took the vigilance of the NAACP Legal Defense and Education Fund and the Office of Civil Rights, a Kennedy-Johnson era initiative, to make mainstream institutions stop using discriminatory standards to keep Blacks out.

But it is critically important to remember that Black colleges are just as much a testament to the determination of America's Blacks to overcome all obstacles as they are reminders of the discrimination of the past. Building on that determination, historically Black colleges and universities became centers of excellence from which to challenge all those obstacles that remain in the path to full equality in American society. Although their faculties traditionally have been more racially diverse than mainstream institutions' – a third or more of Black-college faculty members are not Black – HBCUs remain the biggest repositories of Black intellectual and managerial talent in American society. Their loss would be irreplaceable.

No Bypassing this Point

For to say the hurdles that Blacks have faced have been extreme is to put it mildly. The reason there is an annual Black Engineer of the Year Award, in the middle of Black History Month, is that American society too frequently glosses over or ignores altogether the hostility and opposition Blacks have had to face in trying to reach the high levels of accomplishment promised to those who strive in this society of supposed equals. The reason this book was written is to lay bare that story, and to show how critical civil rights successes were and are in opening up the doors so that today's technical high achievers can prosper.

Aggie Climb

Poorly informed observers often assume graduates of historically Black colleges and universities will not be prepared to compete on the front rank, but Dr. Mitchell's career illustrates why they are so wrong.

Dr. Mitchell, the 1993 Black Engineer of the Year, found ready acceptance at AT&T Bell Laboratories after he completed his Iowa State Ph.D. in 1970, a time at which the revolution in civil rights, still in full swing, was running out of steam. Bell Labs, a center of much scientific excitement during the 1960s and 1970s, had after all experienced the precedent-shattering careers of both Lincoln Hawkins and James West, Blacks whose discoveries were immediately put to use building the Information Revolution.

In 1965 when Dr. Mitchell finished at A& T, his future employer had just released the No. 1 Electronic Switching System, the first "stored-program" telephone switch. Telephone system technicians knew the No. 1 and No. 5 "Crossbar" Central Office switches used since the 1930s were technologically advanced, wired-logic computers, but the innovation of putting a transistorized, stored-program digital computer at the heart of telephone switching made it possible to offer a near-incredible array of new services. It also opened up the communications industry to entire classes of newcomers from non-traditional Bell System backgrounds.

Three years earlier Bell Labs, then still part of an integrated

155

monopoly, had also produced the T-1 Carrier digital multiplex transmission system for voice and data. Telstar I, the first active communications satellite, had opened the era of real-time global telephony, data communications and TV broadcasting in 1962, and other Bell Labs staffers were investigating a new short-range wireless communications concept called "cellular radio," which would multiply by orders of magnitude the market for mobile phones.[5]

Organically Inorganic

Dr. Mitchell entered Bell Labs' heady atmosphere of discovery as a member of the Technical Staff, then quickly rose to supervisor of the Inorganic Analytical Chemistry Research Group, then head of the department. Under Dr. Mitchell, Analytical Chemistry became a world-renowned organization, producing a string of first-time accomplishments in the development of new methods of production and the design of unique instrumentation to characterize materials for electronic and photonic waveguides, structures and devices. Much of today's fiber-optic communications systems owe their capabilities to the cutting-edge research Dr. Mitchell's teams performed.

The production of optical fibers requires levels of purity that far exceeds that of the silicon used in semiconductor devices. Dr. Mitchell's forte is extreme high-resolution materials analysis and characterization of trace elements, and he was a key player in Bell Labs' leadership in the push to move high-bandwidth communications onto optical fiber cables. He and his collaborators pioneered development of X-ray fluorescence methods to determine part-per-billion trace element inclusion. He also is a major innovator in high-accuracy activation methods for ultra-trace analysis, and he designed and prototyped the first laser intra-cavity spectrophotometer for high-accuracy, practical determinations of sub-part-per-billion levels of trace impurities.

Still going strong, Dr. Mitchell invented a cryogenic sublimation technique for ultra-purification of liquid analytical reagents and chemicals for fabricating optical waveguides.

Such leadership propelled the entire industry forward and forced the scientific establishment to rewrite what it knew about materials science. For these achievements, which established the characterization chemistry of optical waveguide technology and became the underpinning of Bell Labs' early development of low-loss materials for optical waveguide research and development, Dr. Mitchell was named a Bell Labs Fellow in 1985. The National Academy of Engineering inducted him into its Materials Engineering section in 1989.

In 1994, Dr. Mitchell moved over to lead the Process Chemical Engineering Research Department, and three years later he stepped up to run the Materials Processing Research Laboratory. In 2001, Dr. Mitchell became vice president of the Communications Materials Technology Research Laboratory.

Spun-off Survival
Recall that in 1983 a federal court order broke AT&T's telecommunications empire into many parts, causing widespread dislocations as the former "Baby Bell" operating companies vied for breathing space in a newly deregulated

market, causing suppliers like the spun-off Lucent Technologies Bell Labs to rethink their business models. It also freed Bell Labs to offer its products, competitively priced, to companies far beyond the confines of the old Bell System.

Mitchell-led teams worked with the business units of AT&T and Lucent Technologies to implement innovations that assured the reliability of Lucent switching equipment in global markets, enhanced the throughput and yield of manufacture of photonic and wireless components and greatly increased the manufacturing throughput of high-end optical fiber by implementing "acoustic" process-control methods. Still not stopping, he led development of chip-scale power module technology for Agere Corp.'s Analogue Product's Division, and his research contributions affected every major product line of the Power Systems business unit.

In other words, Dr. Mitchell's research contributions enhanced the knowledge base of characterization science, while the research units he directed innovated technology that considerably enhanced Lucent Technologies' Bottom Line while, not coincidentally, dramatically advancing the cutting edge of the Information Revolution for businesses and individual consumers.

Endnotes

1. Dr. Decatur Rogers, Dean of engineering at historically Black Tennessee State University, in a Deans' Roundtable session at the 2005 Black Engineer of the Year Awards Conference, estimated that the then 11 HBCU schools of engineering (since expanded to 13 with the addition of Norfolk State and Virginia State universities) produced between 33 and 35 percent of the annual graduating classes of Black engineers. The Council of HBCU

Engineering Deans, a recognized body of the American Society for Engineering Education, encompasses all 13 ABET-accredited institutions, and AMIE (Advancing Minorities' Interest in Engineering), a collaboration organized by the Council, works as a corporate-academic partnership to increase resources available to the schools . In addition to the Council of Deans schools, several other HBCUs, such as Alcorn A&M College, Grambling State University, Savannah State University, Texas Southern University and the University of Maryland-Eastern Shore contribute to the engineering workforce through strong programs in engineering technology. Still others, such as Morehouse, Spelman and Talledega colleges, produce engineers under "dual-degree" programs, through which their students complete three years at the home institutions, then move to the Georgia Institute of Technology for another two years, graduating with HBCU degrees in basic science and Georgia Tech degrees in engineering.

2. See also *www.soulofamerica.com/colleges/overview.html; http://www.pbs.org/itvs/fromswastikatojimcrow/blackcolleges_2.html; http://www.thehighschoolgraduate.com/editorial/UShbcu.htm*

See also *http://www.graduatingengineer.com/articles/20050519/Historically-Black-Colleges-and-Uni...*

3. *U.S. v. Fordice*, 505 U.S. 717 (1992). The ruling incorporated the lawsuit of *Jake Ayers v. Mabus*, which had prompted the federal complaint. Ayers, represented by Alvin Chambliss of the Southern Poverty Law Center, argued that differential funding for historically Black colleges and universities constituted differential treatment of Black college aspirants, and thus, it constituted racial discrimination. The Supreme Court held that a state that had *de jure* segregation could not discharge its duty to provide equal protection under the 14th Amendment "until it eradicated policies and practices traceable to its prior de jure dual system that continues to foster segregation." Race-neutral admissions are not sufficiently corrective. One result of the decades-long legal battle was the strengthening of historically Black Jackson State University to make it attractive to whites as well as Blacks, including the establishment of a new School of Engineering and Computer Science. The settlement also provided new resources and program enhancements for Mississippi Valley and Alcorn A&M colleges.

4. See also www.stanford.edu/group/King/chronology/details/56026.htm; *www.americaslibrary.gov/ cgi-bin/page.cgi/aa/leaders/marshallthrgd/lucy;* and *www.ccom.ua.edu/od/article_foster.shtml.*

5. For an idea of just how many innovations were spun out, how fast, look at *http://www-out.bell-labs.com/history/heritage/innovation.html.*

Chapter 9

From Segregation's Depths to Dizzying Heights

William Wiley grew up in Oxford, Mississippi, where he could admire the students attending the state's flagship university, "Ole Miss," and dream of one day joining them. The Wiley family's taxes supported Ole Miss like all citizens, but when young William applied in 1950, Admissions turned him away, just as it had all other Black applicants.

Medgar Evers, the World War II veteran who later organized the fight to help James Meredith desegregate the university, was still a student at historically Black Alcorn A&M.

Thurgood Marshall, a graduate of historically Black Lincoln (Pa.) and Howard universities, could understand exactly what Wiley was feeling. Growing up in segregated Baltimore, Marshall had been racially excluded from Maryland's only law school, at its flagship university, in his home city, too. Vowing to end segregation, Marshall and Charles Hamilton Houston had just won a major battle over Black law school admissions in Texas, but *Sweatt v. Painter* had not yet resonated across the segregated South.

Thus, the future Black Engineer of the Year for 1994, shunned, enrolled instead at Tougaloo College, a historically

161

Black school that a few years later also graduated a young New Yorker named Eugene DeLoatch, who went on to chair the Electrical Engineering Department at Howard before stepping up to be the Founding Dean of historically Black Morgan State University's Mitchell School of Engineering.[1] Wiley, a football scholarship winner, graduated *magna cum laude* with a degree in chemistry in 1954. Dr. DeLoatch, whose drive as an educator put him in a pivotal role in promoting the growth of the Black engineering community as head of the Council of Deans of Historically Black College and University Engineering Schools and later president of the American Society for Engineering Education, won his scholarship for track and field.

For a While, the Law Seemed Truly Blind

If Southern Blacks' seemingly meek acceptance of the racial domination of the first half of the 20th Century is difficult to understand today, the stark background of violent repression that enforced it explains their response. Racial segregation, written into state law below the Mason Dixon Line and supported by brutal riots, lynchings and official denials of human rights in many areas, was illegal according to the U.S. Constitution, whose 13th Amendment abolished slavery, whose 14th Amendment required equal treatment before the law, and whose 15th Amendment granted full citizenship after the Civil War. It also was illegal under the Civil Rights Act of 1866,
which prohibited oppression by persons "acting under color of law."

But in 1896, in an environment of harsh reaction to the

162

emancipation of Blacks, the U.S. Supreme Court refused to enforce the Constitution. Confronted with an appeal in *Plessy v.*

Ferguson that clearly presented a 14th-Amendment challenge to the segregation laws being enacted across the South and in some Northern states as well, the Supreme Court turned away from its duty. Shocking Blacks, the high court ruled that segregation was legal, so long as "separate but equal" public facilities were provided for Blacks. That put a fig leaf over what was really going on – former Confederate states' blatantly advertised disenfranchisement of the men and women who had just been freed by the bloodiest conflict in American history.

Historians make much of the South's entrenched racial "mores" during the pre-Civil Rights era, but the hard fact is that Jim Crow segregation was merely the politest face of a bloody regime of terror. The forces of law simply looked the other way or, when pushed, offered lame attempts to legitimize the brutality.

Dawn Came after 1945

That all changed when Medgar Evers and the generation who fought World War II came back from overseas. Soldiers who have faced down bitter enemies on battlefields ripped apart by artillery blasts and got up to charge forward under the merciless hammering of opposing machine guns are not easily reacclimatized to backing down before a threat, and Evers and a generation of Black ex-combat soldiers now were tempered by that experience.

White historians minimize the role of the men who drove

163

the "Red Ball Express," often under hostile fire, served in the supply battalions, combat engineer forces and medical corps that accompanied – and frequently fought beside – whites during Patton's race across the Continent, or of the Black Seabees who fought with the Navy and Marines in the Pacific. But those returnees, few as percentages of the overall combat force, were still numerous enough to add a backbone of steel to the drive to break segregation.

Many, thanks to the postwar G.I. Bill, also had the education and skills they needed to develop effective campaigns.[2] Evers, a prime exemplar, had fought at Normandy and battled across the Continent to end the Nazis' holocaust in Europe – the very word "racism" was coined because Nazi Germany's extreme xenophobia exceeded anyone's ability to describe it – and Evers came home imbued with the spirit of that fight for Roosevelt's Four Freedoms. And like many other Black ex-G.I.s , Evers came home more than sure he was the equal of any man.

But even Medgar Evers' self-confidence and determination could not alone defeat segregation. The depth of the legacy of violent repression Blacks had to overcome, difficult to imagine today, cannot be overstated. The key here was that the forces of law – especially in the federal government – turned a blind eye to the terror. It took decades of struggle to force the federal government to reverse that nationwide denial of human rights.

Terrorizing the Generations

As stated, it was a denial that had its roots in terror. Beginning right after the Civil War the Ku Klux Klan, founded by ex-Confederate officers led by Nathan Bedford Forrest, began the domestic terror campaign. The Klan was the most visible, but other terror groups also arose, including the Red Shirts, the League of the White Camellia, and Regulators. Violent attacks on the just-freed Blacks and their Republican allies were unremitting:

• In 1870, bands of whites, outraged at losing elections to Republican "carpetbaggers" and freed Blacks in Laurens County, S.C., drove 150 Blacks from their homes and murdered 13 people.[3]

• White League agitation against Black voting power in Louisiana erupted in a pogrom at Colfax, Grant Parish, in 1872, producing the slaughter of 50 Black Civil War veterans and militiamen, among other killings.[4]

• In 1874 the White League "arrested" and murdered six Republican activists, assassinated the brother-in-law of prominent Reconstruction politician Marshall Harvey Twitchell and tried to kill Twitchell, who lost both his arms in the fight.[5]

• In New Orleans, two infamous gun battles erupted between the Metropolitan Police, supported by an integrated militia, and the White League. The first, in 1873, halted a violent attempt to overthrow Gov. William Pitt Kellogg, a Republican. The second saw 600 police and 3,000 Black militiamen defeated by 8,400 White Leaguers, with 27 people killed on both sides. President Ulysses S. Grant had to send federal troops from Mississippi to restore order.[6] It thus was no coincidence that former Army Gen. Edwin Walker,[7] who in 1962 led the mob storming "Ole Miss" to block the federally enforced enrollment of James Meredith, went to New Orleans to produce his now-infamous TV broadcast urging Southern attorneys general to begin waging "massive resistance" to desegregation.

• Red Shirts started a bloody pogrom in Hamburg, South Carolina, on July 4, 1876,[8] incited by two men who tried and failed to break up an Independence Day parade of Black militiamen. Repulsed, the Red Shirts, led by ex-Confederate Matthew Butler, raced through town, burning the homes and businesses of Blacks who had turned the sleepy settlement across the Savannah River from Augusta, Ga., into a prosperous enclave where they elected their own government. At the pogrom's callous height Red Shirts burned down a church on top of the Black men, women and children inside.

• The 1898 massacre in Wilmington, North Carolina, covered in the preceding chapter, disenfranchised Blacks politically and encouraged segregationists all over the South to make Jim Crow the law of the land.

Hatred in Politics

Southern politicians justified the violence. "Pitchfork" Ben Tillman, founder of the terrorist Sabre Rifle Company which spearheaded the Red Shirts' Hamburg pogrom, rose to governor of South Carolina in 1892 and went on to a 24-year career in the U.S. Senate. Years later, on the Senate floor, Tillman recalled the campaign to destroy Black voting rights:

"We stuffed ballot boxes. We shot them (Blacks). We are not ashamed of it." The Black man, Tillman said, "must remain subordinate or be exterminated." Tillman kept his Senate post until he died in 1918, succeeded by Dixiecrat

Strom Thurmond.[9]

From the 1890s through the first third of the 20th Century, a time of recent, livid memory for the grandfathers and mothers, parents, uncles, aunts and family friends who raised William Wiley's generation, that violence continued.

Packing Up and Getting Out

Not all Blacks accepted the South's repressive racial order, despite the terror campaigns, even during the worst years. By 1877, many disgusted Blacks began a spontaneous mass exodus from the South over the Oregon Trail.[10] Many went to Kansas, settled before the Civil War by Massachusetts abolitionists.

The territory across the Missouri River had been the scene of bloody battles between transplanted Northern abolitionists and Missouri "Jayhawkers" terrorizing them before the war. During the war, Quantrill's raiders burned the town of Lawrence, now home to the University of Kansas, because of its role as a center of abolitionist agitation.

Freed Blacks, aware they could own land under federal Western settlement provisions, founded towns in Kansas and Oklahoma. Many went all the way to the Pacific Coast.

Estimates range from 20,000 leaving Louisiana to more than 70,000 Blacks leaving that state and Mississippi, but many uncounted others quit South Carolina, Alabama, Georgia, Virginia and other former Confederate states. Whites, unable to stop them, derided the Black Exodus, calling the emigrants "Exodusters" because of the dust clouds raised by their wagon trains.

Beginning Segregation's End

Those who remained labored in a society determined to rescind the freedom promised by the Emancipation Proclamation and enshrined in the Constitution. The success of that reactionary drive, almost celebrated by Northern white commentators remarking on how well Southern whites and Blacks "understood" each other, continued into the 20th Century until the post-World War II period, when Black soldiers like Medgar Evers came home just as determined to end it.

Evers, an insurance agent after his 1952 graduation from Alcorn A&M, moved quickly to fight segregation. Evers began organizing boycotts over discrimination and investigating attacks on Blacks seeking to exercise their rights. Shortly after the Supreme Court reversed *Plessy* in the 1954 *Brown v. Board of Education* ruling, Evers applied to the University of Mississippi's law school, but was turned away on racial grounds. Like Thurgood Marshall 20 years earlier, Evers did not take the slap lightly.

A campus leader and student newspaper reporter at Alcorn A&M, Evers had become an NAACP activist by the time he finished college. The NAACP national office appointed him state Field Secretary, and a 1960 boycott he led in Jackson drew national press coverage. Evers also kept pushing to desegregate the University of Mississippi.[11]

International Counterpoint

But that's getting ahead of things. The postwar struggle for civil rights in America also was affected by the ripening struggle against colonialism in Africa and the developing world and the Soviet Union's competitive threat in the Cold War. Soviet Russians had cobbled together an empire in Eastern Europe and now were contending for access to the natural resources and allegiance of the emerging "Third World."[12]

• India, with prompting from U.S. Office of Strategic Services agents during World War II, threw off the British Raj and became an independent nation under Jawaharlal Nehru in 1947. After the Bandung Conference, Nehru and Josip Broz "Tito" of Yugoslavia began arguing for a "Third Way" for developing nations not aligned with either the American-led West or the Soviet-led East. Mohandas K. Gandhi, who had led India to freedom with his epic civil disobedience campaign, was shot to death while completing a series of lectures about the struggle for Black civil rights in America, which he called the vital proving ground for his philosophy of non-violent struggle against oppression.

• Kwame Nkrumah, born in Africa and educated in England and the U.S., organized a Pan African Congress in 1945, with the express purpose of finding ways to free Africa from colonial domination. Nkrumah was jailed in 1950 by British Gold Coast authorities, but freed when his Convention People's Party swept the 1951 elections. Nkrumah's complaints against British racism and discrimination in Africa echoed Blacks' complaints in America, and were deeply troubling to Western leaders. In 1957, Nkrumah led his country to independence as the free nation of Ghana. It was the same year the Soviet Union orbited Sputnik I and shattered America's complacency about the intense technological and political competition it had entered.

169

• Nnamdi Azikiwe, a contemporary of Thurgood Marshall and Langston Hughes at Pennsylvania's Lincoln University, was back in Africa, founding a chain of newspapers and running for office in his homeland. Threatened with imprisonment for writing a "treasonous" article about discrimination in a Gold Coast newspaper, "Zik" was acquitted at trial and returned to Nigeria. In 1954, the year William Wiley finished his baccalaureate at Tougaloo, Azikiwe won election as prime minister of Eastern Nigeria.

Bitter Resistance at Home

Back in Mississippi, William Wiley, like all Southern Blacks, knew the racial score. Next door in Alabama, Autherine Lucy had walked into a vortex of hatred with a simple attempt to enroll in graduate school. She had to sue to get into the University of Alabama, and was expelled after three days when crowds of whites followed her on campus, threatening to kill her.

The record of the great Tuskegee chemurgist George Washington Carver, who used his Iowa State Agricultural School master's degree to promote agricultural improvements that directly benefitted Alabama's economy, should have been a mighty inducement to end the cruel policy of segregation in education. Whites also might have taken counsel for change from the story of the great chemist Percy Julian, another Alabamian, who was denied the opportunity to go to high school in Montgomery but completed his education in the North. Dr. Julian's glaucoma medication *esserine*, his many patented inventions and the synthetic hydrocortisone he developed improved the health of

170

Americans everywhere, even as Jim Crow segregation restricted his social mobility in his home state.

Thus, 40 years after Dr. Julian left his hometown of Montgomery, the young Dr. Martin Luther King found himself using the same boycott tactics Medgar Evers was using in Mississippi in the fight against segregation in public accommodations.

Violence Continued

Emmett Till was killed by white racists in a Delta hamlet, one year after William Wiley finished undergrad school. Wiley was in the Army then, on a two-year tour of duty from 1954 to 1956. Experiences on a military base at that time, just after Harry Truman desegregated the armed forces, gave the young scientist Wiley a taste of what life could be like in a world unrestricted by segregation.. Then, returning home to be a civilian electronics and radar repair instructor at Keesler Air Force Base, the young Dr. Wiley-to-be had a ringside seat to watch the painful convulsions of a dying era.

The Montgomery Bus Boycott shook up the entire South, and Dr. King's victory – detailed in his electrifying book, "Stride Toward Freedom" – energized Blacks all over the country. In 1957 in Arkansas, the nation was transfixed by televised pictures of jeering crowds surrounding the nine brave Black schoolchildren who dared desegregate Little Rock's Central High School.

Some Stayed and Fought, Some Just Left

But it was still a bitter time. Segregationists did not give up easily. Thus, In 1958, as Carver and Dr. Julian had done earlier,

William Wiley went out of state to complete his education. He may not have seen this as an act of social upheaval, but he had joined the second half of the Great Migration,[13] during which five and a half million Blacks left the South for new lives in the North and West. Wiley won a Rockefeller Foundation Fellowship, and began master's-degree studies in microbiology at the University of Illinois. Then he went on to Washington State University, where he completed a doctoral degree in bacteriology, with a minor in biochemistry, in 1965. And he never moved back.

While Wiley was gone, the rebellion against segregation was gathering steam. In 1960, four North Carolina A&T freshmen held a sit-in at a Greensboro F.W. Woolworth's lunch counter.[14] The students told reporters, "We believe, since we buy books and papers in the other part of the store, we should get served in this part."

The students stayed until the store closed, un-served but undeterred. The next day they returned, joined by organizers from national civil rights organizations, with wide press coverage. In two weeks, students were holding sit-ins in 11 cities, primarily at "Dime store" store lunch counters. James J. Kilpatrick, the segregationist editor of the *Richmond News Leader*, was troubled by the contrast between the disciplined Black students and their white antagonists in his city:

"Here were the colored students, in coats, white shirts, ties, and one of them was reading Goethe and one was taking notes from a biology text. And here, on the sidewalk outside was a gang of white boys come to heckle, a ragtag rabble, slack-jawed, black-jacketed, grinning fit to kill, and some of them, God save the mark, were waving the proud and

172

honored flag of the Southern States in the last war fought by gentlemen. Eheu! It gives one pause."

Unease Over Africa

American whites also were disturbed over the events unfolding in the Belgian Congo. Patrice Lumumba, a former postal worker and trade union leader, had embraced Pan-Africanism at the All-Africa People's Conference in Accra, Ghana, in 1958, the year William Wiley left Mississippi for Illinois. In 1959, though imprisoned for his speeches advocating independence, Lumumba and his party won by large margins in Congolese local elections.

When the Belgians convened a Round Table Conference on political change in January 1960, Lumumba's Congolese National Movement refused to participate without him, so he was flown to Brussels. Despite all attempts to prevent it by the Belgians and Lumumba opponents Joseph Kasavubu and Moise Tshombe, the Congolese National Movement swept the May national elections and Lumumba took the helm of Congo's newly independent government.

Lumumba's rise struck fear into the *apartheid* regime in South Africa. The Sharpeville Massacre of Blacks peacefully protesting racial domination in their African homeland spread ugly headlines and TV pictures all over the world in 1960, and the African National Congress, representing the oppressed Blacks, had declared war.

The Big Red Scare

The possibility of a government led by African militants in neighboring Congo was thus daunting to the Pretoria regime.

Even though Lumumba, the Big Boogeyman, preached independence from "imported" ideologies of either the capitalist West or the Communist East, he was not afraid to play one side against the other. Thus, his call for Soviet help in ending Tshombe's power grab in mineral-rich Katanga Province sparked more alarm, and U.S. authorities labeled him a Communist "puppet."

U.S. troops intervened, ostensibly to protect American lives, and Western intelligence agencies collaborated to undermine Lumumba. In one of the Cold War's sorriest excesses, covert operators helped Joseph Mobutu capture Lumumba and turn him over to Tshombe's forces to be executed. American Blacks, avidly following the news, were horrified.

U.S. Black Rebellion Grows

Meanwhile, the sit-ins continued in America. By August 1961, more than 70,000 people had joined in, hampered by more than 3,000 arrests. Sit-ins also were supported by boycotts in the North, where Blacks and sympathetic whites protested against segregation by companies with stores and plants in the South.

Then the students came up with another strategy: Freedom Rides.[15] It had first been tried in 1947, after the Supreme Court reversed a key part of its infamous 1896 *Plessy v. Ferguson* railway segregation ruling, now declaring unconstitutional the segregated seating of interstate passengers.

The Congress of Racial Equality (CORE) had sent an interracial group of bus passengers on a Southern "Journey of Reconciliation," but met virulent hostility. North Carolina authorities sent the group to prison, actually putting some on a chain gang.

In 1961, however, with John F. Kennedy in the White House and his brother Robert serving as attorney general, CORE organized a new Journey, a Greyhound "Freedom Ride" from Washington D.C. to New Orleans, with the whites sitting in the rear and Blacks in front, determined to use the "other race" facilities in segregated bus stations and restaurants.

In Anniston, Alabama, 200 outraged whites stoned the first bus and slashed its tires, then firebombed it when the driver stopped to change tires. In Birmingham, another mob severely beat the second group. One white 'Rider needed 50 stitches, but vowed to continue. Greyhound halted the ride, saying drivers feared for their lives, and the 'Riders instead flew to New Orleans.

More Students Join In

College students in Nashville heard of this, and went to Birmingham to continue the ride. When Robert F. Kennedy tried to intervene, Birmingham police arrested the students and dumped them across the state line in Tennessee. But the students went back and, pressured by the attorney general, Greyhound made a bus available and Alabama State Police protected it on the 90-mile drive to Montgomery. The police then disappeared and a mob attacked in the bus station, beating and kicking one 'Rider while the rest slipped away. The mob left a U.S. Justice Department official unconscious in the street for trying to help one Freedom Rider.

The Rev. Martin Luther King arrived and held a mass meeting supporting the 'Riders in a church surrounded by

175

federal marshals, themselves surrounded by thousands of jeering whites. After a tense, overnight standoff, National Guard troops finally dispersed the mob. Then the 'Riders went on to Mississippi, Dr. Wiley's home state. In Jackson, each was arrested and sentenced to 60 days in prison, but Freedom Riders kept coming. More than 300 spent their summer behind bars, many with serious injuries from beatings.

Winning by Losing

The 'Riders never made it to New Orleans, but won anyway. The steady drumbeat of anti-colonial agitation in Africa and Asia, stridently cheered on by Soviet communists eager to contrast the illegitimacy of Western racism with the "colorblindness" of Communist ideology, meant no U.S. administration could ignore the international implications of violent denials of human rights within its borders. Pushed by the Kennedy White House, the Interstate Commerce Commission outlawed segregation in interstate travel.

'Ole Miss' Doors Cracked Open

In 1962, three years before Dr. Wiley got his Ph.D., Medgar Evers helped James Meredith get federal help to desegregate Ole Miss, the university that refused entry to Wiley and Evers. After intense negotiations, U.S. marshals finally escorted Meredith onto the campus, to be met by rioting crowds led by retired Gen. Edwin Walker, who had left the Army to fight desegregation.

Two federal officers were shot and two other people died during a day and night of swirling riots, but the crowd was finally broken up by federalized National Guardsmen.

The Terrible Bloom of Backlash

The South's violent throes continued. On June 12, 1963, Medgar Evers was shot to death by white supremacist Byron de la Beckwith, who had to be tried three times before he was finally sent to life in prison in 1994. National leaders from across the nation attended Evers' funeral, and he was buried in Arlington National Cemetery like the hero he was.

Then in Birmingham, Ala., on September 15, 1963, in the city's 21st terror bombing attack in eight years – the fourth in four weeks[16] – the 16th Street Baptist Church was blown up in broad daylight. The church, a regular meeting place for civil rights leaders, had drawn the Ku Klux Klan's hatred. Blacks, led by the Rev. Fred Shuttlesworth, were campaigning for voting rights and school desegregation, and the church was a favorite meeting place. This time, however, the bombing killed four girls there for Sunday School. Twenty-three other people were also injured.

Blood on His Hands

Civil rights leaders noted that Gov. George Wallace had opined in a *New York Times* interview that to stop integration, Alabama needed "a few first-class funerals." Dr. King wired Gov. Wallace that "the blood of four little children . . . is on your hands. Your irresponsible and misguided actions have created in Birmingham and Alabama the atmosphere that has induced continued violence and now murder."

Poor Blacks, less committed to Ghandian nonviolence, took to the streets. National news reports said that in addition to the church bombing, police found at least five suspicious fires

177

at Black-owned business establishments, one clearly touched off by gasoline, and the Blacks' anger boiled over.

More than 2,000 Blacks rushed to the bombed church and threw rocks and bottles at police, who fired rifles over their heads, and killed two teenagers on the streets in separate incidents, claiming they did not halt as ordered. Police also had to break up a demonstration by white students protesting school desegregation and intercept a busload of white supremacists supporting them.

Desperate Words, Desperate Acts

NAACP chief Roy Wilkins telegraphed President Kennedy: Unless the U.S. government offers more than "picayune and piecemeal aid against this type of bestiality," Blacks would "employ such methods as our desperation may dictate in defense of the lives of our people."

Geopolitical realities helped to force Kennedy's hand. Succeeding Dwight Eisenhower, who had watched France endure the bitter loss of its Indochina colonies after its debacle at Dien Bien Phu in 1954, Kennedy had sent American "military advisors" to take over the battle against the nationalistic Communist Ho chi Min's attempt to conquer South Vietnam. As the Rev. Shuttlesworth said, at a time Americans were struggling to win the "hearts and minds" of Southeast Asians, the U.S. could ill afford to let violence continue to fester in the South.

Kennedy resolved the immediate crisis by federalizing Alabama National Guard troops and sending them to enforce desegregation orders in Birmingham, Mobile and Tuskegee. Then on November 22, 1963, John F. Kennedy himself was slain during a motorcade in Dallas, and Lyndon Baines Johnson took over in the White House.

More Outrage

The violence continued. In Philadelphia, Miss., in June of 1964, three activists promoting a voter registration drive were abducted and killed, sparking a national outcry. James Earl Chaney, Michael Schwerner, and Andrew Goodman were working in the Congress of Racial Equality's Freedom Summer Project, on their way to investigate a church bombing when carloads of whites, including local police officers, abducted and killed them, hiding the bodies in an earthen dam. Forty-four days later, the FBI found the bodies and filed indictments against the Neshoba County deputy sheriff and 16 others. Seven of the men were convicted.

Finally shocked into action by that spectacle, which generated new headlines about America's racial problems all over the world, Congress passed the Civil Rights Act of 1964, putting new teeth into the enforcement of civil rights laws across the United States.

Climbing Out of the Southern Box

William Wiley, with family back in Mississippi, could not ignore what was happening in his home state. But he did not go back. He completed his Ph.D. at Washington State University and joined Battelle Memorial Institute, a not-for-profit corporation operating the Atomic Energy Commission's Pacific Northwest Laboratory in southeast Washington.

Four years after joining Battelle, Dr. Wiley rose to manager of the Cellular and Molecular Biology Section, where he

179

supervised 25 scientists studying the effects of nuclear radiation on cell functions. Three years later Dr. Wiley got promoted again, to associate manager of the Biology Department. Now he coordinated the work of Pacific Northwest Laboratory scientists with efforts by Battelle scientists in Columbus, Ohio, Geneva, Switzerland, and Frankfurt, Germany.

Segregationists in Mississippi could not have imagined this young man holding such a post after they kept him out of their state's flagship university, but there he was, running projects devoted to the study of the molecular basis of homeostasis, cell surface, membrane receptors, cancer, metabolic inter-conversions and the cellular basis of brain dysfunction.

Once Free, He Flew

Like Percy Julian before him, Dr. Wiley continued to climb, once education lifted him out of the stratified society segregation imposed, benefitting the entire nation.

Dr. Wiley rose to Biology Department manager at Battelle, then director of research, now with a staff of more than 700 looking into atmospheric, geochemical, geophysical, genetic engineering, biomedical, ecological, physical and chemical sciences. The department expanded in 1983 to include chemical process technology, energy systems, engineering physics, and material sciences.

Then in 1984, Dr. Wiley beat out other top candidates to become director of the Pacific Northwest Division, taking over management of the entire Pacific Northwest Laboratory, now under the U.S. Department of Energy.

In a move that surely would vex Gen. Edwin Walker and have the dead Sen. Tilllman turning over in his grave, Battelle had given the Mississippi-born Dr. Wiley authority over more than 4,400 scientists, engineers, technicians and support personnel, with an operating budget greater than $500 million. The Black scholar once turned away by the University of Mississippi now was managing a facility whose land, buildings and equipment were valued at more than $460 million. In addition to facilities on Energy Department land, Battelle Northwest's private holdings included its Richland (Wash.) Research Complex, the Seattle Research Center and a Marine Sciences Laboratory on Washington's Olympic Peninsula.

Environmental Awakening

Rachel Carson's 1962 book "Silent Spring" awakened environmental consciousness all over the world. In the United States, as Upton Sinclair had done six decades earlier with "The Jungle," Carson's advocacy sparked governmental change. The U.S. Environmental Protection Agency was founded as a direct response, but federal and state lawmakers also were inspired to require stringent protections in legislation covering areas in which environmental considerations once were thought irrelevant. This included not only civilian industrial activities, but even the production and testing of weapons and the use of solvents, fuels and chemicals on military bases.

It also brought into sharper focus much of the pioneering research being done in places like the Pacific Northwest Laboratory, where Dr. Wiley led science teams to

181

international leadership in molecular science, environmental restoration and waste management, and global climate change.

Leadership for Empowerment

But Dr. Wiley, who grew up under segregation, also paid close attention to the need to open doors to others. In the words of D.E. Oleson, president and Chief Executive Officer of Battelle Memorial Institute, "Bill also has fostered a cultural environment where innovation and creativity are recognized and rewarded, where staff diversity and affirmative action have real meaning, and where education is a vital partnership – not only between institutions but also between people.

"Because of its impact on his own life, Bill has always been a strong advocate of education, calling it '. . . the salvation of the world, the least expensive option we have for world peace and prosperity.' His message to business leaders, educators and students is that we must keep young men and women, especially members of traditionally under-represented minorities, in the science and engineering educational pipeline because they are essential to our nation's global economic competitiveness."

Not only did Dr. Wiley take the lead in establishing a Washington State University Tri-Cities Branch Campus in 1991, he also was the first national laboratory director to join the Council of Government-University-Industry Research Roundtable, which reports directly to the presidents of the National Academies of Science and Engineering and the Institute of Medicine.

Reaching Out for Business

In addition to serving on the Washington State Governor's Citizen Cabinet and the Economic Development and Environmental Enhancement Task Force, Dr. Wiley sat as a director of the Seattle Branch of the Federal Reserve Bank of San Francisco, was president of the Board of Regents of Washington State University, and a trustee of the Fred Hutchinson Cancer Research Center. He also was a director of the Tri-City Industrial Development Council and helped to raise $1.7 million for the council's Renaissance Project to strengthen the local economy.

Dr. Wiley often told people, "there is nothing more powerful than the belief that you can personally contribute to making a better future," His life exemplified the principle.

Endnotes

1. DeLoatch, a "Blue Chip" track and field recruit from the urban North, continued on to a nationally significant career in historically Black institutions. He spent a quarter of a century teaching electrical engineering at Howard University, and also developed national reach as a key advisor to the National Society of Black Engineers. Recruited to Baltimore's Morgan State University, Dr. DeLoatch became the Founding Dean of the Clarence Mitchell School of Engineering and head of the Council of Deans of the HBCU Engineering Schools, a recognized body of the American Society for Engineering Education. A member of the National Academy of Engineering, DeLoatch also served, in 2004, as president of the ASEE.

2. See also *www.olemiss.edu/depts/english/ ms-writers/div/evers_medgar;*

www.africawithin.com/bios/medgar_evers.htm;
www.gale.com/free_resources/bhm/bio/evers_m.htm

3. See the excellent Reconstruction Period Research Forum documents at www.afrigeneas.com/forum-reconstruction for even more gory details.

4. See "The Cabildo: Reconstruction: A State Divided, at www.lsm.crt.state.la.us/ cabildo/cab11.htm

5. Ibid.

6. Ibid.

7. See "The Strange Case of Maj. General Edwin A. Walker," at www.textiles.com/conspiracy/walker/text.

8. See http://www.arete-designs.com/hamburg, retrieved from http://en.wikipedia.org/wiki/Hamburg%2C_Aiken_County_South_Carolina. See also www.scencyclopedia.com/chamberlain.htm.

9. See www.afrigeneas.com/forum-reconstruction/, supra. See also Report of the Special Committee of the House of Representatives of SC, adopted Dec. 21, 1876; sources in E. Baker, "Under the Rope: Lynching and Memory in Laurens County, S.C. Eric Foner, "Reconstruction in America"; Fox Butterfield, "All God's Children."

10. See "Black Exodus, 1879," at www.college.hmco.com/history/readers.com /ycah/htm/rc_010100_blackexodus.htm; also http://rs6.loc.gov/ammem/aaohtml/exhibit/aopart5.html.

11. See www.olemiss.edu/depts/english/, Supra.

12. Jawaharlal Nehru, the first prime minister of India, coined the term when he and the Yugoslavian strongman Josip "Broz" Tito, seeking a "Third Way" for developing nations not aligned with either the capitalist West or the Communist East. During the Cold War years of the 1950s and 1960s, both camps were contending for development rights, access to mineral and

agricultural resources, and political sway in the developing lands.

13. See Lemann, Nicholas, *The Promised Land: The Great Migration and How it Changed America.* Vintage Books, 1991.
14. See *http://watson.org/~lisa/ blackhistory/civilrights-55-65/sit-ins.html.*

15. *http://watson.org/, ibid.*

16.   See   *http://www.english.uiuc.edu/ maps/poets/m_r/randall/birmingham.htm.*

Chapter 10

Another Proof of the Bounty of Immigration

The official profile put out by the Boeing Company on Walt W. Braithwaite says that he was born in Jamaica in 1945, made his way to the United States and graduated from the American Institute of Engineering and Technology, Chicago, Illinois, in 1965. But that represents the tiniest tip of a mostly untold story: The swelling ranks of Black immigrants and the strengths they bring to America's shores.

Braithwaite, an electrical engineer with a master's degree in computer science from the University of Washington, is an example of that migration, mostly of Black Caribbean islanders but also of growing numbers of Africans, whose drive for education and careers challenges popular notions of "model minorities." Despite the prominence of Colin Powell, the first Black chairman of the Joint Chiefs of Staff and then

186

the first Black to be Secretary of State, the growing presence of Caribbean islanders and Africans has been ignored in the swirl of debate about the burgeoning Hispanic migration across the Mexican border. But that Black migration continues: 15 percent of Black America's population growth came from immigration on the 1990 Census, swelling to 25 percent in 2000.

Roots in the Canal

This Black immigration stream actually started long ago, but now has grown to major proportions Theodore Roosevelt's project to build the Panama Canal moved a quarter of a million Blacks from English-speaking Caribbean countries to Central America, and they stayed, mostly on the eastern side of the isthmus. The continued American presence in the Canal Zone throughout the 20th Century, increased greatly during the two world wars and the Cold War that came afterward, spread an American cultural cast over the entire region.

That influence continues. The close proximity of Caribbean islands to the U.S. mainland and the continuing dominance of American film, cable TV and music exports in world markets means people in Caribbean countries receive much of the same entertainment programming as U.S. audiences. John Logan, professor of sociology at the State University of New York at Albany, says this U.S. cultural influence has been greater in the Caribbean than in other parts of the world. Thus, this pervasive cultural presence, and the extensive networks of kinship, ethnic relationship, and employment induce people to look toward settlement in U.S. cities the way people in other lands look to their own metropolitan capitals.

Economics is the biggest factor. Between 1881 and 1921, 156,000 people left Braithwaite's Jamaican homeland for work on Central American sugar cane and banana plantations, in the Panama Canal Zone, and jobs in the rapidly expanding industries on the U.S. mainland. The Great Depression torpedoed sugar and fruit prices, curtailing plantation work, but significant percentages of Jamaicans remained here, benefitting from Franklin Roosevelt's New Deal.

Industrial Pull

World War II, with its dramatic expansion of war industries, opened the door for many more Caribbean immigrants. American industry was turning out 100,000 warplanes a year by the end of the war, and ships were being built in every major harbor. The auto industry was turning out thousands of tanks, trucks and other vehicles, and all those plants needed imported help while American-born men were off fighting. Thus, between 1941 and 1950 nearly 50,000 Caribbean islanders came here, laboring in 1,500 localities in 36 states.

Walt Braithwaite, born just as World War II was ending, thus was joining an established tradition when he signed on to work in American industry in 1965.

Political Speed Bump

The McCarran-Walter Immigration and Nationality Act of 1952, passed at a time of heightened anxiety over the Cold War, temporarily slowed the growth of Caribbean immigration to the U.S., and 300,000 English-speaking islanders instead headed off to Great Britain. But American-

188

born Blacks complained loudly about the restrictions on Black West Indians in an era when whites were being welcomed from war-torn Europe, and civil rights campaigns pointedly noted that the Statue of Liberty's welcome never seemed as open for people of color. Lyndon Johnson based his appeal to Black voters in the 1964 presidential race on the twin pillars of civil rights and immigration reform. And true to his word to continue the path laid by the slain John F. Kennedy, Johnson linked passage of the Civil Rights Acts of 1964 and 1965 with forging a racially more equitable immigration policy.

Braithwaite graduated from the American Institute of Engineering and Technology in 1965, the same year the Hart-Celler Act passed, liberalizing U.S. immigration again. Great Britain had shut off most Black Caribbean immigration in 1962, but Fidel Castro's 1959 Cuban revolution had changed the equation in the Americas.

Spilloff Benefits

Tourism bloomed on the English-speaking West Indies after Castro shut down the Cuban casinos, hotels and tourist resorts to which Americans and many Europeans had flocked for generations. Mobsters from the U.S. mainland controlled many of those enterprises, and the bribes and skullduggery with which they corrupted Cuban officialdom had been one of the burning issues behind the Cuban revolution. Still, it is important to remember that the tourist impulse did not come from mobsters, but from ordinary Americans.

Thus, those seeking sunny beach resorts in which to spend the cash earned in an expanding post-war economy continued to travel south to the Caribbean, just off the coast of Florida, on boats, ships and planes. When they found Cuba no longer welcoming, they simply moved to other islands.

Castro made it worse when he vocally embraced Soviet-style Communism, nationalized private property and made the Soviet Union his ally, precipitating a nuclear crisis when he allowed the Soviet military to begin setting up intermediate range ballistic missile bases. John Kennedy's bravest act was facing down Soviet Premier Nikita Khrushchev in 1962 with a naval blockade and the very real, very visible preparations for an invasion to force the removal of those missiles. The U.S. economic embargo on Castro's regime that followed that standoff ensured that tourism would grow everywhere but Cuba.

Ready and Waiting
Increased tourism in Caribbean countries produced an immediate boost in the spread of American culture, as well as new connections to American society. Thus, with the door opened by the Hart-Celler Act, U.S. Caribbean immigration grew from 123,000 in the 1950s to 470,000 who came during the 1960s with Walt Braithwaite.

Many of those newcomers were Cubans, educated émigrés who fled Castro's revolution and brought their money with them to build new homes and businesses. The multi-hued *Cubanos* quickly dominated the social and political landscape in South Florida and became a force to be reckoned with in presidential races. But close to 75,000 people also made it to the United States from Jamaica, and their number kept growing. From 1971 to1980, 140,000 Jamaicans arrived, and their numbers reached 208,000 between 1981-1990. That was nearly a quarter of the 872,000 Caribbean emigrants who entered the U.S. during the decade. Braithwaite was in good company.

The Digital Demi-Urge

The young Walt Braithwaite was about to join an entirely different revolution from the political one brewing in Havana. He came to the United States during a time of wide experimentation with digital computers in American industry. The desktop machines that have so reshaped America's business, education and leisure activities had not yet been built, but the large systems we now call mainframes were making serious inroads into all areas of commerce.

IBM's all-transistor 1401 "second-generation" machine had taken over corporate accounting functions during the early 1960s, leading to a "third generation" that propelled IBM to the forefront of competitors racing to computerize America's largest enterprises.

In industry and in academia, smaller computers from the Digital Equipment Corporation were opening up all kinds of new uses. Mainframe computers were big and expensive, and thus were shared by many users to spread the costs. Digital's PDP-5, introduced in 1963, was inexpensive enough to be used by smaller users such as research laboratories, and its PDP-8, the first true minicomputer, introduced in 1964, revolutionized industry. The 12-bit PDP-8 was small enough to fit on a cart, it was simple enough to be used in many different roles, and it cost only $16,000, a paltry sum compared to the big mainframes.

End users in every kind of industry bought PDP-8s, because the machines permitted them to eliminate the delays of getting on a big data center's schedule and the expense of building a complex infrastructure to handle them. PDP-8s could be purchased to fill specific needs, and they were sold in large numbers to laboratories, railroad companies, and manufacturing centers.

Dialed-Up Magic

In communications, AT&T Bell Laboratories had just developed the No.1 Electronic Switching System, the first stored-program controlled telephone switch, and Bell operating companies were racing to install it in switching centers around the country. Stored-program switches – big digital computers operating telephone networks through peripheral switchframes – could provide a range of services not easily duplicated with wired-logic systems, and the No.1ESS system ushered in a new era of flexibility in the design and implementation of services to businesses.

AT&T also had introduced the T-1 Carrier time-division multiplex transmission system in 1962. T-1, which was tailor-made for data transfer, had the added advantage of reducing wire congestion in cable runs, since it put twenty-four 64-kilobit-per-second voice channels on a single pair of wires.

T-1 circuits made it easy to switch between voice and data transmission, or to mix voice and data channels on the same pair of wires. That flexibility propelled business data communications to a new level.

Rolling Up His Sleeves

Walt Braithwaite finished undergraduate school in 1965, just as American industry was beginning to react and adapt to the new capabilities. He joined Boeing in 1966 as an associate tool engineer in Boeing's Fabrication Division, deep in the guts of the world's largest maker of jet airliners. He moved to the West Coast for master's degree studies in computer science, continuing his association with Boeing while he updated his knowledge of the new computer environment, and he graduated from the University of Washington in 1975.

The middle 1970s were when the wheels seemed to be coming off American industry. Foreign producers, especially on the Pacific Rim, were out-producing American steelmakers with new, more efficient Basic Oxygen furnaces. Building on that success, foreign shipbuilders were using the lower-cost, high-quality steel to beat American yards on price and quality with new, modular shipbuilding techniques. Japanese electronics manufacturers were swamping American markets with low-cost, high-quality consumer products, wiping out the American makers of TVs, stereos and radios.

The auto manufacturers, bedrock in American industry, were being mauled by twin horrors: Japanese competitors using new, statistical quality control techniques were beating Detroit products in the market with well-made, fuel-efficient cars, at a time when boycotts and price gouging by the Organization of Petroleum Exporting Countries was forcing all American industries to focus on energy efficiency.

Aviation had its Inertia

Braithwaite was in the aviation industry, where factory

193

automation badly lagged the progress in many other manufacturing enterprises and airliners were still being assembled by hand. But that is not to say that computers and automation had made no inroads at all. American engineers had figured out that the real key to efficiency in the modern factory was control of information. Programmable controllers, embedded microchips, minicomputers and big mainframes became tools that allowed factory managers to see everything that was happening on their shop floors, and to reach out and control the operation of machines all over the plant.

Auto manufacturers were early adopters of computer-driven flexible manufacturing systems, but aircraft makers were not far behind, even if their final assembly process was still accomplished by manual labor. The sophisticated flyers modern aircraft designers were producing required machined parts made to exacting tolerances. Numerically controlled milling machines, computer-controlled lathes and metal cutters, and microprocessor-controlled devices abounded on the factory floor at Boeing and other aircraft makers, crafting subassemblies for the planes that filled the world's skies.

Right Man, Right Time

Braithwaite's computer-science degree was exactly what manufacturers like Boeing needed when these devices and the new, computer-controlled duplexers, head indexers and flexible manufacturing centers were introduced to produce the castings, mountings, fittings, and other machined parts for their products.

Braithwaite's master's thesis was on "An Interactive Three

Dimensional Graphic Display System" at the University of Washington, and he followed that with a paper he co-authored on "The Concept of an Interactive Graphic Design System with Distributed Computing," for publication at the AIAA Conference in August 1975. He also made a presentation to the National Research Council's Assembly of Engineering Committee on Computer Aided Manufacturing on "Interfacing Heterogeneous Application Modules and Systems (1979)."

Braithwaite's experience working with computer-aided manufacturing stood him in good stead when he moved to Boeing's Everett (Wash.) Division, where he was lead engineer in computer aided design, Engineering Division lead engineer in computer-assisted design development, and chief engineer responsible for the integration of computer-assisted design with computer-assisted manufacturing.

Braithwaite was the technical lead in developing the CAD/CAM Integration Information Network (CIIN) and the Geometric Data Base Management System (GBDMS), which became the foundation for Boeing's computer-aided design/computer-aided manufacturing activities.

Core Products

In 1985, Boeing named Braithwaite director of computing systems in the Everett Division, where giant 747 wide-bodies and 767 aircraft are assembled, and from 1986 to 1991, he was director of program management in Renton, Washington, where the Boeing 737 and 757 are produced. Another paper he produced, "Integrated Computer Systems in Aircraft Design and Manufacture: Difficulties and Implications," presented before the 31st Annual Israel Conference on Aviation and Astronautics in February 1990, foreshadowed his later exploits in computer integration.

In 1991 Braithwaite rose to vice president for information systems and architecture, and in May 1994 he stepped up to vice president of all Information Systems activities for the Boeing Commercial Aircraft Group. The format his team developed for Boeing's CAD/CAM Integration Information Network was further developed to become the Initial Graphic Exchange Standard and Product Data Exchange Specification, which allows disparate computer-aided design systems to exchange data in realtime.

That new data exchange standard permitted the Boeing Company's engineers to put aside old design methodologies and time frames in designing the 777 aircraft, which cut years off the design and testing phase for aircraft licensed to carry passengers in the United States.

Gift to the Nation

That achievement was turned into a national standard, Y14-26M (IGES), by the National Institute of Standards and Technology, and Braithwaite was hailed for his leadership both inside and outside Boeing. In 1987 the Association of Integrated Manufacturing Technology presented Braithwaite, Lehigh University professor Roger Nagel and General Electric scientist Philip Kennicott with its highest honor, the Joseph Marie Jacquard Award, for their work in developing the standard.

The award is named after the French inventor of the "Flying Shuttle" punch-card controlled loom, a mid-17th Century invention that with the steam engine, the British "Spinning Jenny" textile mill, iron rolling mill and canal transport systems helped kick off the Industrial Revolution in Europe. The Jacquard Award is not presented annually; it's given only when the international organization's board of directors feels an important breakthrough has been made in manufacturing technology. The award had been given only 13 times in the 25 years before Braithwaite won it.

Growing Importance

The importance of Braithwaite's contributions to computer-aided design cannot be overestimated. Not only did his new graphic exchange standard revolutionize aircraft design, it later was adapted for use in ship design.

The demise of the Soviet Union as a military threat and the rise of a "multi-polar" world left the U.S. Navy in a quandary. The world's biggest maritime force, the Navy now found itself confronting hostile or potentially hostile forces in "brown water," close to foreign shores instead of the "blue water," open ocean on which its forces had expected to meet Soviet fleets.

It always was true that nuclear submarines were used as primary intelligence gathering platforms during the Cold War, but the technological tools that pried open Soviet secrets were of little avail against countries without much of a developed industrial infrastructure. Today's Navy and Marine Corps – the forces most likely to be first to confront hostile activity in faraway lands – need solid intelligence from troops watching those hostile forces on the ground.

Moreover, the increased use of "asymmetrical warfare,"

197

guerrilla and terror tactics, against U.S. and Western targets by irregular groups such as al Qaida in turn has boosted the role of the Special Forces troops U.S. authorities send to meet such threats. What was needed was a new class of low-observable vehicle, a "Stealth" submarine that could outperform the new quiet diesel-electric and air-independent propulsion subs being bought in Europe by the less-developed nations that are home to the terrorist organizations.

New-Style Shipbuilding

Electric Boat Co., the General Dynamics unit famous for building submarines since World War II, won the bidding to build this new class of attack submarine. But E.B., based in Groton, Connecticut, was challenged by budget and time constraints it had never faced in developing a new class of submarine. So its executives took two unusual steps:

1. They contacted Boeing, an aircraft maker, to learn more about its system using the Y14-26M (IGES) standard. Boeing's design team, under Braithwaite's direction, uses the standard and their in-house developed add-ons to produce plans for market-leading airliners. Their refinement of long-used passenger planes to carry freight – and their addition of new, fuel-efficient engines – have allowed Boeing to overtake archrival Airbus Industrie in sales to airlines and air freight carriers.

Airbus' own woes completing the design and manufacturing setup for its planned 747-killer also are notable here. The computer-design tools Boeing uses would have forestalled the manufacturing glitches Airbus experienced in getting its plane to market -- German engineers used 3-D software to design the fuselage, but French designers used 2-D tools, and the two camps put wire runs in different places, with different gages of wiring harness, among other problems -- but Braithwaite didn't work for Airbus, and Airbus parent EADS Corp. didn't adopt the U.S. Y14-26M(IGES) data interchange standard.

Back across the ocean, General Dynamics, which had never designed a submarine by computer, decided to use the Boeing-customized integrated design system to allow its ship designers to see what each other were doing, as they did it, to speed the design process. For the first time, engineers developing a particular subsystem could see the layout and dimensions of other subsystems going into the overall design, avoiding the space conflicts and interoperability problems that used to require so much rethought and redesign as a new class of submarine took shape.

2. Next, General Dynamics took the completely unprecedented step of asking to do the ship's design and construction as a joint venture with its major competitor, Newport News Shipbuilding and Drydock Co. Newport News, one of a small club including Bath Iron Works, of the world's premier builders of nuclear submarines, was used to managing very different techniques to arrive at a design for a new vessel. But General Dynamics was working against critically tight deadlines and sharp budget cutoffs, with less development money than it normally had in a defense contract, and its leaders made the decision that they had to work through the differences in corporate culture and outlook – and share the benefits of using the Boeing system – with Newport News or see the project die on the ways. General

Dynamics bowed to necessity, and Newport News signed on.

The USS Virginia, the ninth U.S. Navy ship to carry that name, was the product of that collaboration. The ship, laid down in 1999 and commissioned in 2003, set new standards in quietness of operation, a key requirement in the close-inshore environment. It also has the capability to deliver Special Forces troops right to enemy shores and recover them undetected, via special facilities and a new-design mini-submersible carried on the Virginia's deck.

None of that would have been possible without the insight, drive and innovations of one Walt Braithwaite, a Caribbean immigrant who exemplifies the best reason America's borders need to stay open for the talent pressing in from abroad.

Supplemental Notes

1. Negative Population Growth, an organization opposed to increasing immigration, closely watches the phenomenon of Caribbean out-migration to the United States. Its Web site, *www.npg.org*, carries an article on "The Caribbean Immigration Centrifuge" that discusses the increasing numbers of recent immigrants coming to the United States.

2. See also *www.unc.edu/depts/afriafam AnniversaryConference/charles.htm*

3. See also *www.gaston.umb.edu/factsheethtml.html* for a more balanced discussion of the issues and timelines of immigration.

4. *People's Weekly World*, an online newspaper, also offers an extensive discussion of Caribbean and African in-migration, among other things listing the immigration numbers from many countries. The newspaper's Web site, *http://www.pww.org/article/view/7359/1/277*, also carries extensive discussion of the cultural and historical factors involved.

Chapter 11

Edmonds Builds and Shapes the Digital Age

Popular media writers date the Information Age from 1977, when new, desktop-sized computers – the Apple II, Tandy TRS-80 and Commodore's PET – brought computing to the consumer market. It is easy to see why, but they are as wrong about the Information Revolution as they are right about the excitement the new computers generated. Leaders like Albert J. Edmonds, a career Air Force officer who grew up with the revolution digital technology propelled, were already at work laying the groundwork for what became known as the National Information Infrastructure well before 1977.

The collection of electronic tinkerers, phone phreaks and gadgeteers who formed Homebrew Computer Club and started Silicon Valley's mad climb onto the world stage – kudos to their own creativity – could not have gotten very far past the hobbyist stage without the hard, out-of-the-spotlight work of dedicated engineers and managers who built the infrastructure of modern data communications, and Edmonds, who retired at the rank of lieutenant general, was a key player at the highest levels in planning, building and managing that infrastructure.

The World Wide Web, today a market force propelling dramatic shifts in business, politics and social organization, could not have become such a pervasive presence if Edmonds and his colleagues at the Defense Information Systems Agency had failed in their quest to design and install an entirely new scheme of communications for the U.S. military and its civilian overlords.

First, He Learned to Communicate

But that's getting ahead of the story. The Defense Information Systems Agency, DISA for short, did not exist when Albert J. Edmonds graduated from historically Black Morris Brown College in 1964 with a degree in chemistry and headed off to Texas' Lackland Air force Base for Officer's Candidate School. Military communications were still a vast mix of analogue systems then, with teletype gear communicating via audio modulation of high-frequency radio signals for mobile units and large data centers communicating via modems, mostly over copper telephone cables and microwave relay systems. Military satellites were in orbit after Telstar, AT&T's revolutionary international communications satellite, began operations in 1962, but they were not yet the focus of routine, real-time communications between distant units in disparate theaters.

Crisis Brought Big Changes

The Cuban Missile Crisis of 1962, during which President John F. Kennedy sent U.S. naval forces to blockade Fidel Castro's Cuba to force removal of Soviet launchers, personnel and intermediate range ballistic missiles from the Caribbean island, had brought into sharp focus the need for a National Communications System. Satellite surveillance and military spy plane overflights had revealed the missile emplacements, and other surveillance photos showed that Soviet vessels were approaching the island with still more missiles.

The Navy sent the aircraft carrier Essex, its associated cruiser and destroyer escorts, supply and munitions ships rushing to intercept the vessels before they could land their ominous cargoes, and the task force's own sensors revealed the presence of Soviet submarines in the waters surrounding Cuba.

Kennedy, Commander-in-Chief of the U.S. military, needed up-to-the-minute, real-time communications with the fleet officers running that blockade, with the Pentagon and with the Army and Air Force units staging at bases on the Gulf Coast, in preparation for a possible invasion. Sitting in the Situation Room beneath the White House, he needed instantaneous communications with congressional leaders and members of his own Cabinet – especially those away from Washington on official business – and with other key civilian leaders as well.

Developments in the tense standoff with Soviet Prime Minister Nikita Khrushchev were rapid and fluid. U-2 overflights showed Soviet and Cuban technicians continuing work on the missile sites as Soviet cargo ships steamed closer and closer to the forbidden zone announced by U.S. forces. Carrier planes were overflying the cargo vessels, "buzzing" low to let their captains know U.S. forces meant business; destroyers were steaming rapidly toward them. Ship-based, megawatt-powered sonar systems were blasting away at submarines we now know were armed with nuclear missiles, letting their skippers know the anti-sub forces knew exactly where they were. Those subs' missiles were primed for targets in the fleet and on the American mainland, but no American leaders had any idea what the Soviets had ordered done with them.

Strategic Air Command bombers were in the air, cruising at altitudes from which they could quickly swoop in to attack the Soviet Union. U.S. missile silos were on alert, and U.S. forces all over the world were in a state of high readiness, should they be needed in an all-out conflict.

Kennedy's National Security Council, working through analog radio systems, secure teletype networks and the switched telephone system, had to maintain real-time communications with all those units while the political drama played out.

Pulling Communications Together

After the crisis had eased and the weapons crews stood down, analysis pointed out the weaknesses of the patchwork communications system through which Kennedy directed the armed forces' response. Out of that analysis, the National Communications System was launched, pulling together 23 federal agencies under one umbrella to address the full range of national security and emergency preparedness issues.

Headquartered in Arlington, Va., the NCS began building the capability to meet the demonstrated needs for real-time, world-wide communications with far-flung fleet units, military bases and command leadership, as well as with civilian emergency preparedness coordinators, state and local authorities and elected government leaders at all levels.

Meanwhile, the young Al Edmonds was working his way up the command ladder as a communications officer, learning the basics of radio and satellite communications, how the large computer systems in use at the time functioned as communications hubs, watching the progress of advances in wired telecommunications systems, learning about communications security.

A Revolution Advanced, Unnoticed by Civilians

On the ground, telecommunications systems were going through a revolution whose implications had not yet become clear to the civilian world. Touch-Tone telephony, introduced in 1964, the same year Edmonds completed Officer Training School, used push-buttons and frequency codes to replace the rotary dials in use since 1927, ushering in a new generation of custom calling features controlled by software embedded in communications networks. The following year, as 2d Lieutenant Edmonds was beginning his 33-year climb as an Air Force communications officer, AT&T introduced the No. 1 Electronic Switching System, the first stored-program central office telephone switch.

Building on the capabilities of No. 1 ESS, the T-1 Carrier digital multiplex and other innovations, the Defense Department set up its own national telephone system for

205

military users. Its capabilities went far beyond what the civilian, non-defense-industry world was seeing. And that was just the beginning. Satellite communications, rapidly expanded after Telstar first flew, let national command authorities connect directly to U.S. military units wherever they were on the globe, in real time. And Al Edmonds, working his way up the career ladder, saw everything come on line, helping to develop many of the technologies he saw being born.

In 1969 AT&T Bell Laboratories scientists released the Unix operating system, an elegant time-sharing software system for minicomputers that could be used for text editing, general computing, switching system operations and trouble reporting. Because Bell Labs was working to perfect control systems for the vast and variegated switching operation handling America's telecommunications needs, Unix came with a number of innovations that gave it the capability to be run on many different kinds of computer setups, and it migrated across the country as university professors and research scientists made it the staple of academic computing. Still later, after Bell Labs relinquished proprietary control, Unix became the foundation for the Internet.

Goosing the Transmission Speeds

In 1973, new innovations in the manufacture of ultra-transparent glass fiber, made through a modified chemical vapor deposition technique, ramped up the transmission speed of voice, data and video traffic. Lasers, which had been invented in 1958, made it possible to push those transmissions mile after mile, through underground conduits and under the oceans, at speeds only imagined in science fiction stories earlier.

Alexander Graham Bell and Lewis Latimer, the Black inventor who built the first central office telephone and power systems, had patented optical communications systems in the 19th Century, but the technology did not exist to make practical use of their discoveries. The first full-service optical fiber communications system began operation in Chicago, Ill., in 1977, the same year the first eight-bit desktop computers began streaming into consumer markets and sneaking through the back door into corporate offices, to the consternation of the official data processing staff. Eleven years later, the first transatlantic optical fiber cable was laid, linking North America to Europe over a distance of 3,148 miles. It could handle 40,000 simultaneous telephone conversations. Four years after that, in 1992, Bell Labs and a Japanese telecommunications firm tested an in-line 9,000-kilometer, optically amplified fiber communication system with an error-free transmission rate of 5 billion bits a second.

The Military Was Watching

Defense specialists such as Edmonds began to experiment with optical fiber transmission systems as soon as they became available.

Edmonds' predecessor at the Defense Information Systems Agency, Army Lt. Gen. Alonzo Short, became the first chief of the agency that took over the national command infrastructure after a distinguished career as a warfighter. General Short, a graduate of historically Black Virginia State University, had begun his military career two years ahead of

Edmonds, rising to platoon leader and staff officer at Fort Riley, Kan., and he later led a battalion of 101st Airborne troopers through two combat tours in Vietnam.

By 1991, when the Persian Gulf War began, Gen. Short was commander of the U.S. Army Information Systems, a worldwide military communications system that put 5,000 Army specialists on the ground to set up real-time or near-real-time communications for the half a million U.S. troops fighting in Iraq and Kuwait. Art Johnson, who was named Black Engineer of the Year for 1997, also participated in the delivery of Gulf War communications as a Lockheed Martin senior executive, driving civilian teams that supported the Gulf's warriors.

The setup became the first large-scale proving ground for warfighters' use of the Global Positioning System. The satellites allowed coalition forces to navigate accurately through the trackless, forbidding deserts of southern Iraq. Computer networks and digital radio links between moving vehicles kept the coalition's commanders constantly updated on the locations of their rapidly moving forces, updating them as well on contacts with enemy forces.

Opponents Outdone

The Iraqis, for their part, were completely flummoxed by the Americans' superior ability to find and move around their forces, so much so that afterward, they asked how it was done.

As *US Black Engineer* magazine said in a 1996 article, when shown the networked, military-grade laptop computers and the small, handheld devices that pinpointed U.S. forces' locations, the Iraqi officers were astonished that even low-ranking soldiers had access to such sophisticated technology. That surpassing battlefield communications capability was one of the reasons Chinese military observers, surveying the carnage close at hand as U.S. and coalition forces routed one of the world's largest and best-equipped armies, concluded that their own country's forces would be no match for Americans' technology in a conventional conflict.

Lt. Gen. Short, also a Black Engineer of the Year honoree, returned from the Gulf War with major kudos from Colin Powell, chairman of the Joint Chiefs of Staff, and Gen. Norman Schwarzkopf, the allied forces commander, who credited the rapidity and dependability of Desert Storm communications – which even reached soldiers in the field via secure networks – with invaluable contributions to the swift victory over Iraqi forces. Gen. Short then stepped up to command the then-new Defense Information Systems Agency, preparing the way for the changes carried through when Lt. Gen. Edmonds took over.

Reaching for Higher Skies

Edmonds had to complete a few more assignments before he assumed command in his biggest role. He served as deputy chief of staff for communications and computer systems for the Tactical Air Command, also commanding the Air Force Communications Command's Tactical Communications Division; was assistant Chief of Staff, systems, for command, control, communications and computers (C4I) at Air Force headquarters; and head of the C4I Directorate for the Joint Staff. Gen. Edmonds is the only officer who has served as senior communications officer in the Air Staff, Joint Staff, and

209

the Defense Information Systems Agency.

At DISA, Lt. General Edmonds retired the World Wide Military Command and Control System he inherited and brought in cutting-edge technology with the new Global Command Control System, which simultaneously modernized the existing system and promoted interoperability between the formerly separate Army, Navy and Air Force communications systems.

The Global Command and Control System (GCCS) is the realization of the Joint Staff's goal to provide a seamless, interoperable command and control structure that uses a mix of commercial and government-developed hardware and software that puts real-world functionality in the hands of soldiers at all levels. Proof of its potency was shown during Operation Uphold Democracy, when U.S. forces charged into Haiti to restore the popularly elected President Aristide to the office from which he had been forced by a military coup.

Opening their Eyes

"The secretary of Defense and the chairman of the Joint Chiefs of Staff saw first-hand an operational system providing a true picture of the evolving battlespace in real time from the Pentagon," Gen. Edmonds told *US Black Engineer.* "GCCS . . . gives the warfighters an ability to order, respond, and coordinate horizontally and vertically to the degree necessary to prosecute our mission in that battlespace. [Its] capabilities include crisis planning, force deployment, logistics, force status, intelligence, positions and direct operations.

"GCCS takes advantage of military satellite communications, commercial satellite communications, [data networks providing] asynchronous transfer mode and synchronous optical network leading-edge technology, and other terrestrial communications capabilities."

What he described has several key elements:

• Physical facilities to collect, distribute, store, process, and display voice, data, and imagery;

• The applications and data engineering practices (tools methods and processes) to build and maintain the software that allows control and communications, intelligence and mission support users to access and manipulate, organize and digest proliferating quantities of information;

• Standards and protocols that facilitate interconnection and interoperation among networks and systems and that provide security for the information carried;

• People and assets that provide the integrating design, management and operation of the Defense Information Infrastructure, develop the applications and services, construct the facilities, and train others in its capabilities and uses.

General Edmonds' initiative converted the military's single-service, "stovepipe" information systems into a globally integrated, widely distributed, user-driven interface, something that large integrated corporations such as IBM, Lockheed Martin, or General Motors work toward, but involving hundreds of thousands more active participants than even such mega-corporations can muster. And the system connects to key defense suppliers as well.

How it Paid Off

Observers of Operation Iraqi Freedom could watch that

211

seamless capability at work, when U.S. forces stormed up the Tigris and Euphrates valleys, sweeping up Saddam Hussein's forces before they ever got a chance to confront the Americans for the set-piece battles they had been trained to expect. In Afghanistan, where the internal communications infrastructure is mostly nonexistent, that satellite capability has meant the difference between life and death for U.S. military personnel operating in rugged, remote areas whose terrain had doomed invading armies for thousands of years.

In the modern era, Soviet forces fought 10 years but met defeat at the hands of ragtag bands of guerrillas, operating with near-impunity in narrow mountain passes, over trails no modern vehicle could follow. But after 9/11 U.S. troops, with their masterly command of communications and satellite location systems, with air forces that could reach over distances impossible for Soviet counterparts, took apart the repressive Taliban regime and dismantled the network of troop training camps run by its al-Qaida allies in months.

And thanks to Lt. Gen. Edmonds, the inter-service communications failures that marred the victory in Desert Storm were gone altogether. U.S. Navy planes flying off carries in the Indian Ocean answered radio calls from embattled Army Special Forces troops in quick-time, summoned by Air Force forward spotters on the ground and in the air, vectored in by Air Force AWACS and Navy E-2C Hawkeye command and control aircraft. Air Force fighters and bombers coming from as far away as the U.S. mainland joined them in denying the Taliban fighters the mountain hiding places, weapons stockpiles and mobility they had used so well against the Soviets.

A 'Most Powerful' Person

While he was at DISA, *Network World* magazine named Lt. Gen. Edmonds one of the Top 25 Most Powerful People in Networking, according to the following categories:

1. Power of the Purse
2. Power of Vision
3. Power of Market Presence
4. Power Over Technology, and
5. Power of Partners.

Gen. Edmonds' upgrade of the Defense Information Infrastructure, involving a $5.5 billion program to construct a private Asynchronous Transfer Mode backbone network to provide secure voice, video, data and multimedia services to government users, was described by Warren Suss, president of Warren H. Suss Associates, as determining the future of networks. That, Suss said, was because what happened under Edmonds' watch had a dramatic effect on the entire industry.

Among other credits, Gen. Edmonds oversaw the successful start of a $6.9 billion Intranet project for the Navy and Marine Corps, a ground-breaking system that tied the sea services' operations together in ways never before experienced.

Enhancing Civilian Capabilities

But warfighter support is only part of the job at DISA. As agency chief, Lt. Gen. Edmonds also was manager of the civilian National Communications System, responsible for providing command, control, communications, computer and intelligence support to civilian authorities at all levels. DISA is where the Defense Information Infrastructure intersects with

213

the civilian National Information Infrastructure, the Information Superhighway. In fact, because DISA's development and management of national standards and its funding and promotion of satellite and optical fiber communications for the military, DISA actually drove telecommunications providers' own plans for installation of state-of-the-art digital signal handling gear. In other words, Lt. Gen. Edmonds built or caused to be built the backbone for much of today's Information Superhighway, making possible the manifold uses which civilians all over the world are developing for the World Wide Web.

Lt. General Edmonds, a distinguished graduate of the Air War College in 1980, also has a master's degree in counseling from Hampton University. He completed the national security program for senior officers at Harvard University in 1987, and has an honorary doctor of science degree from his *alma mater*, Morris Brown.

Keeping His Hand In

Gen. Edmond's career did not end when he left the Air Force in 1997 after nearly 33 years, however. He joined TRI-COR Industries, where he directed daily operations and managed new business development. Then he moved to Electronic Data Systems Corp. as president of U.S. government solutions, with more than 11,000 employees supporting federal, state and local agencies nationwide.

Today, Gen. Edmonds is senior advisor for technology at Dimensions International, an Alexandria, Va.-based, minority owned technology company that serves government, military and corporate clients in the United States and worldwide. Lt.

Gen. Edmonds works directly with the chairman, Dr. Russell T. Wright. Former Army Gen. Johnnie Wilson, the Army's "Chief Technology Officer" when he served as leader of the Army Materiel Command, just retired as Dimensions International's president and Chief Operating Officer, now that Dimensions has became part of Honeywell.

Chapter 12

Rise of the Corporate Mountain-Climber

An often-repeated complaint in Black America – particularly loud during annual Black History Month – is that there are no empire builders: Where are the Black Michael Dells? Where is the next Reginald Lewis? With all the brainpower displayed by the world-beaters in this book, why isn't one of them striking out on his or her own to become the next Lee Iacocca? Why are Rap moguls like Damon Dash, Jay-Z, and Russell Simmons and Cable TV pioneer Robert Johnson the only ones creating wealth for the next generation?

But like many another widely spattered truism about Black

Americans, it's a bogus complaint. It takes big resources to develop a new automotive product, to build a new jet airliner, or design the next generation Navy ship.

The Black-owned Patterson buggy-whip company turned out good cars at the beginning of the automobile age, but it took the resources of the industry-leading Motorola Corp. to capitalize the United Motor Company that Alfred P. Sloan turned into General Motors in the first decades of the 20th Century. Patterson's cars, cranked out in a Cleveland, Ohio, factory had a good reputation during the decades when Americans fell in love with the automobile, but now are long gone and long forgotten.

Leaders Don't Have to Shout

Not everyone can be a Lee Iacocca. Nor should everyone try to be. Alfred P. Sloan never turned into a media hero, but his handiwork in turning GM into a world leader in the efficient management of manufacturing, marketing and servicing of automotive products – technology products, that is – has lasted more than a century. It is well worth emulation.

And lest we forget, Lee Iacocca built his career at Ford Motor Co., where he was the father of the Mustang, before getting shoved out by Henry Ford II and moving over to save Chrysler Corp. And as Iacocca showed, climbing a corporate mountain has its own rewards. Among others, it lets the mountain-climber produce jobs for many more others. Not incidentally, Black corporate mountain-climbers get into positions where they can do much good for the careers of many other Black climbers. For Black and female managers who rise to corporate leadership are vastly much more likely to mentor and promote people whose backgrounds parallel their own. "Comfort zones" are not only applicable to white executives.

Disbelievers should take note of the Dec. 7, 2006 announcement by Robert J. Stevens, chairman and Chief Executive Officer of Lockheed Martin, the biggest defense contractor in the world:

> "*I am pleased to announce the appointment of Linda R. Gooden as Executive Vice President of our Information & Technology Services (I&TS) Business Area, effective January 1, 2007. . . .*
>
> "*Linda has served as President of Lockheed Martin Information Technology since 1997, growing that business from a small, one-customer, one-contract division to a 14,000-employee enterprise providing IT services to federal agencies across the U.S. in more than 60 major locations and in 18 foreign countries. Linda took on additional responsibilities when she was appointed Deputy Executive Vice President for I&TS. She also is an Officer of the Corporation, elected in April 2001. . . .*
>
> "*Linda has a long record of achievement for which she has earned national recognition, including, most recently, being named Black Engineer of the Year by U.S. Black Engineer and Information Technology magazine. She also actively supports many professional, academic, and civic organizations, and serves on numerous executive boards including Armed forces Communications and Electronics Association (AFCEA) International; Information Technology*

Association of America (ITAA); University of Maryland's A. James Clark School of Engineering and Robert H. Smith School of Business' Center for Electronic Markets & Enterprises; University of Maryland, Baltimore County; Prince George's Community College Foundation; Maryland Business Roundtable for Education; and Executive Leadership Council. . . .

"Please join me in congratulating Linda on her new role and in giving her your full support as she leads the I&TS team."

With that memo, Stevens promoted Gooden to head the division which is transforming Lockheed Martin's business. Instead of merely a producer of high-tech military hardware, the company now is as deeply engaged in providing software and services. Gooden, a manager whose career matured growing that business, now was named to head a division with 52,000 workers, scattered over multiple countries. Complainers, take note: She's not the only Big League corporate champion out there.

Like-Minded Climbers

With the blinders off, thoughtful observers can see a whole tier of Black mountain climbers from the engineering ranks, whose corporate access and authority will affect the economic chances of thousands of Black Americans working in companies supporting the biggest economy of the world.

– Look again at Ed Welburn, a Black Philadelphian whose 1958 visit to an auto show inspired him to become a car designer, is working where he should be: as chief of design at

General Motors, where his styling decisions for Hummers, Chevrolets and Saturn cars can be realized in competitive products to save the fortunes of the biggest automaker in the world. GM has had its challenges in the financial meltdown of 2008-9, but the news of the Welburn-led redesign of its product lines has not escaped the watchful eyes of automotive enthusiasts.

– Thus, Ralph Gilles, the Haitian-American designer of the Chrysler 300C, is working where he should be: At the newly privatized Chrysler, doing battle in the big leagues of the North American market.

– Thus, Rodney O'Neal, who won 2002 laurels as Black Engineer of the Year running the biggest part of the biggest auto-parts maker in the world, went right where he should have gone: To Delphi Automotive, which O'Neal helped to spin off into an independent company and at which he became Chief Operating Officer, then Chief Executive. Delphi, hobbled like its former parent GM by expensive union contract obligations and heavy pension requirements coming due as its aging workforce steps down, faces still more critical financial challenges as its chief customer, General Motors, struggles to find its footing in a market full of nimbler foreign rivals whose labor costs are smaller and whose product lines have captured American hearts. But that cannot dim O'Neal's achievements as an engineer and manager.

It takes big backing to revolutionize the world with an IBM PC, as Phil Estridge did with Mark Dean and the team at Boca Raton, Florida, much of it from sources outside the original producer's pockets Or did everyone forget Lotus 1-2-3? Jim Manzi put together a multi-million-dollar financing package at Lotus Development Corp. to market the spreadsheet that put IBM Personal Computers on every business desktop in America.

Backward Myopia

Let's say it again, loudly: The complainers are looking in the wrong direction. There are champions out there building companies and forging new pathways to success, but the lack of public attention to Blacks in technology means few Black Americans can see them. Some of those new Black business pioneers, such as Linda Gooden and IBM's Al Zollar and his colleague Rodney Adkins, are *intra*preneuers, working within established corporate structures to make the big business deals and build executive empires. Alfred P. Sloan did it, why can't they?

• Rodney Hunt, who used a $5,000 loan and a lot of ideas and energy to build RSIS Information Systems into a $300 million company before selling it to a bigger competitor, is certainly admirable, but he is not the only Black technology leader who can make $100-million deals. Linda Gooden, who built an $8-billion computer consulting enterprise within Lockheed Martin, makes such deals almost every month.

• William Smith, the president of America's oldest and largest engineering consulting firm, Parsons, Brinckerhoff, Quade & Douglas, Inc., is another big deal-maker. Parsons Brinckerhoff builds mega-projects like San Francisco's Bay Area Rapid Transit systems and the Dallas-Fort Worth Airport. Now under Smith's leadership, Parsons Brinckerhoff is building a new mass-transit system for Charlotte, North Carolina, and is engaged in hundreds of other projects with price tags ranging from $50,000 into the billions.. Smith, a 1965 graduate of North Carolina A&T State University, joined the Air Force during the turbulent Vietnam War years, traveling to the Far East to supervise the installation and maintenance of military navigation aids, communications gear, and Air Traffic Control centers.

When he got out, Smith joined Kaiser Aluminum and Chemical Corp., then Bechtel Corporation, flying across the world to oversee mining projects and rock quarrying, expanding his cultural horizons in Latin America as he expanded the range of his technology projects. One project was a first-of-its-kind solar cell power project for Pacific Gas and Electric Co. Another project, in Latin America, developed the world's longest mine conveyor system, a gargantuan, electric-powered affair serving an even more gargantuan open-face extraction project.

At Parsons Brinckerhoff, Smith developed power systems for the Lawrence Livermore National Laboratory, the University of California at Davis, and an uninterruptible power system for the Biosphere sealed-environment research project. After serving as chief electrical engineer for the now-canceled Superconducting Super Collider particle accelerator, Smith became Texas area manager for PB Facilities Services, then in 1996, area manager or the San Francisco and Oakland offices, responsible for a technical staff serving 40 public agency clients, including the Bay Area Rapid Transit District.

When Smith was selected the 2005 Black Engineer of the Year, *USBE* noted that he was running an operating company with 3,000 staffers managing 1,700 contracts ranging in size from $50,000 to $14 billion.

• Reginald Van Lee, the 2008 Black Engineer of the year, works at the intersection of business, technology and health-care policy. As Senior Vice President at Booz Allen Hamilton, he leads business efforts in the Public Health and Non-Profit sectors. If that sounds not so technical, remember that the progress of health care policy depends on the progress of scientific discovery and technological developments. Remember also that the National Academy of Engineering identified solving critical health problems as one of the "Grand Challenges in Engineering." Van Lee holds B.S. and M.S. degrees from MIT as well as an MBA from Harvard, and is a recognized expert in determining how global organizations can build capabilities to make them resilient to shocks. An expert in public-private partnerships, Van Lee co-wrote the book "Megacommunities," laying out how government, business and non-profit leaders can tackle global challenges together.

• Al Zollar, until recently general manager of IBM's Tivoli Software unit, also headed Lotus Development Corp. after IBM took the company over, and brought it back from near-death in its market struggle with the Microsoft Office.

• Rodney Adkins now heads IBM's Systems Group Development, responsible for a wide range of hardware and software products for the IBM's server and data storage portfolio. Adkins, who joined IBM in 1981, now holds what former IBM CEO Lou Gerstner called "the biggest development job in technology," managing roughly half of IBM's $6-billion-a-year R&D budget. Adkins sits on the Board of Governors of the prestigious IBM Academy of Technology and is one of the giant computer maker's top 40 executives.

• In 1999, when Adkins was general manager of the RS/6000 computational science unit, he landed a deal to provide the next-generation supercomputer to be used by U.S. Energy Department's National Energy Research Scientific Computing Center at the famed Lawrence Berkeley National Laboratory. The RS/6000 SP won against its competitors because of its ability to handle scientific codes and tests to ensure its capability as a full-production computing system, the center said. The Center's announcement said the tests indicated that the system, when fully implemented, would provide four to five times the center's current computational power. When you realize that the National Energy Research Scientific Computing Center already was one of the world's most powerful supercomputing sites, that was a major mouthful. The five-year, $33-million job was the largest single procurement in the 68-year history of the Berkeley Lab.

Adkins was upbeat. The National Energy Research Scientific Computing Center provides high-performance computing and data storage resources to 2,500 researchers at national laboratories, universities and industries across the United States working on Energy Department programs such as combustion, climate modeling, fusion energy, materials science and computational biology. The Center's seven supercomputers, the largest of which was then a Cray teramonster, are used 24 hours a day, seven days a week, so reliability was an absolute must.

• Adkins' press statement about the contract exemplified the approach of a man who also had signed on early on to be the principal corporate evangelist for the national Black

Family Technology Awareness Week, and returned every year:

"The continuing partnership between IBM and the Department of Energy is further testimony to what can be accomplished when two leaders in the field of computational science push the boundaries of conventional thinking. I can't think of anything more noble than being a part of making lives better, whether it's through helping design cleaner engines or increasing life-saving knowledge about our environment through climate modeling. As always, the knowledge we gain from this initiative will also benefit our commercial customers around the world through powerful business solutions."

Wrong-Way Vision

Reginald Lewis was a Wall Street *wunderkind* with his leveraged buyout at Beatrice Foods and his success electrified Blacks everywhere, but the average reader probably has never heard of those Black engineer-executives named above. That is because Blacks who have stepped into leadership roles in technology businesses are ignored every day, while sports and entertainment figures – whose activity fits more into the 6-o'clock TV broadcast's image of successful Blacks – are thrust to the forefront.

Here's a small example, within the same family: Damon Dash is a Hip-Hop mogul, into fashion, music and film, and admired by young people everywhere. But how many know about his relative Darien, a University of Southern California grad who charged out of the cable TV business in the mid-1990s to create the first publicly traded Black dot-com? Dash

225

used his business skills to make a *jiu-jitsu* takeover of a publicly traded company and get listed on the New York Stock Exchange – it got the attention of President Bill Clinton, who sought Dash's advice on how to close the Digital Divide – and signed a major contract with America Online before Dash and his cohorts watched DME Interactive Holdings' stock tank during the turn-of-the-21st Century dot-com meltdown. Unlike many other dot-commers, however, Darien hung in. Now DME Interactive is breaking new ground in wireless communications, creating text-messaging contests around Latino entertainment venues and promoting artists with interactive Web presentations.

Quiet Builders, But Ground-Shakers

Black America does not have to wait for another Reginald Lewis. By preparing the next generation to take its place among the technology pioneers whose enterprise really drives the economy, Blacks can expand the opportunities available to even line workers whose futures depend on the health of America's corporations.

And by the way, there really is no shortage of entrepreneurial go-getters out there.

Russell T. Wright, another technology leader most Blacks never heard of, is one. Wright grew up helping his father, Dr. Robert L. Wright, build Dimensions International into a multi-million-dollar engineering consulting firm.

Then in 2004 the younger Wright, a business major from Morehouse College with an MBA from Keller Graduate School and another master's degree from the George Washington University School of Business and Public Management, took

226

Dimensions to another level by engineering the friendly takeover of Sentel, a Black-owned technology consulting competitor.

The combined units turned Dimensions International into a $100-million company providing engineering and systems integration solutions to military and other government customers. The combination forged a team with major-league experience and top-level contacts:

- Sentel Founder James F. Garrett stayed on board as division chief. According to *US Black Engineer & IT* magazine, Garrett, the son of a Southern sharecropper, had co-founded Sentel in 1987 with a $33,000 subcontract and managed its growth into a company with more than 300 workers in 14 locations across the country, with some $42 million in annual revenues. Garrett, a graduate of North Carolina A&T State University, won such respect for the company it was selected to do mission-critical work for the Defense Department, NASA, the Federal Aviation Administration, and other agencies. Ernst &Young named Garrett Technology Entrepreneur of the Year for the Washington area in 1999, and he won a Black Engineer of the Year Award for entrepreneurship in 2000.
- Gen. Johnnie E. Wilson, who joined the U.S. Army as a buck private and worked his way up the ranks to four stars as the service's chief technology officer leading the Army Materiel Command, came on board as Dimensions International Chief Operating Officer.

227

- Dimensions International Founder Dr. Robert L. Wright is Chairman Emeritus.

Among other exploits, Dimensions International developed a Radar Analysis Display and Recording System which provides the interface for FAA radar terminals. Another product, the Arts Collection and Editing System, is an interface to Air Traffic Control computer systems and radars. It collects relevant data on flight tracks and related flight plan data. It also correlates, stores, and filters the data to meet FAA security requirements and forwards it to other government agencies, such as the Department of Homeland Security. One of the newest products is a receiver/decoder for the analysis of the aircraft Identification Friend or Foe (IFF) interrogator/transponder environment. This includes the Automatic Dependent Surveillance-Broadcast (ADS-B) system, described by the company as an emerging technology that will revolutionize Air Traffic Control.

Playing in a Bigger Arena

Dimensions International is a relatively small company, as capable and praiseworthy as Dimensions and Rodney Hunt's RSIS are. It would be folly to suggest that there could be something wrong with sending many of the best and brightest young Black engineers to work for Big Industrial Company USA, when there is just as much opportunity to grow there – and to direct corporate resources to the support of community development efforts, à là Art Carter at Boeing – as anywhere.

Let's be realistic: As praiseworthy as they are, Dimensions

International's and RSIS' contracting swath are small change compared to the Lockheed Martin division run by Linda Gooden, and their success made them acquisition targets for larger companies -- Honeywell, in the case of Dimensions. So let's look at how she got to today's eminent heights.

Gooden took her degree in computer technology from Youngstown State University and did graduate work at San Diego State University. She joined General Dynamics as a software engineer, then moved to Lockheed in 1980. Gooden worked her way up in data systems until she rose to vice president of the Software Services Support unit, where in the early 1990s she hit on the idea of "un-bundling" the computer services Lockheed sells to government agencies.

By 1997, Gooden's division, which started out with a few hundred workers, had become a full-blown business unit. In 2001 it became Lockheed Martin Information Technology, now a 14,000-worker enterprise, with Gooden as top honcho. Today, with Gooden making what *Washington Technology* magazine calls "bolt-on acquisitions," Lockheed Martin Information Technology has become the fastest-growing part of the $35-billion-a-year defense giant.

'Bolt-on' Growth

Take a look at that "bolt-on" business. As *Washington Technology* details, In November 2004 Gooden's firm bought the federal contracting unit of Affiliated Computer Services, Inc., and created a 2,000-worker unit dedicated to business process outsourcing. For uninitiates, business process outsourcing involves private companies taking over a government agency's back-office functions such as invoicing, human resources, payroll, finance, procurement and customer service. The private firms also provide the manpower needed to input data and handle the accompanying management processes.

Gooden told the magazine that private companies and state and local governments had been using such outsourcing services for years, but that the federal government was just getting its feet wet. "ACS had an initial capability in that area, and what we plan to do is to leverage that into a new business are for Lockheed Martin Information Technology," she said. The Dallas, Texas-based ACS was working a handful of major outsourcing contracts and several smaller ones, worth more than $100 million total. The largest one supplies Information Technology services, personnel management, materials, and administration to support the Defense Finance and Accounting Service. Gooden's division took it all over, minus some defense work, some existing contracts with state and local governments, and a student loan processing contract with the U.S. Department of Education.

• Lockheed Martin does not publicly report Gooden's division's revenues, but she told *Washington Technology* in July 2005 that IT work raked in more than $8 billion, out of $31.8 billion in total 2004 revenues.

The bolting-on spree continues, so expect the earnings to keep climbing.

• In March 2005 Lockheed Martin spent $440 million to take over Doylestown, Pa.,-based Sytex Group Inc., a provider of IT solutions and technical support services to the Defense Department. It also bought Sippican Holdings, a Massachusetts-based supplier of naval electrical systems. It also signed an agreement to buy Stasys Ltd., a British company specializing in military communications. And in December 2004, Lockheed Martin had taken over Soflinx Corp., a San Diego, California-based company that makes wireless sensors for detection of biochemical agents. The prices for these takeovers were not announced.

• Among other big contracts Gooden's division won in 2004, Lockheed Martin Information Technology garnered a $2-billion contract for the U.S. Postal Service's Universal Computing Connectivity initiative. It also won a $980 million "blanket purchase agreement" for IT support services, as well as a $700 million IT Solutions Environmental Systems Engineering contract with the Environmental Protection Agency.

• In March 2006, the FBI awarded Gooden's division a $305 million contract to modernize its IT infrastructure. Lockheed Martin Information Technology was hired to manage the Sentinel Project, an initiative to shift from a paper-based, case-by-case records system to a comprehensive electronic network to share and store information. The FBI said the whole project would cost $425 million. Under the six-year contract, Lockheed Martin is to develop and deploy the Sentinel framework. FBI Chief Information Officer Zalmai Azmi said the first phase of the project, which includes the building of a "one-stop shop" Web portal providing access to the FBI's older systems, would be completed in 2007. The full system is to be completed by 2009.

GovExec.com, the online newsletter that reported the deal, noted that earlier efforts to upgrade the FBI's IT capabilities had been "riddled with financial and technical problems," forcing FBI Director Robert Mueller to scrap a $170-million upgrade program. This time, with Gooden's division on the case, Azmi expressed confidence it would be done on time and on budget.

Gooden was even more confident: "Success is not an option," she told *GovExec.com*. "It is a mandate."

• In May 2006 *Contract Center Today* reported that Lockheed Martin Information Technology won a five-year, $120-million contract to run two call centers for the Department of Homeland Security's U.S. Citizenship and Immigration Services Directorate. Aspen Systems Corp. had originally won the contract to operate the immigration agency's National Customer Service Center, which serves 10 million callers a year, but Gooden's division took over Aspen Systems in January 2006, putting Gooden in charge.

Gooden's comment was that "expanding our ability to provide business process management services to government customers was a major advantage of the Aspen Systems combination."

• Don't think that Gooden operates only in the safe, comfortable confines of the Executive Suite. As *Black Enterprise* tells it, on September 11, 2001, after al-Qaida's hijackers rammed an airliner into the Pentagon, Gooden led a staff of 200 people back into the smouldering building to make sure its vital data and communications links could keep operating. "There wasn't a lot of introspection," Gooden told the magazine. "We just acted and did what needed to be done to bring the Pentagon back online."

So let the complainers shut up, once and for all. The business of technology advance – and of opening doors so other minority workers can advance too – needs leaders of all sizes, sprinkled throughout the economy, kicking over the traces wherever they are.

Chapter 13

Art Johnson, Space Age Information Warrior

Arthur Johnson, another mountain climber, grew up with the Space Race. His career path has been a dizzying footrace through various parts of the military-industrial complex that builds the hardware, software and personnel expertise that sustains America's reach beyond the Earth's atmosphere and gravity well.

Dizzying, to be sure, not least because of the executive heights Johnson has attained: He's a corporate vice president at defense giant Lockheed Martin, running parts of the company that develop technology for homeland security, design and build computer systems for submarines and the ships, helicopters and planes that hunt them, and manage vast development programs for projects such as the joint Strike Fighter.

But even more dizzying spin went into Johnson's career because of the rapid changes, consolidations and mergers in the defense industry after the end of the Cold War. Johnson, as consummate a survivor as he is a career climber, managed to hold onto positions even as his employers, repeatedly, were merged out of existence.

The military dimension of the Space Race explains how Johnson wound up as a Defense industry mover and shaker when so much of his early career was in support of the ostensibly civilian space exploration program. It's so easy to forget, now that the Cold War is officially over, that the military component of space activity is alive and well.

Today, U.S. astronauts regularly join Russian cosmonauts and astronauts of other nations on orbital jaunts; remotely piloted vehicles send home thrilling pictures of the outer planets, asteroids, and even comets; and robot rovers stretch the boundaries of human imagination crawling across the surface of Mars.

Military Reach

At its core, however, the Space Race from beginning to end was a Hell-bent-for-leather exercise in extending national military capabilities out into the distance between the planets, for fear that others would get their first and send back threats America could not meet. Or as the National Air and Space Museum's excellent summary of space milestones puts it, "The Space Race became a symbol of the broad ideological and political contest between two rival world powers."

When scientists heard Sputnik I's "Beep! Beep! Beep!" beaming down from a stable orbit in 1957, they heard another thing altogether, however. Sputnik ignited a national sense of crisis in the United States, driving forth a whole panoply of federal initiatives in education, research and development, because it was plain that the rocket that shot Sputnik into orbit could just as easily loft a nuclear bomb at the United States. Nothing in the U.S. arsenal could stop it from landing precisely where Soviet planners had aimed it.

Rivalries in Uniform

Americans eventually separated their space programs into civilian and military agencies, but at the beginning, the serious U.S. programs were all military. The Army, Navy and Air Force each had its own space projects, competing in a big-stakes rivalry over who should manage U.S. space efforts. And even today, it bears repeating that the Global Positioning System (GPS) satellites whose signals are prized by pilots, hikers, boaters, golfers, "geocaching" treasure hunters and automobile road-mapping systems, as well as commercial logistics managers, were developed and launched for military uses. Those uses still are extant, as the Afghan Taliban guerillas can attest to their chagrin, reeling as U.S. Special Forces troops direct weapons onto their positions from platforms on bombers and fighter planes, helicopters and even unmanned air vehicles.

Iraqi army officers learned about GPS the hard way when U.S. tanks and troops found their formations even in blinding dust clouds during Desert Storm and Iraqi Freedom. Spy satellites still peer down on former Soviet missile sites in Russia, and on American ones, as well. They also look down onto suspected terrorist training camps in South Asia, drug cartel headquarters in South America, and on the military preparations of nations all over the world.

Growing Up in the Age of Space

Art Johnson was still in school when Sputnik I lifted off, scaring U.S. authorities into a major push to produce more engineers and scientists to meet the challenge of Soviet education, which seemed poised to deliver enough technical professionals to outperform the vaunted industrial base of the United States. American engineers and manufacturers had so outclassed their German and Japanese counterparts in World War II that even Europeans named the 20th "the American Century." But now the Communist system seemed poised to carry out former Prime Minister Nikita Khrushchev's threat to "bury" America and the West under a flood of Soviet technical achievements.

Growing up in North Carolina and watching the Soviet leader's antics on television like many of his schoolmates, Johnson probably was just as puzzled as his grown-up relatives in trying to figure out why there was so much hullabaloo. One positive result of all that national anxiety, however, was that for the first time in American history, U.S. educators, government officials and industrialists began to spend serious money on improving the public schools, even

237

those populated by Blacks and other minority students, in their efforts to boost science and math education. That search for brilliant technologists who could answer the Soviet challenge managed to open many doors that earlier had been closed to Blacks.

The Army shot off the first successful U.S. satellite, Explorer I, in 1958, using a solid-rocket Redstone Missile booster, putting an end to Americans' embarrassing failures to get into space. But then the Soviets put the first man into space, Col. Yuri Gagarin, in a one-orbit flight aboard Vostok I, in 1961. Young Art Johnson was pursuing his science degree at historically Black Morehouse College then, and was probably electrified like the rest of America when Alan Sheppard made his first sub-orbital flight shortly afterward, flying in a Mercury space vehicle that plunged into the sea, to be retrieved by jubilant U.S. Navy sailors.

Southern Dichotomy

Johnson grew up in an era when Southern states like his native North Carolina were in turmoil, roiled by demonstrations and counter-demonstrations in the fight against racial segregation. Sit-ins actually began in Greensboro, North Carolina, and spread to other states after students from historically Black North Carolina A&T made their fateful move at a Woolworth's store lunch counter.

Johnson, who went to high school not far away in Durham, was in a position to watch such developments close at hand, looking toward a future when segregation would not hobble his dreams. He probably would not have been surprised to learn that the National Advisory Commission for Aeronautics, the fore-runner of NASA, was segregated right from its beginning. That enforced racial divide, a historical curiosity today but a critical matter for Black technical professionals then, was the product of the strict segregation installed in the federal bureaucracy by Woodrow Wilson, another Southerner with North Carolina roots, who headed Princeton University before his accession to the White House. It was part of an unsavory Wilsonian legacy many historians might like to forget today, but it was still in force during the early stages of the Space Race.

Talents Unchecked

Segregation was a mindset, but talent is an undeniable fact of life. Segregated attitudes did not stop NACA from using the brilliance of Black scientists like Linwood Wright to invent the turbofan engine; or Robert Shurney, whose "Vomit Comet" program taught astronauts how to handle weightlessness; or the mathematical genius of Katherine Johnson and Sally Richmond to actually calculate the orbits that sent aloft not only Alan Sheppard but also Gus Grissom and John Glenn, and to land Neal Armstrong safely on the surface of the Moon. The Space Race had its own priorities, among them a hunt for talent whose intensity of demand eventually overpowered the segregated mores of NASA's founders and the politicians who controlled its funding.

Starting the Corporate Climb

Art Johnson graduated from Morehouse and joined IBM, the world's largest computer maker, during the heady days of the 1960s. Working his way up the ranks in IBM's Federal Systems

239

Division, Johnson moved between assignments in Westlake, Calif., Manassas, Va., and Houston, Texas, providing critical support for the computer systems and data terminals so regularly shown on TV as NASA controllers and engineers handle major space shots. For not all of the specialists and engineers working the terminals at Johnson Space Flight Center, or at Cape Canaveral, are NASA personnel, even if news reports fail to mention it. NASA could not function without the direct support of the many technology firms that design and build its tools, and the companies' technical representatives are always on the scene.

Western Electric Company, the manufacturing subsidiary of pre-breakup AT&T, had been the prime contractor on the first control rooms at NASA's space centers, but IBM provided the computer expertise and Arthur Johnson, who learned his math and computer skills at Morehouse, was deep into the guts of the Johnson Space Flight Center systems as the Mercury program morphed into Gemini and finally Apollo, which reached the Moon before participating in the famous Apollo-Soyuz handshake in space.

Climbing to the Corporate Stratosphere

Along the way Johnson, who spent many years in the trenches of high technology, metamorphosed as well into a top manager. By the 1980s, he was being groomed for executive-level assignments. In 1983, Johnson was named administrative assistant to the president and Chief Operating Officer of IBM Federal Systems, a post he likens to a training assignment.

"They had a tradition," Johnson said in a *US Black Engineer &*

Information Technology magazine interview. "You worked as an administrative assistant, and that's where you saw how everything worked."

Off to MIT, then to War
But a big part of getting to be one of the most powerful executives in the aerospace industry is also going back to school. In 1986-87, Johnson took time off to be an MIT Foreign Policy XXI Seminar Fellow. Then he returned to Cambridge, Massachusetts, for training in the Harvard Business School's advanced management program. He completed that program in 1990.

Another upper-level apprenticeship, this time as executive assistant to then-IBM Chairman John Akers, led to Johnson's being named to lead the Federal Systems Division. But he also went to war with the troops in Desert Storm in 1991. Deployed to the Persian Gulf with a team of technical representatives and managers supporting the rapid implementation of a state-of-the-art computer network that could reach down to individual unit commanders in the field, Johnson worked closely with Army Lt. Gen. Alonzo Short, then commander of U.S. Army Information Systems.

TV reporters broadcast back amazing stories of the capabilities of the U.S. system, with Technical Operations Centers displaying flat-screen maps of troop deployments and captains, lieutenants and even sergeants keeping close touch with their superiors via laptop computers hooked to secure networks that worked even under the extreme conditions seen in the Arabian Desert. Here's what Gen. Short had to say:

"I became aware of Mr. Johnson's extraordinary talents when elements of the Army Information Systems Command were required to mobilize, deploy and serve during Desert Storm. . . . When the call went out for innovative information systems technology solutions and approaches for utilization in the difficult and hostile terrains of the Middle East, the IBM Federal Systems elements under the direction of Mr. Johnson responded quickly and with practical solutions which greatly contributed to the many successes enjoyed by the U.S. and allied forces. Art Johnson and his people clearly demonstrated that they are key players in this industry."

Two years later, President Bill Clinton named Johnson to a three-year term on the Defense Science Board, and the next year Johnson also joined the Presidential Advisory Council on Historically Black Colleges. Johnson also has sat on the Board of Visitors for the University of Maryland's School of Engineering, as well as the Board of Governors of the Electronics Industries Association and of the Armed Forces Communications Association. A former trustee and vice chair of the National Security Industrial Association, Johnson was the first Black American on the National Security Advisory Committee, experiences that stand him in good stead in the post-9/11 era of concern for homeland security.

Broken-Field Running

But Johnson first had to survive major corporate shakeups to get to his current exalted status. The end of the Cold War prompted the U.S. Defense Department to re-think its approach to contracting. Rather than support a large field of companies competing to produce the next generation of weapons, aircraft, ships and military equipment, the Defense planners, under pressure from budget-cutters in Congress, prodded the civilian companies in the Defense Industry to consolidate. That prompted a flurry of mergers.

IBM Federal Systems Division was sold to Loral Corporation during the early 1990s, and Johnson, its leader and an IBM group vice president, stayed on. By the time he got used to running things under Loral, a merger swept the division into Lockheed Martin. Johnson stayed on again, working his way up the corporate ladder in an entirely new enterprise, and emerged as corporate vice president and division president, in 1996 running a unit with nearly 8,000 employees, developing electronics gear and providing services that brought in $2.2 billion in revenues.

Still Showing Flashy Moves

Today, with new responsibilities in homeland security – and billions of contract dollars available through the new Department of Homeland Security – Johnson's mastery of information technology puts him back on the forefront of technology development.

Looking at the needs of the new department for improved security at airports and borders, transportation terminals and seaports – even for large public venues such as sports arenas, racetracks and entertainment stages – Lockheed Martin's Systems Integration division is poised to gain its share of lucrative contracts for technology developments in non-intrusive sensing for contraband chemicals and explosives, biometric identification systems and secure databases for intelligence and law enforcement as well as military users.

And after the fiasco that followed in the wake of Hurricane Katrina on the Gulf Coast, senior federal administrators are looking to the major players in Defense for help in providing logistical support for civilian emergency preparedness agencies as well as military forces.

Lockheed, one of the largest of the integrated manufacturing concerns, now is looking to partner with traditional logistics providers such as UPS and FedEx. Look for Art Johnson, now one of the key players exploring growth strategies for one of the biggest corporations in the world, to be in the middle of that mix as well. For in the end, it all comes down to passing the data, efficiently and securely, with computers. And as General Short said, with Information Technology, Art Johnson is The Man.

Chapter 14

Ballard Joins Black History's Military March

Like thousands of other youths of the 1960s, Joseph N. Ballard was a war baby. And like so many others, he grew up surrounded by Black war veterans, hearing the stories of their experiences overseas and learning what it takes to be a man among men. The Korean War blew up just as the young Joe Ballard began elementary school, and drew even more young men from across the country into uniformed service, to return with many more tales.

Young Ballard probably had no idea he himself would be thrown onto the Hellish proving ground of combat in a foreign land, but he grew to maturity at the height of the Cold War, and Vietnam beckoned. As Ballard himself said in a 1993 *St.*

Louis Post-Dispatch interview, he had no intention of going out to fight in Southeast Asia when he matriculated at historically Black Southern University. But the university required freshmen and sophomores to participate in Reserve Officer Training Corps activities, and when Ballard graduated with his degree in electrical engineering in 1965, he accompanied a friend who wanted to take the exam for military service. The stage was set for a reluctant warrior to make his own entry into history.

Ballard's friend "was gung-ho Army, and I was anything but," Ballard said. "I just went along for the ride."

Fate intervened. When the two young graduates arrived at the recruiting station, the tester told Ballard that if he was not there to take a test, he'd have to wait for his friend outside. "It was cold out there," Ballard recalled, "so I went ahead and took the test."

An Accidental Soldier Stepped Up

The friend did not pass the test, but Ballard marched through with flying colors. They were still flying, albeit very much higher on the pole, when Lt. General Joe Ballard stepped forward to take command of the Army Corps of Engineers in 1996, the first Black officer to lead the oldest engineering organization in the United States. Ballard, an electrical engineering graduate, had to go back to school, in the Army and in the hard classroom of combat, where the first mistake you make is likely to be the last thing you ever get to think about. But he survived that hard school and emerged decades later to lead the largest engineering, construction and real-estate programs in the world, with a total value of $211 billion, involving a total workforce of more than 290,000 people scattered all over the globe.

"This man reaches right into your life," *US Black Engineer & Information Technology* magazine said in 1998, reflecting on the way Corps of Engineers reach and authority permeates economic activities in America through its command of shoreline development, wetlands and environmental protection, management of flood control and storm-damage mediation efforts, port development programs, and even parks and recreational waterways.

Career Building Steps

In so many ways, Lt. General Ballard's career presents a classic illustration of the less-visible dimension of the Black tradition of military service: The making of careers that very frequently take Black professionals right past the traditional barriers to executive rank in American business, and to leadership rank in society. The young engineer Ballard didn't know it then, but he had just taken his first step on a journey whose endpoint would have been unimaginable to the Black veterans he met growing up in Oakdale, Louisiana.

Young people in military service quickly find themselves in charge of equipment worth millions of dollars, with command authority over personnel whose work may put them in harm's way on a daily basis, even in times of ostensible peace, for the skills of a combat soldier quickly atrophy if not practiced under conditions as close to combat as the training commands can take them. Moreover, the equipment itself often is large, powerful and capable of causing major injuries or death if not handled with utmost care and attention.

Leadership Preparation

Thus even in training, a military commander makes decisions that often make the difference between life and death for the people under his command, a practice that demands high-order leadership skills. Those skills, taught in the hard schools behind the barbed-wire fences that keep civilians out, honed in the fields, jungles and out on the oceans surrounding foreign lands, become increasingly valued the higher the officer rises. They are just as highly prized once that officer leaves the military and ventures out into the business world. In a time of war such as the Vietnam years, the pace of learning is rapid, for the alternative is that the troops and their commander fall victim to leadership on the opposition's team, and get wounded, captured or killed in action.

But that's getting ahead of the story. After training in the Engineer Officer School and a training tour at Fort Dix, New Jersey, Ballard received orders for South Vietnam. It hadn't been Ballard's idea of a bright future, but he was joining a tradition of military service by Black Americans that goes all the way back to the founding of the United States. Actually, long before:

A Long Tradition of Service

• It's well-known that Black Africans arrived in America as enslaved captives, first landing at Jamestown, Va., in 1619, then at New Amsterdam (New York) in 1626, and Salem, Massachusetts, in 1636. But it is singularly less well-known that they quickly found themselves pressed into military

248

service during the colonial wars against Native Americans. In 1641 New Amsterdam authorized Black men to carry "tomy hawks" and half pikes in the fighting. Plymouth Colony listed on its rolls Abraham Pearse, a Black man, as being capable of bearing arms. Later in the Massachusetts Colony, "all Negroes and Indians from sixteen to sixty" were enjoined to attend militia training, and free Blacks were generally allowed to volunteer.

• In New York, Blacks fought in the Tuscarora War in 1711, and again in the Yamassee War in 1715. Southern colonies, more dependent on enslaved labor and fearful of uprisings, restricted Blacks from bearing arms. Still, in emergencies, all hands were needed. Thus, French colonists in Louisiana enlisted Blacks to fight the Natchez Indians in 1730. Continued Natchez unrest prompted the Spanish to assemble a company of Blacks, officered by free Blacks, to join a larger force moving out to do battle near Mobile. It was the first time Blacks served as officers in an American militia unit.

• Geopolitics spurred new openings for Blacks during the 18th Century, just as the Cold War did for Blacks during the 20th. During the French and Indian War, a precursor to the American Revolution, Black militiamen served with independent militia commands from several colonies and as scouts, wagonneers and laborers with the English army. Black troopers won recognition for valor in some of these campaigns. In one instance, "Negro Mountain" in Maryland was named in honor of a Black militiaman killed by Native Americans in a battle of local fame.

• Eyewitness reports credit Crispus Attucks, famously slain in the Boston Massacre, with shaping and dominating the

249

action before he fell. When the other colonists faltered, Attucks is said to have been the one who rallied them to stand their ground. Other Black militiamen fought at Lexington and Concord as early as April 1775, and in that same year British officers began extending an offer of freedom to enslaved Blacks who joined His Majesty's troops battling to put down the Revolution. By December 1775 some 300 Blacks had joined Lord Dunmore's "Ethiopian Regiment," their uniforms emblazoned, "Liberty to Slaves."

• By 1778, each integrated colonial brigade had in its ranks an average of 42 Black soldiers. Later, Rhode Island, Boston and Connecticut formed all-Black units. One of these units fought the Battle of Rhode Island on Aquidneck Island in August 1778, holding its line for four hours against repeated assaults by the British and their Hessian mercenaries. The Blacks' courage enabled the rest of the American Army to escape a trap, and grateful Yankees later erected a monument to commemorate the Blacks' stand in Portsmouth, Rhode Island.

• The Continental Army counted some 5,000 Black men among its 300,000 soldiers, many of whom elicited praise and honors from their commanders. The smaller Continental Navy had no Black captains on its ships, but it did enroll many Black pilots, and several of the 13 states paid bonuses or granted freedom to enslaved Blacks who joined the warships' crews.

Many Marched Before Him

By the time Joe Ballard joined the Army, much of that history had been forgotten. But the memory of the 13,000 -

plus Blacks who fought in the Spanish American War was still alive. The 23 Black sailors on the doomed gunship Maine went anonymously into the dustbin of obscurity with their shipmates when the ship blew up in Havana harbor, but the 10th Cavalry "Buffalo Soldiers" gallantly fighting up the San Juan Heights with Teddy Roosevelt's "Rough Riders" carved their names into Army history.

In an incident never duplicated in combat, the 10th Cavalry standard-bearer saw the standard-bearer for the all-white 3rd Cavalry shot down climbing the hill, and ran to retrieve it. Waving both pennants to rally the troops, the 10th's standard bearer led the cheering men together the rest of the way to the crest of the Heights, and was hoisted on the shoulders of the 3rd Cavalry soldiers who reached him first.

A number of Black horse soldiers were still alive in the post-World War II era when Ballard was a boy and could tell their own stories, even if the stories of the more than 150,000 Black soldiers and 30,000 Black sailors who fought in the Civil War had long been buried by whites in Southern states such as his native Louisiana.

Going 'Over There'

Some 404,000 Blacks went to war with John J. Pershing in World War I, and many of these men were still alive, wearing their old uniforms and telling stories about their time "Over There" when Ballard was toiling his way through elementary school. So were men from among the half a million Blacks who served in the Army, Navy and Marine Corps during World War II. Many of those men also fought in Korea, where Blacks were 13 percent of the U.S. troops.

When Southern University graduate Ballard entered Officer Candidate training, he could not have been unaware of this tradition of service, his own immediate lack of military career plans notwithstanding. Like so many Black youths of his generation, he probably had been hearing about it since the day he took his first, halting toddler steps.

But the truth is that the stories of Black heroism trotted out during Black History Month and quickly forgotten weeks afterward tell only part of the story. Service in combat has always propelled white Americans to high public regard, but their Black comrades in arms have had to battle even longer after the guns went silent to gain the respect and opportunities their own heroism should have earned.

Invisible in the Silence after the Shots

Thus, George Washington became America's first president after his leadership in the Revolutionary War, but the Black Continental Army troops who suffered with him at Valley Forge, crossed the Delaware for the Christmas Surprise at Trenton, and humbled the British troops at Yorktown became faceless men after the war.

A handful of black Civil War veterans like Martin R. Delaney went on to distinguish themselves in public service nearly a century later, but the rest were forgotten in history.

John J. Pershing famously saluted his Black troops after they finished fighting "Over There," but James Reese Europe was the biggest Black name to come out of the Great War, and he was a bandleader. Eugene Bullard, the "Black Swallow" of the *Lafayette Escadrille*, was not acknowledged until Eleanor

252

Roosevelt wrote about him in newspaper columns decades afterward. He had rejoined the French army in 1940 and been wounded fighting Nazi troops on the ground in France before returning to the U.S., but wasn't even considered for service with the Tuskegee Airmen, although white World War I fliers were accepted as leading officers in the Army Air Corps.

Dwight Eisenhower became president of the United States after winning the battle of Europe, but the Black tankers of the 761st Battalion went back to anonymous lives after helping him and George S. Patton turn back the fanatical Nazi challenge at the Battle of the Bulge.

Finally, in the latter part of the 20th Century, Blacks who served also could become national leaders and corporate executives, just like their white counterparts.

Activism Changes Things

What was different in the 20th Century was that Black activism came on line at a time fascist propagandist in Europe and imperialist propagandists in Japan were challenging America's claim of being the land of equality, forcing open the doorway to technical specialties and to officer ranks long closed to Blacks. Black warriors have always shown their abilities and courage in a crisis, but access to the officer ranks – as Air Force pilots and commanders, Army and Marine infantry, tank and artillery commanders, and Navy ship officers and fliers – opens up all kinds of post-war opportunities for those shaped in the crucible of combat. Tuskegee Airmen enjoyed high prestige throughout their military careers and went on to become a leadership cadre for Black America as civilians. But the political and social activism

253

of the civil rights campaign that emerged after World War II forced open doorways to opportunity that had never existed for thousands of other Black soldiers, sailors and airmen in the post-war era.

Geopolitical considerations mattered here, too. As the Nazis and Japanese militarists had done in the 1930s and '40s, Soviet Communists challenged American claims of equality of opportunity during the 1950s, '60s and '70s, raising hard questions about the morality of segregation in a land proclaiming itself open to all. Black civil-rights activists had been asking the same pointed questions for generations, but now their campaigns resonated in a multi-colored world emerging from its colonialist past, and America's uniformed military services were not immune to the calls for change.

Officers Move to the Top

The swelling production of Black college graduates during World War II and afterward produced thousands of young Blacks qualified to become military officers, and the tradition of military service they followed has produced bumper crops of senior administrators and executives for the government agencies and corporations positioned to gain benefit from their training and well-honed leadership skills.

Thus it was for the young Captain Joe Ballard after his tours of duty in Southeast Asia. He went to command combat engineers, and found himself in the middle of sharp fighting. When he got there, however, he found lots of company among his Black contemporaries.

Unlike World War I, when white commanders hesitated to commit Black troops to battle, or World War II, when Blacks were mostly shunted into service units, Vietnam was a conflict in which thousands of Black warriors faced hostile fire. Harry S. Truman's Executive Order 9981, prompted by trade union activist A. Phillip Randolph and the NAACP's Charles Hamilton Houston, Walter White and Thurgood Marshall, had established a policy of equality of treatment and opportunity in the armed services for all persons without regard to race, color, religion or national origin, and after 1948 the services had rapidly ended policies and practices that had enforced racial segregation in the ranks.

Very Different Military Scene

By the mid-1960s the results were easily visible to a young military officer. The changes were dramatic, in a military that had always used Blacks in time of national necessity, but until the post-World War II era had rarely found itself capable of treating them as equals.

Henry Ossian Flipper, the first Black West Point graduate in 1877, had spent four years "Silenced" as his 19th-Century U.S. Military Academy classmates refused to speak to him. And to add insult to injury, even four years' successful service with Black cavalry regiments in the West did not put an end to the whites' hostility. In 1881, a conspiracy led by George Armstrong Custer produced trumped-up charges of conduct unbecoming an officer. Custer had been a hero in the Civil War, running J.E.B. Stuart's Confederate cavalry ragged and running Robert E. Lee to ground at Appomattox, but his racial hostility was self-evident.

Custer refused command of the Ninth Cavalry's "Buffalo Soldiers" in the West, saying he'd never go to war with Black

255

troopers, and his antipathy and relentless pursuit of Native Americans earned him their nickname "Hard Backsides." Custer charged into the Battle of the Little Bighorn and got the just desserts of any soldier who so contemptuously dismisses the fighting capacities of people of color, but Flipper died a poor and disgraced civilian. The court-martial Custer engineered ended Flipper's career, and its guilty verdict stood on the books until 1976, when a petition by Wesley A. Brown, the first Black Naval Academy graduate, got the case reopened.

During the run-up to World War II Benjamin O. Davis Jr., the son of the first Black U.S. Army general, went to West Point too, and was "Silenced" like Flipper before he graduated with high grades and went on to become commander of the Tuskegee Airmen. Besides the Airmen, more than 77,000 Black troopers actually served in the Army Air Corps during the war, proving they could handle the technical duties for which extant racial stereotypes deemed them incapable, fueling, arming and equipping the planes and providing skilled maintenance on bases where they were carefully segregated from white troops.

Black Warriors to the Line

Now, with the United States embroiled in yet another intense overseas conflict, such racially discriminatory behavior was outlawed, by presidential fiat and the Civil Rights Act of 1964. In the second half of the 20th Century a new cadre of young Black officers was in the fight on the ground and in the air, and many of them later would make their marks in the civilian world as well. A few stars stand out:

• Joseph Anderson graduated from West Point in 1965 – the same year former Officer Candidate Ballard joined the Army – and was the first Black officer to lead soldiers in combat in Vietnam. Anderson also had spent two months in Uganda through the Crossroads to Africa program in 1964, and was one of only four Blacks in that 1965 Academy class. Assigned as an 82d Airborne Division officer, Anderson served two tours of duty with the 1st Cavalry Division, earning two Silver Stars, five Bronze Stars, three Army Commendation Medals and 11 Air Medals. Anderson also was featured in the 1966 Oscar-winning documentary, "The Anderson Platoon."

A White House Fellow in 1977, Anderson joined Pontiac Motors in 1979 and by 1990 had risen to become general director of its body hardware business unit. Anderson also was runner-up to Air Force Col. Guion Bluford in the 1991 competition for Black Engineer of the Year, but during the 1960s they both were battling Communists in Southeast Asia.

• Guion Bluford, a fighter pilot who became the first Black Shuttle astronaut, was in the mid-1960s meeting Soviet-built MiGs in daily, deadly combat in Southeast Asian skies – 64 missions over North Vietnam during Operation Rolling Thunder – along with a small but growing corps of Black combat pilots that included Daniel "Chappie" James.

• James, a Tuskegee Airman who stayed through the Army Air Corps' transition to an independent Air Force in 1948, had joined the push for an integrated air combat force before World War II. James had completed the pre-war civilian pilot training program, then helped train Tuskegee Airmen, but was frustrated in his desire for a combat role. James finally won assignment to an all-black bomber group at the war's end, only to see it disbanded before it ever got to fight.

James finally got his turn in fighter cockpits during the Korean conflict, and remained in uniform for three decades. During the Vietnam War he flew multiple combat tours, including 78 Rolling Thunder missions over the North. In one memorable incident James and his commander and wingman, Col. Robin Olds, knocked down more MiGs than the combined total of all other pilots in the skies of Vietnam that day. In 1975 James became the first Black four-star general, almost as much a testament to his persistence as to his gallantry in battle. Eugene Bullard would have been proud.

• Lloyd "Fig" Newton was also in the air over Southeast Asia. A 1966 aviation graduate of historically Black Tennessee State University, Newton flew 269 combat missions in Vietnam in 1968, and later joined the Thunderbirds Aerial Demonstration Squadron. In 1978, after his tour with the Thunderbirds, Newton became a liaison officer with the U.S. House of Representatives. Newton commanded three wings and an air division and was assigned to numerous high staff positions. Among other postings, he also was director of operations for the U.S. Special Operations Command. When he won his fourth star in the late 1990s, General Newton culminated his Air Force career as Commander, Air Education and Training Command, responsible for recruiting, training and education for all service personnel. His command contained 13 Air Force bases, 43,000 active-duty personnel, and 14,000 civilians. In the year 2000, Newton retired and joined United Technologies' Pratt & Whitney Military Engines unit as vice president for international programs and business development.

• Another Black air war colleague was Frederick Gregory, an Air Force Academy graduate who flew 550 combat missions. Gregory, who retired as a colonel in 1993, ultimately logged some 7,000 flight hours in more than 50 types of aircraft, including helicopters. A graduate of the Naval Test Pilot School at Patuxent River, Col. Gregory served as an engineering test pilot for the Air Force and for NASA, where he also served as an astronaut, manager of flight safety and launch support programs before being named acting NASA administrator in February 2005.

• Still another Black Vietnam flier was a young U.S. Naval Academy graduate named Charles F. Bolden Jr., a Marine who flew A-6 Intruder medium-range bombers between 1972 and 1973, completing more than 100 combat missions over North and South Vietnam, Laos and Cambodia from a base in Thailand.

Bolden, also a Patuxent River test pilot grad, later went on to qualify as a Space Shuttle pilot-astronaut. During his first spaceflight in 1986, Bolden helped deploy a communications satellite and conducted experiments in astrophysics and materials processing. As pilot of the Space Shuttle Discovery in 1990, Bolden and his crew put the Hubble Space Telescope into orbit from a record-setting altitude of 400 miles. Bolden later commanded Space Shuttle Atlantis on the first SpaceLab "Mission to Planet Earth." In 1994, Bolden returned to command the Shuttle Discovery on a landmark eight-day, first-ever joint U.S./Russian space mission, carrying a Cosmonaut and the Space Habitation Module-2 into orbit.

A Marine Aircraft Wing commander after leaving NASA in 1994 to serve as Deputy Commandant of Annapolis, Bolden, then a brigadier general, led a Marine Expeditionary Force in Kuwait in support of Operation Desert Thunder. In July 1998 Bolden rose to major general and served as Deputy Commander, U.S. Forces Japan.

Sea Change

Change had come to the Navy, too. Blacks had served in Navy blue going all the way back to James Forten, the Philadelphia sailmaker's son who was a cabin boy during the Revolutionary War and became so wealthy running the family business he helped finance U.S. naval efforts in the War of 1812. Blacks died as crewmen aboard the USS Maine, in an incident that inflamed Americans before the Spanish American War, and they served as enlisted ratings during the First World War, but later the 20th Century Navy so restricted Blacks' enlistment that by World War II Blacks were required to prove all over again that they could handle the complicated technologies and discipline of shipboard service.

Never mind the record of 30,000 Black sailors in the Civil War. Never mind the work of the incomparable "Hell-Roarin' Mike Healy," the Black-Irish Revenue Cutter captain who helped turn Alaska into a viable settlement. Healy, who rose through the ranks to command the cutter Bear, was credited with introducing reindeer to provide food for the Alaska settlers while simultaneously helping to build the modern Coast Guard before retiring in 1903, the year Douglas MacArthur graduated from West Point.

Slowly as She Goes, But . . .

During the 1940s Navy men had to be dragged kicking and

screaming to the table of equality, even after Steward's Mate Dorie Miller proved Blacks could fight, shooting down six Japanese planes from the deck of the USS Arizona at Pearl Harbor. Blacks had to prove themselves all over again, and did so aboard ships like the USS Macon, a destroyer escort commanded by white officers and chief petty officers but crewed by Black enlisted ratings.

In the 1960s Samuel L. Gravely, the Macon's first Black officer and later its commander, was still in uniform. Gravely, featured in *Ebony* magazine as an example of the "new" Navy, later became the first Black flag officer and retired as a vice admiral.

Walter J. Davis, a North Carolina farmboy who grew up to drive fighter jets, was flying off carrier decks to battle MiGs in Vietnam's skies, too, part of a group of seagoing inheritors of the Tuskegee Airmen's legacy. Davis, a 1959 Naval ROTC graduate of Ohio State University, completed flight training at Pensacola Naval Station in 1960, the year Bluford finished high school. In 1967, Davis went to Southeast Asia for two combat tours over Vietnam in F-4 Phantom jets. Davis, a graduate of both the Top Gun fighter pilot school and the Naval Test Pilot School, later was Class Desk Officer managing development of the F-14 Tomcat, the Navy's premier air-superiority fighter, and flew Tomcats for the remainder of his career. Davis rose from flight officer to squadron executive officer to commanding officer, then to air group leader. His first ship command was on a munitions ship, and then he became skipper of the USS Ranger, the carrier aboard which the movie "Top Gun" was filmed.

261

Riding the Waves

In 1990, then a rear admiral, Davis took command of Carrier Group Six, flying Tomcats off the decks of the USS Forrestal, the first super-carrier, and the USS America. Among other jobs, Forrestal Battle Group participated in Operation Provide Comfort, denying Saddam Hussein's air force the freedom to harass Kurds over northern Iraq.

In 1992, Davis received his second star and took command as director, Naval Systems Architecture and Engineering, among other things responsible for Space and Electronic Warfare programs. In English, Admiral Davis, like the Air Force's Gen. Edmonds, was running a systems engineering operation, designing the computer-driven integrated battle management systems that have so impressed America's opponents in the Balkans, Afghanistan and Iraq.

When Davis retired in December 1996, he was wearing the three stars of a vice admiral, and he had accumulated more than 3,500 hours and more than 800 carrier landings in fighter planes. He retired on the same day J. Paul Reason became the Navy's first Black four-star admiral.

Grasping the Sword

Reason graduated from Annapolis in 1965, the same year Ballard finished at Southern, and first went to sea as operations officer aboard the destroyer escort USS Blackwood, then steamed twice to the waters around Southeast Asia. His first Asian tour was aboard the nuclear-powered missile cruiser Truxton in 1968, shortly after it was converted from a conventional steam-driven gunship to a nuclear-powered gun and missile cruiser.

The second Southeast Asian tour came aboard the nuclear-powered aircraft carrier Enterprise in 1971, when Rolling Thunder was blasting away at Ho Chi Minh's truculence. After another turn aboard the Truxton, Reason rotated through a number of shipboard and shore stations before rising to become Commander-in-Chief of the Atlantic Fleet. "Hell-Roarin' Mike Healy, looking on from sailor's heaven, probably smiled before barking out new orders to his angel escort.

The Post as Home
On the ground, Blacks, drafted into the military more frequently than their percentage of the population warranted, have tended to stay in the service longer than their white counterparts, and to volunteer in greater percentages for the elite Marines, Army Ranger, Air Cavalry and 101st and 82nd Airborne units. During the Vietnam conflict, Blacks, 11 percent of the population, constituted 16 percent of the draftees. Many who joined, like the college-trained Ballard, distinguished themselves as officers.

• Wilmer Cooksey, a "muscle-car" addict who became the plant manager making Chevrolet Corvettes years after the war, was one such during the 1960s, leading soldiers in Vietnam, as were thousands of young Black college graduates in an Army whose 1968 troop strength was 12 percent Black. Cooksey, who loved Corvettes, bought one when he returned, and later joined General Motors. Now a Ph.D. in mechanical engineering and a certified professional road racer as well as manager of the plant that makes Corvettes and Cadillac's new, 2-seat sports car, Cooksey turned the plant around when GM was considering closing the entire Corvette line.

• The young Colin Powell, who also rose to four-star rank, went to South Vietnam early. Powell was actually in-country before Lyndon Johnson's massive buildup turned the Vietnamese civil war into a superpower proxy war. Powell, who graduated in the same 1958 City College of New York class as Mobil's Arnold Stancell, had joined the Army and served as a military advisor to a unit of the Army of the Republic of Viet Nam. Powell won the respect of his South Vietnamese cohorts when he persuaded them to wear American-made flak jackets, which helped many to survive the Viet Cong ambushes that were decimating their ranks. Powell returned for successive combat tours, experience he later put to good use during Operation Desert Storm when, as chairman of the Joint Chiefs of Staff, he led U.S. forces to victory over the Iraqi invaders of oil-rich Kuwait. Later, as the first Black Secretary of State, Powell became known as a consummate proponent of worldwide democracy.

• Thus, Joe Ballard did not go alone into the hellish arena of combat as he commanded first a company and then a battalion of combat engineers, building roads and structures while defending against enemy attacks in South Vietnam. Unlike in World War I, when only 1,300 of the 404,00 Black soldiers held officer rank, the Vietnam War U.S. military held thousands of Black serving officers. Its soaring Black enrollments still contained disproportionate shares of enlisted versus officer ranks, but it was an entirely different military establishment than the one that fought World War II.

Ballard the Soldier-Constructor
On the ground, Ballard led teams building everything from

rough combat trails and pipelines through Vietnam's notorious jungles to major paving projects.

"We actually built the first ice plant to be built by troops," Ballard recalled in a 1996 *US Black Engineer & Information Technology* interview. "Our Pacific Architecture and Engineering Command ordered it, and we found the site, laid it out and started construction when we discovered we had to find water to supply it. We had to stop and look for water – fortunately there was an underground stream about 50 meters away – and we had to send teams to the U.S. to do research on the saline mix and cooling vats. We built roads, too, as well as a bakery and an ice cream plant."

When he got back from Vietnam, Ballard still doubted he was cut out for a military career. After two combat tours, he thought he was ready for a more peaceful life. Ballard, now married with children, took his family to the Midwest and settled in as a mid-level manager for the Illinois Bell Telephone Company.

But civilian life paled, and Ballard found that his family missed the ordered camaraderie and rhythms of base life. The Army called again, offering him funding for a master's degree program at the school of his choice, and Ballard signed on again, completing a master's degree in engineering management at the University of Missouri at Rolla. He also had completed the Engineer Officer basic and advanced training programs at Fort Dix, and he went on to complete courses at the Army Command and General Staff College and the Army War College.

Large and in Charge

Military service puts Black professionals in charge of large resources, with authority their civilian counterparts often never get to handle. Ballard, a registered professional engineer, has commanded the Army Engineer Center at Fort Leonard Wood, been a special assistant to the Army Chief of Staff, and been commandant of the Army Engineer School at Fort Leonard Wood, a 63,000-acre reservation, managing a 10,000-person staff on a budget that exceeded $100 million.

In Ballard's first year of command, Fort Leonard Wood trained more than 35,000 Active Duty service personnel and another 42,000 members of the National Guard, reservists from the Army, Navy and Marine Corps, college Reserve Officer Training Corps cadets, and members of the Civil Air Patrol. In Fiscal Year 1993, Ft. Leonard Wood's payroll was about $300 million, and it made almost $200 million in purchases. Some $69 million of that purchasing money went to buy things from small, disadvantaged or women-owned enterprises, too, and the hospital and dental clinics on the post, serving military personnel and dependents spread over a five-state area, handled more than 116,000 patient visits that year.

A posting in Europe with the 18th Engineer Brigade in Karlsruhe, Germany – the biggest brigade in the Corps of Engineers – tested Ballard's mettle again, this time dealing with civilian as well as military needs in a country not at war, but in the thick of the Cold War.

On Oct. 1, 1996, Joseph N. Ballard, then a lieutenant general, took command as the 49th leader of the Army Corps of Engineers. For the first time in history, a Black man was wearing the "castle" pins that had been given to a young Douglas MacArthur at his 1903 graduation from West Point by his father, Civil War hero Arthur A. MacArthur, one of the fathers of the modern Army.

A Commander with Bite

Ballard took command of an organization that had, as he put it, lost its focus. With 500 uniformed service men and women and 39,000 civilian engineers, the Corps was managing an annual budget of $11 billion, but its focus on civilian waterways, wetlands protection, management of recreational lands and lakes, and disaster remediation had seemed to take precedence over its military role as real estate agent and construction manager for the Army and Air Force.

When the news arrived that Ballard, an experienced combat engineer who had spent his career in the field and never served at headquarters, would command the nation's oldest engineering organization, *Engineer Update* magazine asked Ballard what he thought of the Corps.

"I've served in the larger Corps, in the Regiment," Ballard said, "but I've never served in the major command called the U.S. Army Corps of Engineers. Primarily, my contact with USACE has been as a customer at small installations, large installations, and communities in Germany, on the receiving end of what the Corps does. My impression of the Corps was that it was a professional organization with fine folks, but a little out of the mainstream of the Army, and didn't always deliver everything they promised. Those perceptions are shared by others outside the Corps, and that's one of the things we have to work on."

Or as H. Martin Lancaster, then Assistant Army Secretary, put it: "The Corps has in the past been seen by some as separate and apart from the war-fighter side. That has not always benefitted us in the Pentagon and in Congress." Ballard, Lancaster said, "has two great strengths. One is the respect that he enjoys among the 'war-fighter' side of the Army. His other big plus is his reputation for being a really strong, take-charge kind of leader."

Shifting the Course

By all accounts, Ballard succeeded in transforming the Corps of Engineers. His Strategic Vision, developed after careful study and consideration of the recommendations of a transition team composed of Pentagon officials, senior Corps personnel and others, dramatically changed the way the Corps of Engineers works, clearing out bureaucratic bottlenecks that had been in place for decades and making the Corps more "customer friendly." Those changes outlasted Ballard's tenure as head of the Corps, and figure prominently in the disaster relief efforts in such places as the U.S. Gulf Coast, where hurricanes Katrina and Rita landed a double whammy whose effects will be felt for years.

Plan Derailed

Ballard had actually put together a plan to rebuild and replace the levees whose failure left New Orleans and many of the surrounding communities suffering from the worst storm-driven floods since the hurricane of 1900 inundated Galveston. But a strange combination of Republican budget-

268

cutters in Congress and environmental activists questioning the propriety of the massive construction project needed for the work killed the plan.

Still Being Heard

Now Ballard, retired and leading a civilian consultancy, is speaking out about what will be needed to rebuild New Orleans and other Gulf Coast cities such as Mobile and Biloxi, and former protégées such as Brig. Gen. Robert Crear, now commander of the Mississippi River Commission, consult him almost daily on remediation efforts.

Congress and the White House, prodded by the daily horror stories coming out about a city flooded over 80 percent of its territory and the biggest forced migration since the Dust Bowl years, are reviewing their stands on what will need to be done. Critics point to the extensive hydraulic works protecting cities such as Amsterdam, the Netherlands, and London, and Ballard's plans should soon be reevaluated.

Ballard, the engineer who honed his skills in the high-adrenalin arena of combat, would be an ideal person to provide consulting services in that effort. He's a warrior who learned to build as well as tear down, under some of the harshest conditions an engineer has faced anywhere.

Endnotes

1. For an excellent discussion of the long struggle to desegregate the armed services, refer to the Defense Studies Series book," Integration of the

Armed Forces 1940-1965," by Morris J. MacGregor, Jr. Available online at *http://www.army.mil/cmh-pg/books/integration/IAF-FM.htm*, the book provides a comprehensive examination of the history of Black participation in the U.S. military services.

2. See also "Proudly We Served: The Men of the USS Mason," by Mary Pat Kelly. US. Naval Institute Press, 1999. 220 pages. See also "Black Company: The Story of Subchaser 1264," by Eric Purdon. Bluejacket Press. The events described in Kelly's book were recreated in the movie "Proud," with famed actor Ossie Davis, in his last role, portraying one of the sailors. It ends with President Bill Clinton awarding a citation to surviving members of the Mason crew, aboard a modern USS Mason, with Davis in attendance.

3. See also *http://www.africanamericans.com/Military.htm*, supra.

Chapter 15

Dean Elbows into the Digital Pantheon

The Desktop Computer Revolution, said to have launched the Information Age via the "Information Superhighway," came to public notice in 1977, when a group of California hobbyists from the Homebrew Computer Club began selling machines produced with the knowledge they gained tinkering with microprocessors.

Or did it? Like so many technological advances – especially those whose rapid spread completely overturned traditional ways of doing business – the reduction of electronic circuitry to the microchip sizes that put supercomputer-like processing power on the average person's desktop actually began

271

decades earlier.

And Dr. Mark Dean, the architect of the "Advanced Technology" Personal Computer IBM used to dethrone the Homebrew Clubbers' Apple IIe, the Commodore Vic-20 and 16 and Tandy Corp.'s TRS-80 computers and push desktop machines into homes, schools, and every kind of business, had plenty of predecessors. The whites are familiar names to those following technology. The Blacks, Dr. Dean's colleagues, competitors and the all-important forerunners on the cutting edge, are very much less so.

Boykin at the Beginning

Otis Boykin was one of those Black predecessors, and his ideas profoundly affected the work of the computer pioneers like Dr. Dean who came after him. Boykin, born in 1920, was a boy during the years of the flappers and the "floy-floy," and he lived through the Great Depression as a teenager. The post-World War I era, for Blacks, was not so fun-filled and prosperous as many whites seem to remember, as pests such as the boll weevil ruined cotton crops, mechanical harvesters began displacing Black labor in vegetable and grain fields, and the spread of the Dust Bowl bankrupted many family farms.

In the industrial cities, labor union organizing – frequently supported by Blacks at inception – all too frequently turned into organized efforts to keep Blacks out of the higher-paying factory jobs after the unions won contracts. The riots observed by Amos Webber in Philadelphia in the 1840s had many parallels in the blue-collar workplace of the early 20th Century, when white immigrants began using violence to eliminate the competition of Black workers for jobs.

272

Still, Otis Boykin's father, a Dallas, Texas, carpenter, prospered and was able to send him to historically Black Fisk University at a time few other Blacks had the money or preparation for college. Boykin graduated from W.E.B. DuBois' *alma mater* in 1941, and joined the Majestic Radio & TV Corporation in Chicago, Ill., working as a lab assistant testing automatic controls for aircraft. At the end of World War II, when the future IBM Master Inventor Dean was not yet a twinkle in his father's eye, Boykin formed his own consulting company, Boykin-Fruth, and took graduate courses at the Illinois Institute of Technology.

Enabling Discoveries
During the 1950s, when many Americans were just beginning to appreciate the benefits coming from the rapidly expanding electronics industry, Boykin was a key player in its advance, developing ever-smaller components that still are used today. In 1959, when the future Dr. Dean was a toddler, Boykin patented a wire precision resistor, used in radios, television sets and, yes, computers today. He also invented thin-film capacitors and methods to make them, thin-film resistors, and many other devices, 26 in all. A polyphem imager Boykin developed became the primary navigational aid for cruise missiles, and his "burglar proof" cash register cut down the risk of theft in stores. His most famous invention, however, was the microprocessor control unit for heart pacemakers, which saved many lives.

Molecular Advance
An even earlier pioneer was Dr. Samuel Elmer Imes, born in

Memphis, Tennessee, in 1883. Imes, another Fisk University alumnus, graduated in 1903 and went on to get his master's degree at the University of Michigan in 1910. Eight years later, he became the second Black American to earn a doctorate in physics, after Edward Bouchet (Yale, 1876). Dr. Imes began work as a consulting chemist in New York, then as a research physicist for the Federal Engineer's Development Corp., before moving on to the Burroughs Magnetic Corporation as a research engineer. Burroughs, a name not so widely known as in earlier years, once was a major competitor in the market for large computer systems, now dominated by IBM.

Dr. Imes' research, published in his dissertation, prompted a complete reevaluation of quantum physics theory: He showed that quantum effects could be traced in the molecular structure of materials.

If that seems esoteric, recall that the invention of the transistor, and all the solid-state technology based on it, were practical applications of scientists' understanding of quantum molecular effects in silicon. It would not have been possible without the research discoveries of Dr. Imes and his generation of scientists.

Semiconductors Jump Out

The point-contact transistor amplifier was invented in 1947 by three AT&T Bell Laboratories scientists, and in 1952, 11 years after Dr. Imes' death, G.W. Drummer of Britain's Royal Radar Establishment continued the work with a technical paper arguing that a solid block of materials could be used to connect electronic components, without externally added wires. That came to pass in 1958-59, when Texas Instruments'

Jack Kilby and Fairchild Semiconductors' Robert Noyce independently developed the solid-state, integrated circuit. Texas Instruments had begun commercial production of silicon transistors in 1954, but Kilby's design used germanium, a substance widely used in diodes. Noyce's implementation used silicon, and Fairchild also developed a "planar" process to crank out commercial quantities. The tools Mark Dean would use to drive a new revolution in technology were thus being forged. Born in Tennessee in 1957, the little revolutionary had some growing up to do before he could take his own place on the front lines of technological advance.

Growing Pains

American society had some growing up to do as well, before it could begin to appreciate the talents and contributions of Black citizens like Mark Dean. The Great Migration of Blacks from the agricultural, still-segregated South, begun during the run-up to the First World War, rapidly accelerated after the second. Mechanical cotton pickers swept through the Deep South from 1947 on, also sweeping to the sidelines generations of Black farmhands whose labor had produced the raw material for the great textile industries of the Northeast and England. Mechanized corn harvesters and huskers, grain-cutting combines and all sorts of gasoline-driven "labor-saving" implements removed Black farmworkers' reason for being on the land in other Southern states.

Global economic developments also played a role. It gets repeated every year that the United States, the world's leading producer of manufactured goods before the two great wars, promptly buried all combatants with war materiel, weapons and an 8-million-man Army, by the end of the Second World War producing 100,000 airplanes a year and building the largest Navy the world had ever seen. But it is just as often forgotten that after the Second World War, the flow of money into America's great industrial enterprises increased again, as the Europeans and Japanese struggled to rebuild their war-torn cities and re-start their own industrial economies. Americans, protected by two great oceans from the bombs, bullets and tanks that so devastated the rest of the developed world, were the suppliers of first resort.

The Magnetic North

With the steel mills, shipbuilding yards, locomotive works, truck and tractor plants, textile mills and industrial manufacturers of all kinds selling everything they could make to the former combatant nations while at the same time building a new world for the returning U.S. soldiers and their newly founded families, the factories of the Northeast, Midwest, and West Coast were taking in all the workers they could find. Black hands, surplus labor in a farm economy increasingly taken over by mechanized "agribusiness," were welcomed in places where Blacks had once been shunned, welcomed also into many of the same unions that once had battled in the streets to keep them out.

Politics, as always, sparked compelling changes. As has been noticed by many observers, 1960 was the year Black voters cast the deciding ballots that moved John F. Kennedy into the White House and sent Vice President Richard Nixon packing. Dr. Martin Luther King and his desegregation marchers were shaking up the conscience of the country from the South at the same time the Rev. Leon Sullivan and his "Philadelphia 400" were challenging corporate leaders to end workplace discrimination in the North. A different challenge came from the Soviet Union's new militaristic stance, its capabilities underscored by Sputnik I and its successors in space, and the jitters that produced ram-charged America's competitive zeal.

Lessons Overseas Applied at Home

Having emerged from the global conflict against fascist, racist empire-builders as the leader of a worldwide coalition espousing Roosevelt's "Four Freedoms," America was determined to show that it was different.

Thus, the programs begun under Franklin Roosevelt's Fair Employment Practices Committees, strengthened under Harry S Truman, gained new vigor under the Kennedy-era Office of Equal Opportunity and the U.S. Labor Department under the activist guidance of Assistant Secretary Arthur Fletcher. Thus, the Black challengers at the gates of higher education, barred from attending the venerable institutions serving the "mainstream" white population, got a new hearing when they demanded entrance for their sons and daughters. Thus, the Black veterans who returned from the world-wide conflict against racist regimes abroad, reinvigorated after breaking segregation in their own uniformed ranks, brought their courage home for the fight against racial domination in their own land.

Thus, the young Mark Dean grew up in a world radically different from the one in which his parents evolved.

Rushing to the Future

Technologically, the pace of change was frenetic. IBM, Mark Dean's future employer, developed its first automatic mass-production transistor foundry in 1960, producing circuitry to be used in "second generation" digital computers such as the all-solid-state 1401.

Two years later, the Teletype Corporation introduced the Model 33 terminal, a keyboard and punched-tape device for computer input and output. Early computer hobbyists adopted Teletype's terminal to program the small systems they designed to use the integrated-circuit "microprocessors" introduced by the brand-new Intel Corporation. But that came much later. The groundwork for the Information Revolution Dr. Dean helped to drive had still to be laid.

The Tools Came First

In 1964, when Dean was a second-grader, two Dartmouth College professors, John Kemeney and Thomas Kurz, developed the Beginners' All-Purpose Symbolic Instruction Code (BASIC) as a simplified, easy-to-learn programming language to introduce their students to the concepts of computer programming. Four years later, Douglas C. Englebart of the Stanford Research Institute electrified a San Francisco Joint Computer Conference audience with a new system for inputting, retrieving and displaying data. It used a keyboard, a numeric keypad, a cathode-ray-tube display, a new tool -- a "mouse," and a windowing interface. Englebart also used a software word processor, a "hypertext" system, and demonstrated remote collaboration with his colleagues.

278

Enter the Microprocessor

About the same time, Robert Noyce and Gordon Moore, dissatisfied at Fairchild Semiconductors, did what many of their colleagues were doing: Struck out on their own with a new company, Intel, for "Integrated Electronics." Noyce typed up a one-page summary of their ideas, and a San Francisco venture capitalist, impressed, promptly raised $2.5 million to fund the new firm.

The next year, the ETI Company, or Busicom as it was known, came calling from Japan. Busicom wanted to market a new line of calculator products, powered by integrated circuits. Busicom wanted 12 custom chips, for keyboard scanning, control of display and printing, and other functions. Intel, lacking the manpower for so many jobs, decided to go another way. Intel's Ted Hoff and his colleagues convinced Busicom they could design a single integrated circuit that could handle all 12 functions, and Busicom agreed to fund the development. Federico Faggin led the design team, with Hoff and Stan Mazor, who wrote the microcode for the new chip, collaborating with Busicom Co.'s Masatoshi Shima.

Tiny But Powerful

The finished product, the world's first microprocessor, was the engine that drove the Information Revolution. At an eighth of an inch wide by a sixth long, the Intel 4004 did not look like a weapon to rattle cages in the biggest businesses of the world. But with its 2,300 metal-oxide semiconductor transistors, the 4004 contained as much computing power as the 18,000 vacuum tubes of ENIAC I, the machine that

279

launched the postwar computer business. Running at a clock speed of 108 Kilohertz, the 4004 supported 45 instructions and could process 60,000 operations a second. To support it, Intel also introduced the 1103 memory chip, the first generally available Dynamic Random Access Memory chip.

Intel, realizing what it had wrought, bought the rights to its design for $60,000. Busicom went bankrupt, but Intel quickly rushed out a marketing plan to encourage development of applications for its fledgling microprocessor. In 1971, it introduced the 4004 to world, the first-ever single-chip, general purpose central processing unit. Within months, manufacturing engineers were using the chip and its successor, the eight-bit 8008, for many different kinds of jobs. When a young Intel consulting engineer named Gary Kildall wrote a "Control Program for Microcomputers (CP/M)" in 1975, the new, improved Intel 8080 microprocessor had a bonafide disk operating system onto which applications could be developed. It was the first multi-platform operating system for the new desktop computers.

Readying for the Leap

Mark Dean was just finishing high school then, but the tools he would use to rewrite technology history were almost ready for his charge onto the field where master innovators play.

Dr. Dean began his collegiate studies at the University of Tennessee, in Knoxville, in 1975. He enrolled as just another student, majoring in electrical engineering. No noisy riots greeted his matriculation, unlike James Meredith at Ole Miss. The Ku Klux Klan did not storm up on horseback, burning crosses to keep him out, and no retired Army generals charged up the steps of the registrar's office. The university, which had voluntarily desegregated in 1961, did not decide it had to dismiss his enrollment "to protect his safety," as the University of Alabama did with Autherine Lucy. But so much had happened in the maturation of American society to let a young Mark Dean make an uneventful step onto the flagship campus of the state where only seven years earlier, Nobel Peace Laureate Dr. Martin Luther King Jr. was shot down for fighting racial domination in the segregationist South.

Drawing the Contrasts

A story told in 1996 by the late Vernon Jarrett, another famous Tennessean, puts the changes into perspective.

Jarrett, a legendary reporter and broadcaster, had begun his career working beside W.E.B. DuBois at the *Chicago Defender* during the 1940s. Then he and the great jazz singer-composer Oscar Brown Jr. initiated the nation's first-ever Black daily radio newscast, in 1948. Jarrett, a lifelong NAACP member who founded the ACT-SO program (Academic, Cultural, Technical and Scientific Olympics) to motivate Black youth to compete in intellectual arenas as they do in sports, also produced a news and commentary show on race relations on Chicago TV station WLS (TV-7). The show carried nearly 2,000 programs, and earned Jarrett the Silver Circle Award from the National Academy of Television Arts and Sciences.

Tireless Journeyman

In 1970 Jarrett joined the *Chicago Tribune* as its first Black syndicated columnist, and five years later he became a founding member of the National Association of Black

281

Journalists, the nation's largest professional group for journalists of color. In 1983 Jarrett moved over to the *Chicago Sun-Times* Editorial Board, and remained until 1994. Allegedly retired after that job, Jarrett began writing columns for the *New York Times'* New American News Syndicate and produced the "Jarrett Journal" news show on the Black-oriented radio station WVON-AM.

Jarrett, even in his twilight years, was known for seizing a microphone to set the record straight in a meeting of Black journalists – or meetings of journalists of any kind, in reality – and the group gave rapt attention when he stormed to the podium at a 1996 NABJ conference, on the campus of historically Black Fisk University.

Remembering From Whence We Came

Fuming over a deprecating speech by Muslim leader Louis Farrakhan, Jarrett delivered an impromptu history lesson. Jarrett, who had not been scheduled to speak, strode to the podium before his collected colleagues during a commemorative session at Jubilee Hall, the first building ever constructed for Black education in America.

> *"Tell Louis Farrakhan Black journalists don't need him to tell us about history; we've lived it and we've covered it. . . .*
>
> *"Here we are in Jubilee Hall, where the Fisk Jubilee Singers stood singing Gospel songs inside while the Ku Klux Klan rode outside, burning crosses. The Jubilee Singers became famous all over the world singing the spirituals and raising money for the university. But they*

had to deal with the Ku Klux Klan at home. And I've sat in these very same pews while they sang their songs with the Ku Klux Klan outside, and they didn't worry about the Ku Klux Klan . . .

"Tell Louis Farrakhan we don't need him to tell us about the struggles Black people have gone through! My grandfather was a slave! And I know the hard road my grandparents had to travel . . .

"My father built this building. I sat in these wrought-iron pews one day and watched my older brother graduate with his master's degree from Fisk, with Dr. Alain Locke delivering the commencement address. My father started babbling, and I was shocked. My parents were schoolteachers, and there was a rule in the Jarrett household – you did not speak during a sermon or an oration – not if you wanted to live! And the great Dr. Alain Locke was delivering the oration.

"But my father was babbling, and when I looked closely, I saw that he was just about crying. He was talking about the days when he worked on the crew that built Jubilee Hall, when he was just a boy.

"When my father worked on that construction crew, he was so poor he didn't have a place to stay. So he became the lockup man, the last one to leave the building for the day. He'd leave a door unlocked, so he could come back in and roll his clothes up into a bedroll and go to sleep. He'd get up early to wash up and get ready to meet the crew when they came back to work the next day.

"And he worked hard, completing the building and

screwing down those wrought-iron pews in Fisk Jubilee Hall.

"My father could not afford to go to Fisk University. Blacks were not allowed to go to white schools like Vanderbilt; they couldn't go to the University of Tennessee. They could only go to Black colleges, and it was his lifelong dream to go to Fisk, but he didn't have the money to go to Fisk. My father went to work for some rich people in Knoxville who promised they'd pay for him to go to college, and he went to Knoxville College. My mother went there. My father could not afford to send his children to Fisk for their undergraduate degrees either, so we went to Knoxville, too.

"But now here he was, sitting on those same wrought-iron pews that he'd screwed down as a young boy, watching his son receive a master's degree from Fisk University. With the great Dr. Alain Locke delivering a speech to the graduates. He was overwhelmed!"

So were hundreds of Black journalists the author included, realizing Jarrett's father had screwed those wrought-iron pews into place 103 years before they arrived. Listening to Jarrett's lesson, we all reflected on how far we all had come.

Shadows of His Forebears

The young Mark Dean may not have known Vernon Jarrett, or heard of Autherine Lucy, William Wiley, Medgar Evers, or the legions of other Blacks who were turned away from state-funded universities in Southern states not much more than a decade before his arrival at the Tennessee Volunteers campus. But the campaign that opened the university doors to Black youths like himself also opened the doors to a new set of capabilities for industrial America, as Dr. Dean's own career demonstrates.

As do those of his Black, highly talented peers.

Dreaming of a 'Net

The year before Dr. Dean arrived in Knoxville, a young Nigerian immigrant named Phillip Emeagwali was busy pursuing a math degree at Oregon State University. Among his reading matter was a 1922 science fiction piece about a way to use 64,000 mathematicians to forecast weather patterns on the entire planet Earth. Emeagwali built on those ideas, constructing a theoretical scheme for using 64,000 computer processors, distributed evenly around the Earth, to do the same thing. He called this system he conceptualized a "HyperBall international network," in a paper now recognized as a prescient discussion of what now is known as the Internet.

Emeagwali went on to graduate studies at George Washington University for two master's degrees – in civil and marine engineering – and another master's in mathematics from the University of Maryland, before completing a doctorate in civil engineering at the University of Michigan. Dr. Emeagwali then went to work on The Connection Machine, the first "massively parallel" system, linking 65,000 processors. When completed in the mid-1980s it was the fastest computer on Earth. The Connection Machine, which could perform 3.1 billion calculations a second, was not Dr.

Emeagwali's invention, but his contributions to its development won the Gordon Bell Prize for 1989; and the work was so influential that many other manufacturers built on it to develop their own multiprocessing computer systems. Dr. Emeagwali, the recipient of many awards from organizations such as the National Technical Association and the World Bank, also was cited as the "Best Scientist in Africa" by the Pan African Broadcasting Company's Heritage Achievement Awards program in 2001. Former President Bill Clinton described him in a televised speech as "one of the great minds of the Information Age."

Another Silicon Pioneer
Other Blacks were contributing their minds and inspirations as well. During the early 1970s when Mark Dean was in high school, Roy L. Clay, Sr., was an engineer in the computer division of Hewlett-Packard, the company whose founding was the beginning of Silicon Valley. One of his colleagues was Tom Perkins, who later left to form Kleiner Perkins, Caulfield & Byers, the venture capital firm that financed the computer startups that turned Silicon Valley into an economic powerhouse. Perkins chose Roy Clay as his go-to guy on technology, evaluating prospective investments for new enterprises including Tandem Computers and Compaq Computer Corporation, whose suitcase-sized "transportable" machine began America's love affair with portable computers, and whose use of IBM's PC bus architecture kicked off the long run of companies making "PC Compatible" computers. Earlier, Clay also had helped persuade Kleiner-Perkins to back Intel, whose

microprocessors made the desktop revolution possible.

High-Octane Engineering

During a high-octane career at H-P, Clay led the team that engineered its first computer, the 2116A, in 1966. As a citation for Clay's induction into the Silicon Valley Hall of Fame states, not only had Clay been the first director of Hewlett-Packard's Research and Development Software and Hardware Group, he was a founding member of the Computer Division of H-P, which had begun its life as a world-class maker of precision electronic test equipment.

After Perkins left to form Kleiner Perkins, Clay was interim general manager before also leaving to form ROD-L Electronics, a world leader in the development of electrical safety testing equipment.

Stepping Up to Bat

Dr. Dean, who's spent his entire career at IBM, knows that the computer industry developed all over the United States, not just in Silicon Valley, however. IBM, headquartered in Armonk, N.Y., supercharged the desktop revolution when it introduced the Personal Computer, developed by a "Skunk Works" team in Boca Raton, Florida in 1981.

Dean, who graduated from Tennessee "with highest honors" in 1979, was a key player on that team. He was lead engineer who developed the original IBM PC's Color Graphics Adapter display, put to industry-leading use by Lotus 1-2-3, the spreadsheet that put PCs on business desks across the world. Next, he became lead engineer to design the bus architecture – now the "Industry Standard Architecture" – for the PC AT

(Advanced Technology), the base layout for "PC Compatible" computers. He set the design for the system board and memory cards, as leader of a 30-person development group, and holds three of the original nine patents for the PC AT.

While in Boca Raton, Dean completed a master's degree program in electrical engineering at Florida Atlantic University, with the graphics adapter as his thesis project.

Dean's next project was the IBM Personal System/2. Still in Boca Raton, he was lead engineer for the architectural definition, design, and test of the PS/2 Model 70-A21 and Model 80 systems, and he also was the chief architect of the Micro Channel, a high-performance bus architecture that IBM wanted to make the primary, proprietary standard for PC products.

Unfortunately for IBM, its own success promoting the more open Industry Standard Architecture made the Micro Channel architecture less appetizing for Corporate America. A technological *tour de force*, it came too late to keep IBM in the lead in desktop computers.

Compaq Storms In

Working in Texas, a small group of engineers – the legendary 30 – in a startup company called Compaq Computer Corp. had studied the PC's open architecture design closely. The desktop computers built by Silicon Valley's entrepreneurs were eight-bit machines, powered by the Intel 8080 microprocessor and its offspring, the Zylog Z-80, or in the case of the industry leading Apple II, the MOSFET 6502 eight-bit processor.

Many businesses used the new desktop machines, but many others were waiting on the sidelines. Corporate Data Processing departments were suspicious of the new machines brought to the office by early adopters using the Visicalc spreadsheet or its main imitator, Microsoft Multiplan, because those systems could not interface with the large systems in the corporate data centers. IBM's entry into the desktop market legitimized the use of small computers in corporate suites, and its use of 16-bit Intel 8808 processors opened vast new vistas for programmers. Sixteen-bit central processors had an address space orders of magnitude greater than that of eight-bit machines, producing graphics and spreadsheet-handling capabilities the Silicon Valley products could not match.

Spotting Their Niche

Compaq's engineers, among them a young, gifted and Black Howard University graduate named Leroy Jones, concluded that IBM's open architecture and its use of outside suppliers' parts and peripherals could safely be copied. IBM might change its product mix and its program approaches, but by making its own products closely compatible to IBM's open architecture, Compaq Computers could benefit from the rush of software developers to market products for the IBM PC. Compaq took the gamble, and IBM, instead of battling the upstart, acted more like it approved, declining to push a competing product in the market for portable computers. After all, it did use IBM software.

Soon other imitators were rushing to market with "IBM Compatible" desktop computers running the "PC-DOS"

289

operating system Bill Gates cobbled together from a CP/M knockoff he bought from a storefront software company named Seattle Micro, and even Compaq began marketing a desktop machine. Costs dropped, to the delight of corporate buyers as well as individuals, and the desktop "PC" – whether made by IBM, another name brand, or even a no-name "clone" maker – showed up on more and more desk tops.

By the time the Micro Channel rolled out, the robust competition among "PC Compatible" makers had ensured a wide spread of desktop machines that could use Lotus 1-2-3, the then industry-leading WordPerfect word processor, and the graphics products developed for the PC. The Micro Channel was a major advance over the Industry Standard Architecture, to be sure. But the standard won out anyway.

Still Moving Upward

Continuing his rapid progress at IBM, Dean rose to be chief engineer of Personal RISC (Reduced Instruction Set Computer) Systems and team leader of the PowerPC development group, building a new family of microprocessors destined to help Apple Computer bring its Macintosh line up to speed against the accelerating Intel/Windows PC-Compatible computers with its excitingly designed G- series Macs. While in that job, Dean also took time out to complete his education at Stanford University.

David L. Dill, a Stanford computer scientist who was one of Dr. Dean's faculty advisors, wrote a letter to the Selection Panel for the Black Engineer of the Year Awards, excerpted here, that said amazing things about him:

"In brief, Mark Dean was one the very best graduate students I have ever known. . . His Ph.D. thesis was of the very highest quality, especially with regards to originality and thoroughness. . .

"Although I was impressed with Mark from the beginning, I realized after a time that I had underestimated him. His style was to be very 'low key,' ask questions, and listen more than he spoke. He would come to my office to present an idea that sounded odd at first.

"When I started asking Mark some probing questions, he would have good answers (unlike most early graduate students, who decide to go think some more). As I would dig deeper, he would begin producing data (and charts and graphs), until I had exhausted all the objections I could raise. In fact, he had thought of all the objections already, made the right measurements, solved the problems, and measured the solutions, all in a few days, before coming to see me (of course, he had actually anticipated more issues than I raised). . .

"In my original recommendation for Mark (ten years ago), I wrote a full page about his research achievements at Stanford. Since that is only a small part of what he has done, I'll summarize more briefly here. He came up with a new encoding for data in

291

speed independent circuits that (like other schemes) used two wires per bit. However, Mark's method required only one signal transition per bit, avoiding the delay and energy consumption of a 'return to zero' transition required in the usual scheme. Another idea was to sense the completion of an operation by sensing when a functional unit stopped consuming current (this idea was subsequently pursued by a number of other researchers).

"His Ph.D. thesis was an amazing effort to speed up a pipelined RISC processor (by a factor of 3!) by judicious use of asynchronous design techniques, while avoiding the overhead of fully asynchronous design styles. All of this work gives several implementation alternatives, with careful simulations and performance estimates. . .

"In summary, Mark is a stellar engineer, and an amazing person. His talents were obvious to me, and I'm glad to see that they have been recognized by IBM (to IBM's benefit, of course). . ."

— *David L. Dill, associate professor, Department of Computer Science, Stanford University*

In 1995 IBM named Dr. Dean an IBM Fellow, the first Black American to be designated on the top tier of technical achievers at the world's largest computer maker. Two years later, the National Inventors Hall of Fame made him the third

Black person it ever recognized . He's now a senior vice president at IBM, and his career continues to zoom, a legacy of the long fight waged by freedmen and women like Vernon Jarrett's grandparents, their children and their children's children to see that talents like Mark Dean's got their chance to stand toe to toe with the very best the world has to offer. And succeed, brilliantly.

Chapter 16

Prof: 'Learn a Trade!' She Chose Science

Growing up in communities marred by the stark facts of discrimination, bright Black students hear a constant refrain: "It's not WHAT you know, but WHO you know that counts." Stated as some great historical truth, the refrain is mostly used as a put-down: *Don't think your academic achievements mean anything, Smarty Pants. What matters most is that you're Black like the rest of us. Your brains won't take you anywhere.*

But that is just a dodge, and it's long past time to lay it to rest. It IS what you know – and what you're made of – as a careful examination of the careers of the Black high-achievers

294

in this book has shown. At bottom, the claimed supremacy of influence over intelligence – most loudly touted by those who show little evidence of either – is a papered-over excuse for a failure to try.

The story of Shirley Ann Jackson, the first Black president of America's oldest private engineering and research university, provides a case in point.

Two Different Worlds

Jackson was born in Washington, D.C., in the post-World War II era, to middle-class parents. White Americans remember the late 1940s as a time of great expectations: The United States had just led the Western Allies to crushing victories over Nazi Germany and Imperial Japan. American forces, backed by the mightiest industrial complex the world had ever seen, were the masters of the air, land and sea. American business was humming on overtime now that the war was over, and consumer "creature comforts" and conspicuous display had quickly replaced the discussion of weapons and strike capabilities in public discourse. Big cities in Europe and Asia were in ruins, but so what? American cities were pristine, untouched by the ravages of war.

Blacks, especially the soldiers who had just returned from fighting a war to protect democracy in lands most of them had never known anything about, knew they lived in a different society and were impatient for change. Segregation was still the law, in places like Washington, D.C., Baltimore just to the north, and all points south. Or stated another way, in the places where most of America's Blacks lived.

295

Banneker's Example

Jackson, like almost all Blacks in her generation, began her education in segregated schools and remained behind segregation's walls through high school. Her mother read stories to her about Benjamin Banneker, the informally educated but still-eminent Black scientist who challenged Thomas Jefferson over the propriety of Black enslavement when Jefferson had proclaimed "all men" to be equal, and the young Shirley Jackson was inspired. During Black History Month, Blacks resurrect the stories about Banneker, whose all-wood mechanical clock was a wonderment in early American society and whose almanac rivaled that of Benjamin Franklin. Schoolteachers repeat the story of how Banneker later played a key role in laying out the city of Washington when the hot-headed Frenchman hired to do the job got fired over a management dispute.

What they should be emphasizing is Banneker's perseverance. Born into an Eighteenth-Century society determined to ignore the brainpower of the Black Africans it was importing to enslave, Banneker grew up in a world in which the idea of schooling for Blacks was preposterous. Sitting in legislatures across the states, slaveholders even banned the teaching of reading and writing to the enslaved. Himself the son and grandson of manumitted slaves, Banneker evaded that obstacle and got an eighth-grade education from a Quaker school before taking over the family farm at 15. The wooden clock Banneker carved as a copy of his white neighbor's imported timepiece brought him renown and, borrowing his neighbor's books, Banneker educated himself in science and mathematics.

Getting the Point

The young Shirley Ann Jackson imbibed that lesson deeply. Her father, a postal supervisor, continually urged her to follow her dreams and a key mentor, the assistant principal for boys at all-Black Roosevelt High School, pointed her toward the Massachusetts Institute of Technology, where few Blacks had gone before.

When she arrived on campus in 1964, legal segregation was history, but the attitudes that perpetuated it were still very much evident, North and South. Abolitionists from Massachusetts were leading lights during the run-up to the Civil War, even founding the town of Lawrence in eastern Kansas and renaming Hogback Ridge "Mount Oread" in honor of home. The Jayhawk wars over the free-state status of the territory of Kansas were precipitating incidents leading up to the war – remember John Brown? – and Kansas' transplanted Northeasterners were leading Republican radicals after the war. Too bad the Irish-dominated white community of Boston had forgotten its predecessors' principled stand.

Walking Ahead, Alone

Jackson found herself ostracized by her fellow students, just as Benjamin O. Davis was ostracized at West Point before the Second World War. Clearly, nothing had changed in the mindset of these Northern whites, even after Davis and his Tuskegee Airmen had blown away any pretense of rationality in the preconceptions about Black abilities in the skies over Germany.

Thus, while other students collaborated in study groups,

297

Jackson studied alone, as Davis had a generation earlier. Jackson, one of fewer than 20 Black students on campus, was the only Black person studying theoretical physics. Whites resented Jackson's presence, and one professor even told her to go "learn a trade." But Jackson, like Banneker and Davis before her, persevered.

Hostile Crowds

On the streets, Jackson was treated to the hostility Autherine Lucy had met a decade earlier. As *Prism*, the magazine of the American Society for Engineering Education reports, whites shouted and spat on the young Black woman as she walked down the street, and in Downtown Boston, someone actually fired a gun at her. Fortunately, the shot missed.

Jackson, undeterred, continued to study. And what she knew began to count, as the students who once shunned her watched her continue to score highly on exams. They sought her out for tutoring and mentoring, and Jackson suddenly found herself invited into the circles of friendship.

Not Backing Down

Living through an extended period of hostility and alienation, far from home, takes a toll. Jackson, determined to stay connected to her roots, volunteered at Boston City Hospital and tutored Black students at the Roxbury YMCA. She also joined with others to found the Black Students Union, whose Task Force on Educational Opportunity prodded MIT's president to open the institution's doors to wider participation by Black students. By the time Jackson left with her doctorate in 1973, MIT had begun a conscious effort to recruit minority students, and the activism of the BSU she co-founded had begun to force changes in their treatment on campus.

Jackson completed her B.S. in 1968 and remained at MIT for graduate studies, becoming the institution's first Black female physics Ph.D. Her perseverance, determination and activism had changed the face her *alma mater* turned to Black students, and now she was about to go forth and do the same thing in theoretical science.

Being Prepared

President Bill Clinton named Dr. Jackson to lead the Nuclear Regulatory Commission in 1995, to the amazement of Blacks who'd never heard of Shirley Jackson, but the precedents for her appointment were laid many years earlier: at Roosevelt High, where the assistant principal for boys took note of her intense interest in science; at home where she collected and experimented on bees; in her dissertation, on "The Study of a Multiperipheral Model with Continued Cross-Channel Unitarity," published in the *Annals of Physics* in 1975. Edward Alexander Bouchet, who went to Philadelphia to run the Institute for Colored Youth (Cheyney University today) after discrimination blocked the science career his 1876 Yale physics Ph.D. should have ensured, would have been inestimably pleased.

Emulating Heroes of the Past

Jackson did research at the Fermi National Accelerator Laboratory in Batavia, Illinois, in 1973 and 1974, fulfilling the legacy of Blacks who had worked in its predecessor, the Manhattan Project. One such was Moddie Daniel Taylor, a Black University of Chicago researcher who demonstrated that fissionable materials could achieve "critical mass" and sustain a chain reaction, one of the key discoveries that helped the Manhattan Project succeed. Another Black nuclear forerunner was the prodigy J. Ernest Wilkins, who completed his undergrad and master's degree studies at 17 and his doctorate in mathematics at Chicago at 19. From 1944 to 1946, Dr. Wilkins worked in the Metallurgical Laboratory with Enrico Fermi, working out principles for designing the Bomb. Dr. Wilkins' mathematical models demonstrated the amount of gamma radiation a given material could absorb, developing shielding against the radiation from nuclear fission.

Dr. Jackson, their successor, journeyed to Switzerland, to be a visiting science associate at the European Center for Nuclear Research (CERN), returning in 1975 to rejoin Fermilab as a research associate. In 1976, she left Fermilab to join AT&T Bell Laboratories' technical staff, and spent a year doing more research at the Stanford Linear Accelerator Center and the Aspen Center for Physics. Such steps are beyond the ken of people who believe in truisms like "it's not what you know," but Dr. Jackson was building the knowledge base that would equip her to run the world's premier nuclear regulatory agency.

Also in 1976, Dr,. Jackson went on the faculty of Rutgers University in Piscataway, N.J., close to the Murray Hill headquarters of Bell Labs. From 1991 to 1995, Dr. Jackson also was a Bell Labs consultant in semiconductor theory.

President Clinton's later appointment of Dr. Jackson to the

NRC chair brought national attention, but she had proven her skills, problem-solving abilities and management acumen much earlier.

Proven Abilities

Prism reports that MIT faculty who were present during the rough years of Dr. Jackson's undergraduate and graduate studies "remember that she never lost her temper, always arguing elegantly and calmly for the merits of changing racist policies." The magazine also says her even-handed treatment of explosive issues at the NRC – an agency many Americans believed to be too close to the nuclear utilities it was supposed to regulate – earned her the respect of public-safety watchdogs and nuclear industry representatives alike.

Dr. Jackson, who had arrived at the agency at one of the lowest points in its history, restored faith in its credibility by toughening safety standards and driving off commissioners who were too lenient, bringing her own broad nuclear knowledge base to bear on the industry's problems. "She is credited with wisely resolving some of the toughest dilemmas the NRC has ever faced," *Prism* said.

Still Pushing for Change

Dr. Jackson, the 2001 Black Engineer of the Year, also remained true to her stated goal of increasing the number of Black students at MIT. She joined the institution's Board of Trustees and, during her 20 years in New Jersey, was a mover and shaker on state task forces promoting science and technology.

301

One of the organizations she helped found, Building Engineering Science and Talent (BEST), produced a persuasive 2002 report, "The Quiet Crisis: Falling Short in Producing American Scientific and Technical Talent," urging new initiatives to bring minorities into the science "mainstream."

Competition is Afoot, Abroad

Emerging countries such as India and China out-produce the United States in graduating scientists and engineers today, at a time when new discoveries and the technologies built on them are radically reshaping world economies. American industry reports continued shortages of creative engineers, and the high numbers of science and engineering graduates coming out of Asia mandates increased investments in research centers there, executives say.

"Out-sourcing" – transferring technical work to centers in India, China and Japan – is a phenomenon that threatens the livelihoods and careers of America's own technical professionals, an example of the a problem Dr. Jackson says "stems from the gap between the nation's growing need for scientists, engineers, and other technically skilled workers and its production of them. . . This 'gap' represents a shortfall in our national scientific and technical abilities."

The answer, BEST argues, is greater emphasis on getting minorities, heretofore under-served, into and through the science and technology pipeline.

Crisis Debated

To be sure, the size of the crisis, and the accuracy of reports on the graduation rates of engineers in India and China, are under debate. A 2004 report by the RAND Corporation questioned the quality of the data on which the BEST report and others were based, and a December 2005 report by Duke University executive in residence Vivek Wadhwa disputes the high graduation rates claimed for India and China and the low rates claimed for Americans.

While the United States is said to produce only 70,000 engineers a year, China claims 600,000, and India some 350,000. Wadhwa, however, believes those number are widely misinterpreted. If the U.S. counted computer science and information technology graduates as engineers, as India does, the real U.S. yearly total would be 134,000, he told *Business Week*. And India's four-year baccalaureate total is 122,000 a year, with the Asian giant's schools producing almost as many three-year graduates, considerably fewer than the claimed 350,000. If true, it means U.S. institutions still outpace India's in per-capita production of engineers.

Ditto for China, Wadhwa says. The definition of an engineer varies from province to province – some authorities even count mechanics as engineers, he says – and other observers say that only about two in five Chinese engineering graduates emerge from their studies prepared for technical work up to the standards of Western corporations.

True to Her Stand

Dr. Jackson, named president of Rensselaer Polytechnic Institute in 1999 – and handed yet another tricky set of problems to solve in rebuilding the nation's oldest private engineering and research university – probably would be heartened by Wadhwa's report.

But as *Business Week* noted, American engineers say Wadhwa's findings do not match the grim reality of downsizing in U.S. research and development laboratories while U.S. corporations invest increasingly large amounts of capital in foreign labs and offshore factories. The American share of scientific papers has fallen to the degree that researchers in other lands are outpacing U.S. scientists, most notably in stem cell research, but foreign specialists also are visibly taking the lead in other areas as well. And federal funding for basic research has fallen off sharply; what remains is narrowly focused on targeted applications.

Dr. Jackson, who served as president of the American Association for the Advancement of Science in 2005 in addition to leading Rensselaer, remains on the side of those arguing for a new urgency in producing more science and engineering talent and opening doors for more minorities to join the pool.

Still Fighting for Diversity

In a speech on "the Beauty of Diverse Talent," appended to the joint AAAS-National Action Council on Minorities in Engineering report "Standing Our Ground: A Guidebook for STEM Educators in the Post-Michigan Era," Dr. Jackson said,

"The demographics of our nation have changed. African Americans and Hispanics now account for a about a quarter of the total U.S. population. Add to that another population segment – women – comprising more than half of our people. Then, groups under-represented in the science, engineering

304

and technical disciplines – are now a majority – what I call the 'new majority' – comprising nearly two-thirds of the entire U.S. workforce.

"There has been another change. For many years we have relied upon – and welcomed and benefitted from – the infusing of talent from abroad, in our colleges and universities, and in our corporate and government laboratories. During the decade of the 1990s, the percentage of foreign-born scientists and engineers in the United States leaped from 24 percent to 38 percent.

With security measures in place since September 11th, 2001, however, that source of talent has been curtailed. A study by the National Science Board found that from 2001 to 2002 the number of temporary worker visas issued for jobs in science and technology plunged from 166,000 to 74,000 – a decline of 55 percent. Similarly, successful visa applications fell from 10 million to 6.5 million. Aside from visa issues, many of the talented scientists and engineers are choosing to study elsewhere in the world, or, are choosing to remain at home – because, increasingly, they can.

"What does this mean for American innovation? How will it affect our nation and our future? What do we need to be doing?

Challenges Outlined

"As those of us here readily know, and take for granted, our nation's prosperity, our quality of life,

305

the very security of our nation relies, in large measure, on the driving forces of scientific and technological discovery and innovation. These national benefits are a direct result of our deep technology base, highly productive workforce, strong research and development capacity, and robust competitive spirit.

"This national capacity has given us an economic engine powered by innovations and discoveries in science, engineering, and technology. It has brought us a quality of life and a global primacy many take for granted.

"This national capacity rests largely on the work of a small segment – scientists and engineers comprise a mere 5 percent of our total workforce.

"This small, but critical segment of our workforce is aging. About half of U.S. science and engineering workers are over 40years old. It is only logical to assume that retirements among science and engineering workers will increase dramatically over the next two decades. The segment, today, is overwhelmingly white and male.

"To replace them when they leave, we must look to the millennium generation of young people, which, as demographics now dictate, comprise the 'new majority.'. . .

"While the United States is experiencing challenges to its production of science and engineering professionals, other nations increasingly are committed to national capacity – i.e., investing,

306

especially, in human capacity – and it has been paying off. A $250 million World Bank loan to India is helping to revamp engineering colleges and technological universities, where more than 100,000 students study. The money is modernizing facilities, upgrading curricula, and training faculty members.

"Collectively, China, India, Japan, South Korea, and Taiwan have more than doubled their production of bachelor's degrees in the natural sciences since 1975, and quadrupled the number of bachelor's degrees in engineering.

"As nations are investing in higher education at home, they also are creating global industries in focused technological areas. Taiwan, Korea, Ireland, Israel, and India are emerging in the pivotal information sector. Scandinavian countries are comparatively strong in telecommunications. Japan and China are investing heavily in science and technology. And, of course, American corporations, experiencing economic pressure to cut costs and to build global networks, are moving a spectrum of jobs overseas.

"It becomes clear that U.S. global primacy is being pressured from the outside by the building competition among both developed and developing nations. From the inside, we are experiencing pressure to replace the graying science and engineering workforce with new talent – educated young scientists and engineers who will make the discoveries and innovations which have paid off so handsomely, to date. This has been called 'the Quiet Crisis.'. . .

"Our nation must galvanize the national commitment, and the national will, to develop and to tap the full spectrum of homegrown talent. With national commitment and will, I believe, we would succeed in finding, nurturing, and developing the talent inherent in our children. We did it before, when the Soviet-launched 'Sputnik' orbited Earth's skies, spurring America to action. We can do it again. . . ."

Dr, Shirley Ann Jackson, a child of segregation who grew up in the Sputnik era, with doors opened for her amid the swirl and activism of the 1960s, is a living example of what happens when under-appreciated Black talent is let free. Even more than her pithy speeches and penetrating reports, her own life story stands as powerful proof of the veracity of her argument.

Supplemental Notes

1. BEST (Building Engineering & Science Talent), is a public-private partnership dedicated to building a stronger, more diverse U.S. workforce in science, engineering and technology by increasing the participation of under-represented groups. Its Board of Directors includes the former vice chairman of NASDAQ, the president and treasurer of Alcoa, the chairmen and CEOs of Qualcomm Corporation, Merisant Corporation, and OpCenter, LLP; the chancellors of North Carolina State University and the San Diego Community College District and the provost of the University of California; a senior vice president of the W.K. Kellogg Foundation; and the president of the Council on Competitiveness, and its National Leadership Council,

Unheralded but Unbowed

chaired by Texas Rep. Eddie-Bernice Johnson, is equally high-profile. See the complete report at www.best.org.

2. Standing Our Ground: A Guidebook for STEM Educators in the Post-Michigan Era, by Shirley M. Malcolm, Daryl E. Chubin, and Jolene K. Jesse, was released in October 2004 by the American Association for the Advancement of Science and the National Action Council for Minorities in Engineering. It is a report summing up discussions at a January 2004 conference by nearly 200 educators, attorneys and science professionals disturbed at the failure of the Bush Administration Department of Justice and the U.S. Department of Education's Office of Civil Rights to provide guidelines and interpretation for educators trying to implement diversity programs in an era of strident attacks against affirmative action by right-wing think tanks and legal foundations seeking to end minority-targeted scholarship programs, special-consideration admissions programs and other efforts to open up the campus to under-served minorities.

As the report notes, the U.S. Supreme Court's decision in the critical lawsuits of *Grutter v. Bollinger*, 539 US 306 (2003) and *Gratz v. Bollinger*, 539 US 244 (2003), "Sanctioned what has been known for decades in higher education admissions offices, in corporate board rooms, and even in military service academies: in this country, diversity can be an essential component of excellence in education. Granting constitutional legitimacy to educational policy makers' pursuit of this ideal is not only respectable as a matter of equity under the law, but is actually essential. Changing demographic patterns and national priorities demand that America fully utilize its greatest resource – its citizenry. Educational policy makers get it. And finally, the U.S. Supreme Court does, too."

Many educators were relieved at the high court's decisions, the Guidebook says, but "In the aftermath . . . the persistent ambiguity that has plagued this area of the law has again begun to rear its ugly head. What do the Supreme Court decisions mean for institutions that use race-conscious decision-making in financial aid assessments and outreach efforts in the pursuit of a diverse class? What do they mean for institutions sponsoring minority-exclusive activities, such as recruitment overnights or academic enrichment programs? Perhaps the most urgent question is what do these decisions mean for institutions outside of the higher education community, including K-12 public and private schools, charter schools, non-profits, and even business and industry. In other words, what do the decisions *really* mean?

Thus, dismayed at the federal failure to assist institutions seeking to develop and justify viable programs, the sponsoring organizations held a conference to work it out for themselves. The results of that conference are published the Guidebook to help educators figure their way through the swamp of anti-affirmative action lawsuits, lobbying and attacks in state legislatures.

Ominously, the Guidebook's Acknowledgement section declined to name many of the people who contributed, because "The climate of intimidation that dominates discussions of policies and programs today on the issue of inclusion (commonly referred to as 'affirmative action') makes it imprudent and risky to highlight their participation lest they and their institutions become subject to harassment and the targets of critics. . . ."

"Many believe that our problems are over and the need for special efforts is long past," the Guidebook says. "The data belie those beliefs; educational preparation and opportunity are not yet evenly distributed by race, ethnicity, gender, and geography. This guidebook can help level the playing field, but we are far from that state of grace. . . ."

Postscript:

Tell the Students How They Can Win

Tables from the federal Bureau of Labor Statistics' annual survey of occupational data tell an amazing story: When you add up all the Black people working in high-technology professions, the total comes to more than 276,000. That's without counting thousands of aircraft mechanics and service technicians, manufacturers' computer-control programmers, computer, ATM and office machine repair technicians, or radio and telecommunications repair techs, too..

Americans are used to saying the Black percentage of workers in the technology enterprise is small – less than one in 20 workers – to the dismay of many Black observers. But that "small" percentage of the several million people making up America's professional and technical, architecture and engineering workforce contains numbers big enough that if

311

all the Blacks decided to emigrate tomorrow to, say, Nigeria or South Africa, it would dramatically upgrade the African nation's ability to compete in world markets and dramatically downgrade America's.

Transplanted, those Capabilities Would . . .
Think not? Then imagine what would happen if 20,000 extra Black civil engineers showed up in Nigeria, a country without much of a road network, poor distribution of clean drinking water, and a highly undeveloped system of dealing with sewerage and garbage, just now trying to figure out how to use the River Niger to open up cargo trade to its interior.

Ditto for the addition of nearly 20,000 Black American electrical and electronics engineers, buttressed by almost 7,000 computer and hardware engineers, into a country such as South Africa, which has an established industrial base but very unevenly developed highway, rail and air transport systems, electric power grid, telephone system, and Internet infrastructure. Add 10,000 incoming industrial engineers, another 8,000 mechanical engineers and 1,700 chemical engineers to that mix in a country with vast natural resources, large amounts of undeveloped land, and several big rivers begging for hydroelectric development, and in 10-20 years you'd see a new economic Tiger rearing its head on the African continent.

It Happened Before – Here
Doubters have only to refer back the United States' own Industrial Revolution, which propelled this country to the world economic leadership it has never relinquished.

In 1790 the newly independent U.S., very much less developed than Nigeria or South Africa is today, received invaluable stolen property: Memorized plans of the steam-driven Arkwright textile mill. Industrial Britain's greatest trade secret had been lifted by the English craftsman Samuel Slater, who became a millionaire industrialist with American copies of the Arkwright mill.

In 10 years the British could barely recognize their former colony. In 20 years, American industries were cranking out products that were better made, more innovative, and cheaper than European competitors could manage. By 1820, 30 years after the purloined intellectual property dropped on America's doorstep, English and European industrialists were traveling to the United States to gain insights on the wealth of inventions, techniques and new factory tools that had made the new industrial *wunderkind* such a manufacturing and trade powerhouse. As the 19th Century wore on, "*Yankee ingenuity*" became a new market buzzword.

Real-World Exploits, Real-World Rewards

A modern mass Black Exodus scenario is not likely to come to fruition, but the point is that those nearly 300,000 Black engineers, computer scientists, software engineers, programmers, architects and technicians already are working technological miracles in the places where they earn their living, in America. The results of their energy, verve and innovation would be more high-profile in a less developed country, but their employers know full well the value of unleashing their talents in the industrial free-for-all of today's multi-polar world. That's why top executives keep showing up

313

each February to extol their achievements at the annual Black Engineer of the Year Awards.

For examples, look at Boeing, America's biggest exporter, whose jetliner sales are taking off all over the world, even as Europe's government-supported Airbus strengthens its own product line.

-- Look at Motorola, whose cell telephone products were badly beaten by Finland's Nokia, but roared back on iDEN technical innovations and a whole new approach to styling.

-- Look at Hewlett Packard, the original Silicon Valley pioneer, whose desktop and laptop computers, cameras and printers continue to lead markets even as other American manufacturers bow out to foreign competitors.

-- Look at IBM, trouncing all comers with innovative servers and consulting services while other former tech fast-movers fall by the wayside.

-- Look at Corning, whose optical fibers continue to be front-runners in the race to connect everyone in the world to the Internet.

-- Look at Lockheed Martin, the world's leader in military weapons systems, fighter aircraft, ship systems and transport aircraft.

-- Look at Chrysler before the 2008 economic meltdown, whose cars, American-designed even under Daimler-Benz, won new market share even as Ford and General Motors retreated before the onslaught of better-designed Japanese, German and Korean cars. The U.S. credit crisis brought Chrysler low, requiring a rescue by yet another European company, but the achievement stands.

314

The Diversity Advantage

All of these companies, and many others not mentioned, employ Blacks in critical positions in research and development, product development, manufacturing and consulting as well as technical sales and marketing, and all are seeing major benefits that they trumpet at annual events such as the Black Engineer of the Year Awards, National Women of Color Technology Awards, Emerald Honors for Minorities in Research Science, and Hispanic Engineer National Achievement Awards.

The discussion on the preceding pages pretty much illustrates that, but it is helpful to remember that the small number of winners in the biggest contest, the Black Engineer of the Year Awards – more than 600 over the last 24 years – represents only the tip of the iceberg. What should be gleaned from stories about the lives and careers of that small sample of today's thousands of high-achieving Black engineers and scientists is that:

1. Black engineers, whatever their percentage in the technology workforce, have broken through many barriers to become essential producers of the innovations that drive American industry. They are not on the periphery of the talent pool, but at the center.

2. Performance at the high levels these exemplars have set gets recognized, and promotions, clout and big paychecks await those who follow the paths they have blazed. Corporate vice presidents make more than movie stars, and as former Mobil executive Bill Granville tells students in his Granville

Academy business-focused motivation and tutoring program, executives' lifetime earnings make even All-Pro athletes look like poor second-raters.

Teach the Children

Black children need to assimilate those two points, for their chances of becoming successful engineers and scientists are far better than their chances of winning success on the playing fields of the National Football League, Major League Baseball, or the NBA, despite the glamour and hoopla that surround professional sports. Ditto for the entertainment world, whose flashy success stories obscure the much greater numbers of busted-out hopefuls who couldn't make it into the Big Time. The cultural predisposition in America is that it takes extreme ability to make it in science, but what it takes mostly is hard work at the books, right through school, with strong support and encouragement from teachers and parents. Too often, however, the Black students who do show ability often are not encouraged to pursue science because, as with the young John Slaughter, no one around them believes they can succeed. That has to change.

The Urgency of Promoting Engineering

Here's why: The U.S. Department of Education's Center for Education Statistics' "Science Indicators 2006" report says that America's manufacturing industries are increasingly shifting to high-tech product lines – aerospace, pharmaceuticals, office and computing equipment, communications equipment, and scientific instruments, to be exact. The United States' share of the world-wide production of this high-technology manufacturing has grown from 25 percent in 1990 to nearly 40 percent in 2003, while the shares of the European Union countries and Japan fell from 25 percent to 18 percent and 11 percent respectively.

That's 40 percent of $3.5 *trillion* worth of manufacturing output, and high-technology products have risen from 12 percent to 30 percent of the total domestic manufacturing output.

All of this points to a continuing need to produce more scientific and technical workers to keep that high-tech enterprise going. Or else watch the business migrate overseas, to the developing technology sectors in India, China and Southeast Asia.

The Changing College Picture

Demographic shifts compel a re-examination of how we promote engineering and science to Black students. The Center for Education Statistics says that colleges and universities enrolled about 422,000 engineering students in 2003, the last year for which figures were available, and that Black students, whose percentage hovered around 5 percent through the 1990s, are increasing their numbers.

The U.S college-age population is increasing, and so is enrollment, but the makeup of that population is changing rapidly. From 12.6 million students in 1983, the student population at U.S. institutions grew to 15.7 million in 2001, but the newest Census figures show that the number of college-aged youths, 20 to 24 years old, is expected to grow from 18.5 million in 2000 to 21.7 million by 2015.

317

Blacks, who regularly surprise Census prognosticators, are projected to see their college-aged population grow by 19 percent, while Hispanics and Asian-Pacific islander youth populations can expect more than 50-percent growth. The white college-aged population is projected to increase slightly through the year 2010, and then decline. Where will we get the new science and technology students? Among women and minorities. Especially among Blacks, whose numbers in four-year baccalaureate programs exceed all other minorities.

Hopeful signs

Black students are showing that they are willing to boost their numbers in math, science and technology programs. While statisticians point to the small percentage of Blacks preparing for science careers, the U.S. Education Department's annual survey of students actually in college, planning their majors, found that 10 percent of Black freshmen aiming for science and engineering in 2004, the same percentage it found in 1983. The final numbers going into science, math and engineering programs are thus smaller than they should be. Another recent study, by the National Institutes of Health shows why:

Blacks and others from under-served communities are regularly being shunted out of the science and engineering pipeline instead of encouraged to stay the course.

That report, by the National Institute of General Medical Science, cautioned educators to stop using "paper credentials rather than ability" to gage Blacks' readiness for science study. Too many capable students are being lost to other careers that way, the Institute said, posing a threat of shortfalls in the critically important research workforce.

Get the Message?

What all this means is that the science and engineering workforce, whose intellectual achievements end up as products, services and techniques that keep American business at the top of the world food chain – 5 percent of the U.S. workers – can only get the new recruits it needs by mining the expanding vein of college-aged youth in the Black community, among women, and in other minority communities. The whites who have dominated science fields are declining as a share of the national population.

The Cold War's end opened up a new world of competition, now that communications satellites, optical fiber cable connections and advances in wireless technology have made it possible for people in developing lands to gain rapid access to information resources once available only to Americans and Europeans. High-tech manufacturing, producing wealth that drives the entire economy, requires lots of high-tech workers. Standing idly by while other countries race to produce new generations of engineers, scientists and technicians and fight to replace America as the world's economic leader is not an option.

Garland L. Thompson
Philadelphia PA, August 2009

Notes

For a trenchant analysis of the potential for recruiting a new science workforce from America's minority youth, see the "Report of the National Institute of General Medical Science Workshop on Achieving Scientific Excellence through Diversity, May 6-7, 2001."

That National Institute report, which can be found at *http://www.nigms.nih.gov/news/reports/diversity_report.html,* said that "Data show that a large population of minority students who enter undergraduate programs lose interest in science in the freshman year. Expanding the pool of potential graduate students is dependent upon building self-confidence and academic skills in the freshman year. Students who successfully make the freshman-sophomore transition are likely to stay in science. . . .

"The pipeline leaks at several places: the freshman-sophomore transition, baccalaureate graduates who choose a medical profession over a research career, and the transitions from Ph.D. to postdoctoral fellow and postdoctoral fellow to faculty. Biomedical scientists have the responsibility to convey the excitement and opportunities that a research career offers, and to convey the importance and relevance of research to society in improving quality of life and reducing health disparities. . . "

The Institute report also noted that "In the past, students were defined as 'at risk' based on the use of [Graduate Record Exam] scores and numerical credentials as predictors for success; however, many programs and mentors now realize that, regardless of whether a student is majority or minority, other indicators (research experience, commitment, letters of recommendation, and interviews) may be more valuable measures and predictors of a student's potential to succeed. In fact, labeling students as 'at risk,' based on paper credentials rather than ability, can create an added obstacle to success by lowering expectations. . . ."

Index

324

329

330

Rodney Adkins, *221, 223*
Rodney Hunt, *221, 228*
Rodney O'Neal, *220*
Roger Nagel, *196*
Rolling Thunder, *258*
Ron Brown, *30*
Ronald McNair, *96*
Roosevelt High School, *297*
Rooseveltian "Four Freedoms",
 148
Rosa Parks, *125*
Roscoe Draper, *42*
Roxbury YMCA, *298*
Roy L. Clay, Sr., *286*
Roy Wilkins, *178*
Russell Simmons, *216*
Russell T. Wright, *226*
Rutgers University, *300*

S

Sally Richmond, *14, 115*
Sally Richmond and Katherine
 Johnson, *67*
Samuel Elmer Imes, *273*
Samuel L. Gravely, *261*
Samuel Slater, *313*
Sandra Laursen, *112*
Saul Alinsky, *55*
segregation, *viii, xv, 3, 4, 7, 9, 12,
 14, 57, 61, 66, 74, 82, 104,
 106, 115, 128, 138, 141, 143,
 149, 150, 159, 161, 162, 163,
 164, 168, 170, 171, 172, 174,
 176, 180, 182, 238, 254, 255,
 277, 296, 297, 308*
Selma University, *152*

Sen. Barry Goldwater, *90*
Sentel, *215*
Servant Leadership, *132*
Sharpeville Massacre, *173*
Sherita Ceasar, *117*
Shirley Ann Jackson, *295, 297,
 308*
Shirley Jackson, *vi, 1, 296, 299*
Siege of Atlanta, *vii*
Silicon Valley, *201, 288*
sit-ins, 82
Some 404,000 Blacks went to
 war with John J. Pershing in
 World War I,, *251*
Southern Company, *29, 31*
Southern University, *146, 246*
Soviet, *11, 14, 39, 43, 44, 72, 85,
 86, 88, 89, 95, 98, 99, 100,
 105, 169, 174, 176, 190, 197,
 203, 204, 212, 236, 237, 254,
 257, 277, 308*
Space Race, *14, 87, 105, 115,
 234, 235, 239*
Space Shuttle, *95, 257, 259*
Space Station Habitat Modules,
 73
Special Forces, *40, 198, 200,
 212, 236*
*Sputnik, 87, 97, 105, 169, 236,
 237, 277, 308*
Stan Mazor, *279*
Stanford Linear Accelerator
 Center, *300*
Stanford Research Institute, *278*
Star Wars, *72, 98*
Steward's Mate Dorie Miller, *261*
Strategic Air Command, *204*

Cuban casinos, *189*
Tuscarora War, *249*
Tuskegee Airmen, *12, 13, 38, 41, 42, 49, 50, 253, 256, 257, 261, 297*
Tuskegee Airmen's legacy, *261*
Tuskegee Institute, *49, 138*
Tuskegee University, *147*

U

U.S. Army Corps of Engineers, *120, 267*
U.S. Energy Department, *224*
U.S. Olympic Committee, *36*
U.S. Postal Service, *231*
U.S. v. Fordice, 150
University of California at Davis, 222
University of Chicago, *300*
University of Illinois, *172*
University of Maryland, *242*
University of Maryland at College Park,, *1*
University of Pittsburgh, *118*
University of Tennessee, *280*
Unix operating system, *206*
USS Arizona, *261*
USS Macon, *261*
USS Ranger, *39, 47, 261*

V

Vernon Jarrett, *281*
Vietnam, *24, 263*
Vietnam War, *222*
Vietnam was a conflict in which

thousands of Black warriors faced hostile fire., *255*
violent takeover of the county seat at Hamburg, South Carolina, *140*
Virginia State College, *106*
Virginia State University, *147, 207*
Vivek Wadhwa, 303

W

W.E.B. DuBois, *58, 66, 273, 281*
Wal-Mart, *115, 116*
Walt Braithwaite, *vi*
Walt Hazzard, *82*
Walt W. Braithwaite, *186*
Walter Davis, *39*
Warren Suss, *213*
Washington State University, *172*
Washington Technology magazine, *229*
Waymon Whiting, *67*
West Virginia State College, *14, 55*
Wharton School, *23, 33*
What happens to, 6
White Americans remember the late 1940s as a time of great expectations, *295*
White League agitation against Black voting power, *165*
Willa Brown, *13, 49*
William Donald Schafer, *7*
William Smith, *221*
William T. Coleman, *106*

Unheralded but Unbowed

Made in the USA
Charleston, SC
23 June 2011